CALIFORNIA STYLE MANUAL

Fourth Edition

A HANDBOOK OF LEGAL STYLE
FOR CALIFORNIA COURTS
AND LAWYERS

By

Edward W. Jessen

Reporter of Decisions
for the Supreme Court and Courts of Appeal

WEST GROUP

San Francisco
2000

ISBN 0-314-23370-9

Page composition by ImageInk, San Francisco
Cover design by Side by Side Designs, San Francisco

Editiorial preparation and manufacturing
West Group, California's Official Legal Publisher

FOREWORD

For almost 60 years, the legal community of California has benefited from the publication of the California Style Manual. The manual provides a guide to standard legal style in the appellate courts, and benefits litigants and jurists alike by establishing a common stylistic base that permits readers to focus readily on substance rather than form.

In the 14 years since publication of the third edition of the Style Manual, much has changed in the processes used for creating legal documents. A personal computer on the desk is now the rule rather than the exception for most lawyers and judges. At the same time, the availability of diverse reference resources has expanded the ease and scope of research. This latest revision of the manual reflects and responds to many of the changes that the legal profession has experienced, while maintaining a steady hold on the practices that have served the courts and the profession so well. I extend my appreciation to the Reporter of Decisions and those who have assisted him in the task of revising this valuable reference tool.

Ronald M. George
Chief Justice of California

SUPREME COURT APPROVAL

To the Reporter of Decisions:

Pursuant to the authority conferred on the Supreme Court of California by Government Code section 68902, the California Style Manual, Fourth Edition, as submitted to this court for review is approved and adopted as the official organ for the styles to be used in the publication of the Official Reports.

Dated: December 21, 1999

Ronald M. George
Chief Justice of California

PREFACE

The fourth edition of the California Style Manual endeavors to continue a tradition started in 1942 by Bernard E. Witkin, as Reporter of Decisions, with the first edition of the manual. In the subsequent 58 years, the California Style Manual has evolved from a guide primarily intended for court staffs, the Reporter of Decisions Office, and the Official Reports publisher to become the standard for legal office style in California. In addition to Bernard E. Witkin, the contributors to this tradition have been William Nankervis, who wrote the second edition in 1961, and Robert E. Formichi, who edited the second revised edition (1976) and the third edition (1986).

Since publication of the third edition in 1986, revolutionary changes have occurred in the nature and sources of legal reference material (e.g., the Internet and other modes of legal research by computer) and in how legal documents are produced by computer. Reflecting these changes and maintaining the style manual as a comprehensive, convenient, and current reference for California appellate styles required a collaborative effort drawing on the experience and expertise of many. Listed below are those who reviewed drafts of various chapters, and those who otherwise contributed to the editing of this fourth edition. Special thanks, however, for the enthusiastic contributions of the Reporter's staff, and for the careful review of all chapters by Peter Belton, the Supreme Court's senior attorney with 40 years of service.

> Peter Belton, Supreme Court Attorney
> Hal Cohen, Supreme Court Attorney
> Guy Colburn, Supreme Court Attorney
> Brenda Cox, Reporter's Office Legal Editor
> Sheila D'Ambrosio, Reporter's Office Legal Editor
> Irene Dieter, Court of Appeal Judicial Assistant
> Robert Dobbs, West Group Copyeditor
> Steve Gilmartin, Contract Copyeditor
> Blair Hoffman, Supreme Court Attorney

Robin D. Kojima, West Group Attorney Editor
Edith V. Lavin, Reporter's Office Legal Editor
Levin, Court of Appeal Attorney
Terry Mead, Supreme Court Attorney
Bennett N. Miller, West Group Editor
Herbert F. Miller, West Group Attorney Editor
Christine Miklas, Administrative Office of the Courts
Iris Okura, West Group Editor
Eric Ratner, Supreme Court Attorney
Geraldine Rausch, Assistant Reporter of Decisions
Robert Reichman, Supreme Court Attorney
Milton Roberts, Reporter's Office Legal Editor
Victor Rowley, Administrative Office of the Courts
Carol D. Sakamoto, Reporter's Office Legal Editor
Jeffrey Shea, West Group Attorney Editor
Alma Sifuentes, Court of Appeal Judicial Assistant
Cynthia Sletto, West Group Director and Managing Editor
Kayko Sonoda, Court of Appeal Judicial Assistant
Ted Stroll, Supreme Court Attorney
Norm Vance, Supreme Court Attorney
Sue Walenta, Supreme Court Judicial Assistant
Katie Willsey, Court of Appeal Judicial Assistant

San Francisco   Edward W. Jessen
January 2000

TABLE OF CONTENTS

TABLE OF FREQUENTLY USED ABBREVIATIONS

The abbreviation table lists usages found in the manual. Some deviation will be noted in specific circumstances (e.g., the manual has adopted the abbreviated general style of "opn." for "opinion," but practice has established that references to the Opinions of the Attorney General of California be styled as "Ops.Cal.Atty.Gen."). The styles provided in this manual generally limit use of abbreviated forms to parenthetical usages, but abbreviated forms of publication names are used for both parenthetical and nonparenthetical usages.

A

Accounts . . . . Accts.
Administrative Office of
   the Courts . . . . AOC
Administration, administrative . . . . admin.
Advance . . . . adv.
Affirmed . . . . affd.
Affirmed by memorandum
   opinion . . . . affd. mem.
Affirmed *per curiam* . . . . . . affd. *per curiam*
Affirmed under the
   name of . . . . affd. *sub nom.*
Affirming . . . . affg.
Alabama . . . . Ala.
Alaska . . . . Alaska
Amendment . . . . amend.
American Annotated Cases . . . . . Ann. Cas.
American and English Annotated
   Cases . . . . Am. & Eng. Ann. Cas.
American Bar Association . . . . ABA
American Decisions . . . . Am.Dec.
American Jurisprudence . . . . Am.Jur.
American Jurisprudence
   Second Am.Jur.2d
American Law Institute . . . . ALI
American Law Reports . . . . A.L.R.
American Law Reports Digest,
   Second Series . . . . A.L.R.2d Dig.

American Law Reports,
   Federal Series . . . . A.L.R.Fed.
American Law Reports,
   Second Series A.L.R.2d
American Law Reports,
   Third Series A.L.R.3d
American Law Reports,
   Fourth Series A.L.R.4th
American Reports . . . . Am.R.
American State Reports . . . . Am.St.R.
And others . . . . et al.
And the following . . . . et seq.
Annotated, annotation . . . . . . ann., annot.
Annual . . . . ann.
Ante meridiem . . . . a.m.
Appeal dismissed . . . . app. dism.
Appeal pending . . . . app. pending
Appellate . . . . App.
Appendix . . . . appen.
April . . . . Apr.
Arbitration . . . . Arb.
Arizona . . . . Ariz.
Arkansas . . . . Ark.
Article, articles . . . . art., arts.
Assembly . . . . Assem.
Assembly Bill Number . . . . Assem. Bill No.

Assembly Concurrent Resolution
Number. . . . . . . Assem. Con. Res. No.
Assembly Constitutional Amendment
Number . . . Assem. Const. Amend. No.
Assembly Joint Resolution
Number. . . . . . . Assem. Joint Res. No.
Assembly Journal. . . . . Assem. J.
Assembly Resolution
Number . . . . Assem. Res. No.
Assistant . . . . Asst.
Association . . . . Assn.
Atlantic Reporter . . . . A.
Atlantic Reporter, Second Series. A.2d
At that place. . . . . op. cit.
At the same place . . . . loc. cit.
Attorney . . . . Atty.
Attorney General . . . . Atty. Gen.
Attorney General
Opinions . . . . Ops.Cal.Atty.Gen.
August. . . . . Aug.
Avenue . . . . Ave.

B

Ballot Pamphlet . . . . Ballot Pamp.
Basic Approved Jury
Instructions . . . . BAJI
Beverly Hills Bar
Journal . . . . Bev. Hills Bar J.
Board. . . . . Bd.
Boulevard . . . . Blvd.
Building . . . . bldg.
Bulletin . . . . Bull.
Bureau . . . . Bur.
Business and Professions
Code. . . . . Bus. & Prof. Code

C

California. . . . . Cal.
California Appellate Reports . . . . Cal.App.
California Appellate Reports,
Second Series Cal.App.2d
California Appellate Reports,
Third Series. Cal.App.3d
California Appellate Reports,
Fourth Series Cal.App.4th
California Appellate Reports
Supplement . . . . Cal.App.Supp.

California Appellate Reports
Supplement, Second
Series. . . . . Cal.App.2d Supp.
California Appellate Reports
Supplement, Third
Series. . . . . Cal.App.3d Supp.
California Appellate Reports Supplement,
Fourth Series . . . . . . Cal.App.4th Supp.
California Attorney General
Opinions . . . . Ops.Cal.Atty.Gen.
California Center for Judicial Education
and Research. . . . . CJER
California Code of Regulations
. . . . Cal. Code. Regs.
California Compensation
Cases. . . . . Cal.Comp.Cases
California Jurisprudence
Third. Cal.Jur.3d
California Jury Instructions,
Civil. . . . . BAJI
California Jury Instructions,
Criminal . . . . CALJIC
California Law Review. . . . . Cal.L.Rev.
California Law Revision
Commission
Report. . . Cal. Law Revision Com. Rep.
California Lawyer. . . . . Cal.Law.
California Public Utilities
Commission . . . . Cal.P.U.C.
California Regulatory Notice
Register . . . . . Cal. Reg. Notice Register
California Reporter . . . . Cal.Rptr.
California Reporter, Second
Series. Cal.Rptr.2d
California Reports . . . . Cal.
California Reports, Second
Series. Cal.2d
California Reports, Third
Series. Cal.3d
California Reports, Fourth
Series Cal.4th
California Rules of
Court . . . . Cal. Rules of Court
California State Bar. . . . . State Bar
California State Bar
Journal . . . . State Bar J.
California Uniform Commercial
Code . . . . Cal. U. Com. Code

California Unreported
   Cases . . . . Cal.Unrep.
California Western Law
   Review. . . . . Cal. Western L.Rev.
Certification, Certifying. . . . . Certif.
Certiorari. . . . . cert.
Certiorari denied. . . . . cert. den.
Certiorari granted . . . . cert. granted
Chapter, chapters . . . . ch., chs.
Chief Justice . . . . C. J.
Circuit . . . . Cir.
Civil Code . . . . Civ. Code
Clause. . . . . cl.
Clerk's transcript. . . . . C.T.
Code of Civil
   Procedure. . . . . Code Civ. Proc.
Code of Federal Regulations . . . . . . C.F.R.
Colorado . . . . Colo.
Column. . . . . col.
Comment, comments . . . . com., coms.
   [except where there is a potential for
   confusion]
Commercial Code . . . . Com. Code
Commission. . . . . Com.
   [except where there is a potential for
   confusion]
Commission on Judicial
   Performance. . . . . . . Com.Jud.Perform.
Commissioners. . . . . Comrs.
Committee. Com.
   [except where there is a potential for
   confusion]
Company . . . . Co.
Compare. . . . . cf.
Compensation . . . . Comp.
Concurring, concurrent. . . . . conc.
Conference, conflict. . . . . conf.
Congress. Cong.
Congressional Record. . . . . . . Cong. Rec.
Connecticut . . . . Conn.
Constitution . . . . Const.
Continuing Education of
   the Bar . . . . Cont.Ed.Bar.
Corporations Code . . . . Corp. Code
Corpus Juris. . . . . C.J.
Corpus Juris Secundum. . . . . C.J.S.
Court . . . . ct.

Court of Appeal . . . . Ct.App.
Criminal . . . . Crim.
Criminal Law Reporter . . . . . Crim.L.Rptr.
Cumulative Subsequent History
   Table . . . . Cum. Sub. Hist. Table

D

December . . . . Dec.
Decision . . . . Dec.
Deering's Advance Legislative Service
   . . . . Deering's Adv. Legis. Service
Deering's Water-Uncodified
   Acts . . . . . Deering's Wat.-Uncod. Acts
Delaware . . . . Del.
Denied. . . . . den.
Department . . . . Dept.
Department of Health, Education
   and Welfare . . . . HEW
Dictionary. Dict.
Digest. . . . . Dig.
Dismissed . . . . dism.
Dismissed per
   stipulation . . . . dism. per stip.
Dissenting. . . . . dis.
District . . . . Dist.
District of Columbia . . . . D.C.
Division . . . . Div.
Docket. . . . . Dock.
Doctor of Medicine. . . . . M.D.
Doctor of Philosophy . . . . Ph.D.
Document. Doc.

E

Ecology Law Quarterly . . . . . Ecology L.Q.
Edition. . . . . ed.
Editor . . . . edit.
Education Code. . . . . Ed. Code
Effective. . . . . eff.
Elections Code . . . . Elec. Code
English Reports . . . . Eng.Rep.
Et cetera . . . . etc.
Evidence Code . . . . Evid. Code
Executive Order . . . . Exec. Order
Ex relator . . . . ex rel.
Extra . . . . ex.
Extraordinary . . . . Ex.

F

Family . . . . Fam.
Family Code . . . . Fam. Code
February . . . . Feb.
Federal Reporter, Second Series F.2d
Federal Reporter, Third Series F.3d
Federal Rules Criminal
    Procedure. . . . . Fed. Rules Crim.Proc.
Federal Rules Decisions . . . . F.R.D.
Federal Rules of Appellate
    Procedure . . . . . . Fed. Rules App.Proc.
Federal Rules of Civil
    Procedure . . . . Fed. Rules Civ.Proc.
Federal Rules of
    Evidence . . . . Fed. Rules Evid.
Federal Supplement . . . . F.Supp.
Federal Supplement, Second
    Series. F.Supp.2d
Financial Code . . . . Fin. Code
First 1st
Fish and Game Code . . . . Fish & G. Code
Florida . . . . Fla.
Following. . . . . foll.
Food and Agricultural
    Code . . . . Food & Agr. Code
Footnote, footnotes . . . . fn., fns.
For example . . . . e.g.

G

General . . . . Gen.
Georgia . . . . Ga.
Glendale Law Review . . . . Glendale L.Rev.
Government Code. . . . . Gov. Code
Government Printing Office Style
    Manual . . . . GPO Manual

H

Harbors and Navigation
    Code . . . . Harb. & Nav. Code
Hastings Constitutional Law
    Quarterly . . . . Hastings Const.L.Q.
Hastings Law Journal . . . . . . Hastings L.J.
Health and Safety
    Code. . . . . Health & Saf. Code
History . . . . Hist.
Honorable . . . . Hon.

House Bill Number. . . . . H.R. No.
House Concurrent Resolution
    Number . . . . H.Con.Res. No.
House Joint Resolution
    Number . . . . H.J.Res. No.
House of Representatives . . . . H.R.
House of Representative
    Journal . . . . H.R.J.
House Resolution
    Number . . . . H.Res. No.
Housing Authority . . . . Housing Auth.

I

Idaho . . . . Idaho
Illinois . . . . Ill.
Illustration . . . . illus.
Immigration . . . . Immig.
Improvidently . . . . improv.
Incorporated. . . . . Inc.
Indiana. . . . . Ind.
Industrial Accident Commission
    of California
    (decisions cite) . . . . I.A.C.
In propria persona . . . . in pro. per.
Institute, institutions . . . . Inst., Insts.
Instructions . . . . Instns.
Insurance Code. . . . . Ins. Code
Internal Revenue Code. . . . . Int.Rev. Code
International. . . . . Internat.
In the same place. . . . . *ibid.*

J

January. . . . . Jan.
Joint. . . . . J.
Journal. . . . . J.
Judge . . . . J.
Judgment . . . . judg.
Judicial. . . . . Jud.
Judicial Council of
    California . . . . Judicial Council of Cal.
Judicial Panel on Multidistrict
    Litigation . . . . J.P.M.L.
Junior . . . . Jr.
Jurisdiction . . . . jur.
Jurisdiction noted. . . . . jur. noted
Justice. . . . . J.

K

Kansas . . . . Kan.
Kentucky . . . . Ky.

L

Labor Code . . . . Lab. Code
Law Revision Commission Reports
. . . . Cal. Law Revision Com. Rep.
Lawyer . . . . Law.
Legislative . . . . Legis.
Legislature . . . . Leg.
Los Angeles . . . . L.A.
Louisiana . . . . La.
Loyola Consumer Protection
    Journal . . . . . Loyola Consumer Prot.J.
Loyola University of Los Angeles Law
    Review . . . . Loyola L.A. L.Rev.

M

Maine . . . . Me.
Majority . . . . maj.
March . . . . Mar.
Maryland . . . . Md.
Massachusetts . . . . Mass.
Memorandum . . . . mem.
Michigan . . . . Mich.
Military and Veterans
    Code . . . . Mil. & Vet. Code
Minimum . . . . min.
[except where there is a potential for
    confusion]
Minnesota . . . . Minn.
Minute, Minutes . . . . min., mins.
[except where there is a potential for
    confusion)
Mississippi . . . . Miss.
Missouri . . . . Mo.
Modified . . . . mod.
Montana . . . . Mont.
Municipal Court . . . . Mun. Ct.

N

Namely . . . . viz.
National, Nationality . . . . Nat.
Nebraska . . . . Neb.
Nevada . . . . Nev.
New Hampshire . . . . N.H.

New Jersey . . . . N.J.
New Mexico . . . . N.M.
New York . . . . N.Y.
New York Supplement . . . . N.Y.S.
New York Supplement, Second
    Series N.Y.S.2d
Nonpublished . . . . nonpub.
North Carolina . . . . N.C.
North Dakota . . . . N.D.
North Eastern Reporter . . . . N.E.
North Eastern Reporter, Second
    Series N.E.2d
North Western Reporter . . . . N.W.
North Western Reporter, Second
    Series N.W.2d
November . . . . Nov.
Number, numbers . . . . No., Nos.

O

October . . . . Oct.
Office . . . . off.
Official . . . . Off.
Ohio . . . . Ohio
Oklahoma . . . . Okla.
Opinion, opinions . . . . opn., opns.
Opinions of Legislative
    Counsel . . . . Ops.Cal.Legis.Counsel
Opinions of the Attorney
    General . . . . Ops.Cal.Atty.Gen.
Oregon . . . . Or.
Ordinance . . . . Ord.

P

Pacific Law Journal . . . . Pacific L.J.
Pacific Reporter . . . . P.
Pacific Reporter, Second Series P.2d
Page, pages . . . . p., pp.
Pamphlet . . . . pamp.
Paragraph . . . . ¶ or par.
Part, parts . . . . pt., pts.
Partially published . . . . par. pub.
Penal Code . . . . Pen. Code
Pennsylvania . . . . Pa.
Pepperdine Law
    Review . . . . Pepperdine L.Rev.
Petition . . . . petn.
Plurality . . . . plur.
Political Code . . . . Pol. Code

Post meridiem . . . . p.m.
Practice . . . . Prac.
President . . . . Pres.
Presidential Proclamation . . . . . Pres.Proc.
Presiding Justice . . . . P. J.
Probable Jurisdiction
   noted . . . . prob. jur. noted
Probate Code . . . . Prob. Code
Professional . . . . Prof.
Proposition . . . . Prop.
Propria person . . . . pro. per.
Public Contract
   Code . . . . Pub. Contract Code
Procedure . . . . Proc.
Public Law . . . . Pub.L.
Public Resources
   Code . . . . Pub. Resources Code
Public Utilities Code . . . . . Pub. Util. Code
Public Utilities Commission . . . . . . P.U.C.
Published . . . . pub.
Puerto Rico . . . . P.R.

Q

Quarterly . . . . Q.

R

Railway . . . . Ry.
Regular Session . . . . Reg. Sess.
Regulating, Regulation,
   Regulatory, Regulations . . . . Reg., Regs.
Rehearing . . . . rehg.
Rehearing denied . . . . rehg. den.
Rehearing granted . . . . rehg. granted
Report . . . . Rep.
Reporter . . . . Rptr.
Reporter's Transcript . . . . R.T.
Resolution . . . . Res.
Restatement . . . . Rest.
Retransferred . . . . retrans.
Revenue and Taxation
   Code . . . . Rev. & Tax. Code
Reversed . . . . revd.
Reversed *per curiam* . . . . . revd. *per curiam*
Reversing . . . . revg.
Review [law reviews] . . . . Rev.
Review denied . . . . review den.
Review granted . . . . review granted
Revised . . . . rev.

Revised edition . . . . rev. ed.
Rhode Island . . . . R.I.
Rules . . [see applicable section for specific
   rules]
Ruling Case Law . . . . R.C.L.

S

Sacramento . . . . Sac.
Same . . . . *id.*
San Diego Law
   Review . . . . San Diego L.Rev.
San Francisco . . . . S.F.
Santa Clara Law
   Review . . . . Santa Clara L.Rev.
Santa Clara Lawyer . . . . . Santa Clara Law.
Second 2d
Secretary . . . . Sect.
Section, sections . . . . . . §, §§ or sec., secs.
Senate . . . . Sen.
Senate Bill Number
   [Cal.] . . . . Sen. Bill No.
Senate Bill Number [Fed.] . . . . . . Sen. No.
Senate Concurrent Resolution
   Number [Cal.] . . . . Sen. Con. Res. No.
Senate Concurrent Resolution Number
   [Fed.] . . . . Sen. Con. Res. No.
Senate Constitutional Amendment
   Number
   [Cal.] . . . . Sen. Const. Amend. No.
Senate Constitutional Amendment
   Number
   [Fed.] . . . . Sen. Const. Amend. No.
Senate Joint Resolution
   Number [Cal.] . . . . . Sen. Joint Res. No.
Senate Joint Resolution
   Number [Fed.] . . . . Sen.J.Res. No.
Senate Journal . . . . Sen. J.
Senate Resolution
   Number [Cal.] . . . . Sen. Res. No.
Senate Resolution
   Number [Fed.] . . . . Sen.Res. No.
Senator . . . . Sen.
Senior . . . . Sr.
September . . . . Sept.
Series . . . . ser.
Session . . . . Sess.
Social Security . . . . Soc. Sec.
South Carolina . . . . S.C.

T

U

V

W

—Notes—

—Notes—

CASE AUTHORITY

B. CALIFORNIA OPINIONS
1. Basic citation styles

2. Effect of California publication rules

A. GENERAL RULES OF CITATION

§ 1:1   Initial references; full citations

[A] Running heads or equivalents

Case citations begin with the opinion title. Follow exactly the shortened title used in the running head of a paper-based reporter or a shortened title shown in a computer-based source. When a running head title, or the computer version equivalent, is not available, exercise discretion in shortening the title while providing sufficient information to identify the opinion. When even a shortened title is unwieldy, an abbreviated form (a short cite) may be used for subsequent references (see [C], below).

[B] Italics for opinion titles

Italicize the opinion title in its entirety, including the "v." and, where relevant, the designation "ex rel." References to trial court and administrative adjudicatory matters should be similarly italicized.

> (*People v. Barton* (1995) 12 Cal.4th 186 [47 Cal.Rptr.2d 569, 906 P.2d 531].)
>
> (*In re Marriage of Gowan* (1997) 54 Cal.App.4th 80 [62 Cal.Rptr. 453].)
>
> in *Adoption of Chad T.* (1995) 39 Cal.App.4th 1107 [46 Cal.Rptr.2d 147], . . .
>
> *Traverso v. People ex rel. Dept. of Transportation* (1996) 46 Cal.App.4th 1197

[C] Short cites; multiple opinions with identical titles

If an opinion title that will be cited often in the document is unwieldy, a shortened form of the case name (a short cite) may be adopted for subsequent references. Although not required to use shortened case names, the author may specifically adopt a shortened form (i.e., by enclosing the shortened form in parentheses immediately after the initial cite), which is then used for all subsequent references to that opinion.

> (*Zamudio v. State of California* (1998) 62 Cal.App.4th 673 [73 Cal.Rptr.2d 79] (hereafter *Zamudio*).) . . . But as the court noted in *Zamudio, supra,* 62 Cal.App.4th at page 677, . . .
>
> The provisions of an insurance policy must be considered in their full context. *(E.g., Waller v. Truck Ins. Exchange, Inc.* (1995) 11 Cal.4th 1, 18–19 [44 Cal.Rptr.2d 370] *(Waller).)* . . . Plaintiffs rely on *Waller, supra,* 11 Cal.4th at page 23, for reversal.

When citing different opinions with identical running heads, insert the last names of real parties in interest (if any) in parentheses to distinguish the cases. When the opinions do not have designated real parties in interest, adopt a short cite incorporating roman numerals to distinguish the two opinions.

> *Los Angeles County Dept. of Children etc. Services v. Superior Court (Charles S.)* (1997) 60 Cal.App.4th 1088 [70 Cal.Rptr.2d 658] and *Los Angeles County Dept. of Children etc. Services v. Superior Court (Shawn B.)* (1996) 51 Cal.App.4th 1257 [59 Cal.Rptr.2d 613] both illustrate . . . .
>
> Appellant relies on *State Compensation Ins. Fund v. Workers' Comp. Appeals Bd. (Brown)* (1982) 130 Cal.App.3d 933 [182 Cal.Rptr. 171] and *State Compensation Ins. Fund v. Workers' Comp. Appeals Bd. (McDowell)* (1977) 76 Cal.App.3d 136 [142 Cal.Rptr. 654].
>
> *(People v. Superior Court (Alvarez)* (1997) 14 Cal.4th 968 [60 Cal.Rptr.2d 93, 928 P.2d 1171].)
>
> *(People v. Superior Court (Romero)* (1996) 13 Cal.4th 497 [53 Cal.Rptr.2d 789, 917 P.2d 628].)
>
> Nevertheless, under the approach of the United States District Court in *Fireman's Fund Ins. Companies v. Ex-Cell-O Corp.* (E.D.Mich. 1992) 790 F.Supp. 1318, 1338 (hereafter *Ex-Cell-O I*), and *Fireman's Fund Ins. Companies v. Ex-Cell-O Corp.* (E.D.Mich. 1992) 790 F.Supp. 1339, 1346 (hereafter *Ex-Cell-O II*) . . . .

[D] Court and date parenthetical

The first time an opinion is cited in full, indicate the year of filing in parentheses immediately following the title. If the court and jurisdiction are not discernible from the citation to the reporter (see [E], below), include the court abbreviation within the parenthetical, before the date. For recently filed opinions for which no reporter citation is available, add the full date and docket number to the parenthetical.

For citing the opinions of other states, see sections 1:28–1:31; for citing recently filed opinions, see sections 1:3, 1:18.

> *People v. Marshall* (1997) 15 Cal.4th 1
> *California v. Romero* (1983) 463 U.S. 992
> *Spurgeon v. Mission State Bank* (8th Cir. 1945) 151 F.2d 702
> *McInnis v. Shapiro* (N.D.Ill. 1968) 293 F.Supp. 327
> *Gressler v. New York Life Ins. Co.* (Utah 1945) 163 P.2d 324
> *English v. State* (Okla.Crim.App. 1969) 462 P.2d 275
> *Bridges v. Robinson* (1959) 24 Cal.Comp.Cases 59
> the recent United States Supreme Court decision in *Kansas v. Hendricks* (June 23, 1997, No. 95-1649) ___ U.S. ___ [65 U.S.L. Week 4564, 1997 WL 338555].

[E] Volume and page numbers

After the court and date parenthetical, complete the citation with a reference to the opinion's location in the relevant reporter. Provide the volume number, reporter abbreviation, and the page number on which the opinion begins. When referring to an opinion as a whole, give the inception page of the case. If discussing or quoting from the opinion, give the inception page *and* the page or pages on which cited material appears (i.e., the point page). If no paper-based reporter citation is available, a citation to a computer version is sufficient (e.g., a Westlaw or Lexis citation). If neither a paper-based nor a computer-based citation is available, see sections 1:3, 1:18, and 1:34[A].

> in *Sheldon Appel Co. v. Albert & Oliker* (1989) 47 Cal.3d 336, 876, . . .
> *Packard v. P.T.&T. Co.* (1970) 71 Cal. P.U.C. 469

[F] Parallel citations

Depending on the jurisdiction, an opinion may appear in multiple paper-based reporters and computer-based sources. Parallel citations are citations to alternate sources for an opinion. Parallel citations follow an official or primary citation and are always enclosed in brackets. Opinion authors are not required to provide parallel citations in opinions; parallel citations are added during editorial preparation of the opinion for Official Reports publication. In some circumstances (e.g., recently filed United States Supreme Court opinions), parallel citations will be available before the official citation (see §§ 1:3, 1:32[B]). In this situation, use the parallel citation throughout, including for point page references.

> (*O'Connor v. Ortega* (1987) 480 U.S. 709 [107 S.Ct. 1492, 94 L.Ed.2d 714].)
> and in *People v. Mayfield* (1997) 14 Cal.4th 668 [60 Cal.Rptr.2d 1, 928 P.2d 485], . . .
> (*Neder v. United States* (1999) ___ U.S. ___ [119 S.Ct. 1827, 1831, 144 L.Ed.2d 35].)

§ 1:2   Subsequent references

[A] In general

After an opinion is first cited in a document, it is not cited in full again. Later references to that opinion use abbreviated citation forms to save space, facilitate the flow and readability of text, and signal that the opinion has been previously introduced.

[B] Subsequent references in different paragraph

Once an opinion is cited in full, the first reference in any subsequent paragraph must include the case name, *supra* (to signal a prior full cite and the omission of some elements of that citation), the reporter, and the volume and page numbers. If the first subsequent reference is to a point page within the opinion, either provide the inception page for the opinion followed by the point page, or use "at page" (or "at p." in parentheses) without the inception page. Some authors prefer mixing the "at page" and inception/point page styles within a lengthy document to periodically provide the inception page throughout.

> (*Silacci v. Abramson, supra,* 45 Cal.App.4th 558.)
> (*Silacci v. Abramson, supra,* 45 Cal.App.4th 558, 562.)
> (*Silacci v. Abramson, supra,* 45 Cal.App.4th at p. 562.)
> *Nasongkhla v. Gonzalez, supra,* 29 Cal.App.4th Supp. 1.
> (*Nasongkhla v. Gonzalez, supra,* 29 Cal.App.4th at pp. Supp. 3–4.)

[C] Subsequent references in same paragraph

To repeat an identical citation to an opinion within the same paragraph, *ibid.* may be used when no intervening authority is cited. To repeat a citation to an opinion with a different point page, *id.* may be used. *Ibid.* and *id.* are used only to refer to the *immediately preceding* citation in the *same paragraph*. Citations within quoted passages do not constitute intervening authority. *Ibid.* and *id.* may not be used when the citation being referred to is one of two or more in a string citation. References within footnotes are styled as references in different paragraphs (see [B], above), not as references in the same text paragraph.

> The conduct of the plaintiff in *Khawar v. Globe Internat., Inc.* (1998) 19 Cal.4th 254, 267 [79 Cal.Rptr. 178] did not make him a public figure. His role in the underlying controversy was "trivial at best." (*Ibid.*)
> The California Supreme Court declined to characterize the plaintiff as a public figure in *Khawar v. Globe Internat., Inc.* (1998)19 Cal.4th 254, 267 [79 Cal.Rptr. 178]. The court also declined to adopt a neutral reportage privilege in that case. (*Id.* at p. 273.)
> (*People v. Flood, supra,* 18 Cal.4th 470, 504–507; *id.* at pp. 548, 550–554 (dis. opn. of Kennard, J.).)

To repeat a case citation in the same paragraph when there is intervening authority, *supra* may be used to signal that the case was cited in full earlier and elements of the full citation have been omitted. A shortened case name followed by a point page reference is also sufficient for second and subsequent references within the same paragraph, whether or not there is intervening authority. Provided no other cases are cited in that paragraph, a subsequent reference may be limited to a volume and point page citation without the case name.

> Burglary is not committed by placing a stolen check in a bank's window chute, based on the court's decision in *People v. Davis* (1998) 18

> Cal.4th 712, 724 (disapproving *People v. Ravenscroft* (1988) 198 Cal.App.3d 639). However, burglary "may be committed by using an instrument to enter a building." (*People v. Davis, supra,* at p. 717.)
> A penalty provision is separate from the underlying offense. (*People v. Wolcott* (1992) 10 Cal.App.4th 1584, 1596–1598; *People v. Bryant* (1983) 34 Cal.3d 92, 101.) The jury does not consider the penalty allegation until it first reaches a verdict on the substantive offense. (*Bryant,* at p. 101.)
> (*Cheong v. Antablin, supra,* at p. 1069.)
> (16 Cal.4th at p. 1069.)
> (*Cheong,* at p. 1069.)

§ 1:3   Citing recently filed opinions; computer-based sources

Many opinions are available very shortly after filing through various computer-based sources, including Westlaw, Lexis, and the Internet. Paper-based versions of opinions are published by California legal newspapers within a day or two of filing. Within a few weeks of filing, officially published opinions, or opinions otherwise designated for inclusion in a paper-based reporter, will generally be available, with editorial enhancements and a permanent volume and page citation, in advance pamphlets for the particular reporter. The rest remain generally available only through computer-based sources.

Use volume and page citations to a paper-based reporter if available. In the interim, and for opinions available only through computer-based sources, follow the styles provided in this section. After the opinion title (see § 1:1[A]), provide the full date and docket number in parentheses. Court and jurisdiction information (see § 1:1[D]) must be provided before the date within the parentheses, unless leaving blanks for the volume and pages on either side of a reporter designation will signal the court and jurisdiction. Do not, however, use blanks with a reporter designation unless it is certain that the opinion will be published therein. Providing docket numbers aids in locating opinions across a broad range of computer-based sources. It is helpful, but not necessary, to provide a citation to the San Francisco Recorder's California Daily Opinion Service (C.D.O.S.), the Los Angeles and San Francisco Daily Journal's Daily Appellate Report (D.A.R.), Westlaw, Lexis, or a similar source (e.g., the Internet URL).

> (*Knowles v. Iowa* (Dec. 8, 1998, No. 97-7597) ___U.S.___ [1998 D.A.R. 12417].)
> (*Knowles v. Iowa* (Dec. 8, 1998, No. 97-7597) ___U.S.___ [1998 C.D.O.S. 8954].)
> (*Knowles v. Iowa* (Dec. 8, 1998, No. 97-7597) ___U.S.___ [1998 WL 840933].)

(*Knowles v. Iowa* (Dec. 8, 1998, No. 97-7597) ___U.S.___
 <http://www.supct.law.cornell.edu/supct>.)

Kansas v. Hendricks (June 23, 1997, No. 95-1649) ___ U.S. ___ [1997 WL
 338555]

(*Process Gas Consumers Group v. Federal Energy Regulatory Commission*
 (D.C. Cir., Oct. 23, 1998, No. 93-1405) ___ F.3d ___ [1998 WL
 735869].)

(*Process Gas Consumers Group v. Federal Energy Regulatory Commission*
 (D.C. Cir., Oct. 23, 1998, No. 93-1405) ___ F.3d ___
 <http://www.ll.georgetown.edu/Fed-Ct/cadc.html>.)

(*Craft v. Campbell Soup* (9th Cir., Dec. 2, 1998, No. 98-15060) ___F.3d
 ___ [1998 WL 828105].)

(*Ghana v. Pierce* (9th Cir., Nov. 5, 1998, No. 97-35588) 1998 WL
 790346.)

(*Washington Metropolitan Transit Authority v. One Parcel of Land* (D.Md.,
 Nov. 23, 1993, Civ. A. No. HAR-88-618) 1993 U.S.Dist. Lexis 18485.)

(*Banks v. Jockey International, Inc.* (N.D. Miss., Mar. 9, 1998, No.
 4:96CV253-S-B) ___ F.Supp. ___ [1998 WL 102752].)

(*Roe v. Kidder Peabody & Co., Inc.* (S.D.N.Y., Apr. 18, 1990, No. 88 Civ.
 8507) 1990 WL 52200.)

(*Roe v. Kidder Peabody & Co., Inc.* (S.D.N.Y., Apr. 9, 1990, No. 88 Civ.
 8507) 1990 U.S. Dist. Lexis 4536.)

(*Macklin v. Retirement Plan for Employees of Kansas Gas and Electric* (U.S.
 Dist. Ct., D.Kan., Nov. 13, 1995, Civ. A. No. 94-2402-GTV) 1995 WL
 708418.)

Shuster v. Lyons (Conn.Super.Ct., Aug. 7, 1997, No. CV9100363025) 1997
 WL 472419

State v. Higgs (Ohio Ct.App., Jan. 12, 1990, No. WD-89-6) 1990 WL 1351

Jones v. State (Tex.App., Nov. 29, 1995, No. 04-95-00334-CR) 1995 WL
 699987

For citing recently filed California opinions, see section 1:18; for administrative agency decisions, see section 1:22; for opinions from other states, see sections 1:28–1:31; for federal opinions, see sections 1:32–1:35.

§ 1:4 Introductory signals: see; cf.; compare with; accord

Introductory signals precede the citation and provide information about the nature and strength of the cited authority. The signal applies to all the cited authorities that it introduces, until another signal appears or the group of citations ends.

When a case is cited as the source of a quotation, or when a case directly supports the proposition stated in the text, no introductory signal is appropriate. Citations to weaker support, however, should be introduced by the word "see." Thus, "see" should precede citations to cases that only indirectly support the text, citations to supporting dicta, and citations to a concurring or dissenting opinion. Never use "see" to support a direct quote. In the latter instances, insert an explanatory parenthetical note indicating "dicta," "conc. opn.," or "dis. opn." (see § 1:10). Secondary authority may be introduced by "see," but need not be.

"See also" may be used to indicate *additional* authority that indirectly supports the proposition. "See generally" introduces helpful background authority. "E.g.," (Latin: *exempli gratia*, meaning "for example") or "see, e.g.," may be used to introduce opinions cited as examples of the stated proposition's application.

The signal "cf." (Latin: *confer*, meaning "compare with") is used to introduce a decision that is sufficiently analogous to lend support to the proposition, as where a cited case applies a similar statute. The word "accord" is a signal used after a primary authority has been cited, and introduces decisions, including those from other jurisdictions, holding squarely in accord. "Accord" is also used when the author wishes to *quote* from one opinion and then cite other supporting authorities.

To contrast decisions, use the form "Compare . . . with . . . ." To cite cases squarely to the contrary of the proposition stated, or the primary authority cited, use the term "contra." "But see" may be used to indicate a holding or dictum that is somewhat contrary to, or inconsistent with, the main authority.

> (*Bennett v. Spear* (1997) 520 U.S. 154.)
> (See *Bennett v. Spear* (1997) 520 U.S. 154, 162.)
> (See *Bennett v. Spear* (1997) 520 U.S. 154,165 [dicta].)
> (See *Chandler v. Miller* (1997) 520 U.S. 305, 323 (dis. opn. of Rehnquist, J.).)
> (See also *Chandler v. Miller* (1997) 520 U.S. 305.)
> (See generally *Chandler v. Miller* (1997) 520 U.S. 305.)
> (See, e.g., *Chandler v. Miller* (1997) 520 U.S. 305.)
> (Cf. *Bennett v. Spear* (1997) 520 U.S. 154, 166.)
> (Compare *Bennett v. Spear* (1997) 520 U.S. 154 with *Chandler v. Miller* (1997) 520 U.S. 305.)
> (Accord, *Bennett v. Spear* (1997) 520 U.S. 154, 166.)
> (Contra, *Bennett v. Spear* (1997) 520 U.S. 154, 166.)
> (But see *Bennett v. Spear* (1997) 520 U.S. 154, 166.)

§ 1:5   Order of cited authority

[A] General rules

The order of cited opinions is not governed by rigid rules. Citation sequence is arranged to best support the proposition stated, generally with the most pertinent case or cases cited first. Customarily, cases are cited in the following order: first, cases that directly support the proposition stated;

second, cases that indirectly support it; third, cases with dicta in accord; fourth, cases that are analogous; fifth, cases with contrary holdings; and last, cases with contrary dicta. When *quoting* from an opinion, always list that opinion first, and include the page number on which the quoted matter appears. If additional opinions that indirectly support the quoted matter follow, they should be preceded with the signal "see also." For the sequence of multiple opinions within any of these categories, see [D], below.

[B] Type of authority

Constitutional and statutory citations generally are given priority over case citations. When a constitutional provision or statute is cited together with cases construing it, the statutory cite should precede the cases. References to secondary authorities should follow citations of constitutions, statutes, and cases.

[C] Date

Cite decisions of the same court in reverse chronological order, with the most recent opinions first. Generally, all panels of a court sit as one court. For example, several Ninth Circuit Court of Appeals opinions would be cited in reverse chronological order, regardless of which panels issued the opinions.

[D] Level of court; federal and out-of-state courts

United States Supreme Court case citations precede all others; California cases generally precede those of other jurisdictions, and California Supreme Court cases precede Court of Appeal cases. Federal cases (except for the United States Supreme Court) come next, followed by citations from other states, in alphabetical order by state. Decisions of the highest court of a jurisdiction should precede those of the lower courts, regardless of the dates of the cases.

§ 1:6 Parenthetical description of case

If helpful, the relationship of a cited opinion to the text discussion can be illuminated by a *short* parenthetical description after the citation. Use parentheses when the citation is part of the main text; use brackets if the citation is within parentheses. The parenthetical comment may describe the holding or facts, or may quote from the opinion. Keep the comment or quote brief for maximum effectiveness. A brief parenthetical generally does not commence with a capital letter unless otherwise required, nor does it conclude with punctuation. Parenthetical comments or quotes that are full sentences or multiple sentences are disfavored. If used, they may commence with or without a capital letter and should conclude without sentence-ending punctuation. Consistent treatment throughout the document is, however, paramount.

> and this conclusion is supported by *People v. Beach* (1983) 147 Cal.App.3d 612 [195 Cal.Rptr. 381] (relocation away from home community as unreasonable condition of probation).
>
> (See *Martin v. Dentfield School Dist.* (1983) 35 Cal.3d 294 [197 Cal.Rptr. 570, 673 P.2d 240] [employment rights of tenured school teacher on reappointment after emergency layoff].)
>
> (Cf. *Ghirardo v. Antonioli* (1996) 14 Cal.4th 39, 51 [57 Cal.Rptr.2d 687, 924 P.2d 996] ["A person is enriched when he receives a benefit at another's expense"].)

§ 1:7   Punctuation in series of citations

In the text, two or more opinions cited in a series may be separated either by commas or by semicolons. Within parentheses, citations should always be separated by semicolons.

> *Douglas v. California* (1963) 372 U.S. 353 [83 S.Ct. 814, 9 L.Ed.2d 811], *Gideon v. Wainwright* (1963) 372 U.S. 335 [83 S.Ct. 79, 29 L.Ed.2d 799], and *Hamilton v. Alabama* (1961) 368 U.S. 52 [82 S.Ct. 15, 77 L.Ed.2d 114] apply.
>
> (Civ. Code, §§ 1430, 1431, 1659, 1660; *Knight v. McMahon* (1994) 26 Cal.App.4th 747, 754, fn. 2 [31 Cal.Rptr.2d 832]; *Fried v. Municipal Court* (1949) 94 Cal.App.2d 376, 378 [210 P.2d 883]; 1 Witkin, Summary of Cal. Law (9th ed. 1987) Contracts, § 213, p. 222; see also 47 Am.Jur.2d (1995) Judgments, § 71, p. 185.)

When citing two opinions dealing with a single cause, separate the cites with a comma, not a semicolon, both in the text and in parentheses.

> (*Domar Electric, Inc. v. City of Los Angeles* (1994) 9 Cal.4th 161 [36 Cal.Rptr.2d 521, 885 P.2d 934], same cause (1995) 41 Cal.App.4th 810 [48 Cal.Rptr.2d 822].)

§ 1:8   Citation to footnote

To refer to a footnote, insert the page number, or numbers, on which it appears, then add "footnote" (or "fn." if cite is in parentheses) and the footnote number. To refer to a footnote *and* to the text it accompanies, use "and," or the ampersand if within parentheses.

> (*People v. Carpenter* (1997) 15 Cal.4th 312, 380, fn. 4 [63 Cal.Rptr. 2d 1, 935 P.2d 708].)

(*In re Kimberly F.* (1997) 56 Cal.App.4th 519, 529, fn. 14 [65 Cal.Rptr. 2d 495].)
(*Granberry v. Islay Investments* (1995) 9 Cal.4th 738, 750 & fn. 7 [38 Cal.Rptr.2d 650, 889 P.2d 970].)
in *Granberry, supra,* 9 Cal.4th at page 750 and footnote 7, the court considered . . . .

§ 1:9   Citation to appendix

To refer to material in an appendix, insert the page number where the material appears, then add "appendix" (or "appen." if in parentheses):

(*Legislature v. Reinecke* (1972) 6 Cal.3d 595, 604–605, appen.)

§ 1:10 Citation of lead, plurality, concurring, or dissenting opinion

When citing to an opinion that is not the majority opinion, identify it as such in parentheses after the cite, by adding "dis. opn.," "conc. opn.," "plur. opn.," "dis. & conc. opn.," or "lead opn." Always use parentheses, whether the cite itself is within parentheses or in the text. The opinion author's name is optional, but is usually included for minority opinions.

An opinion is characterized as a plurality opinion when it has more signatories than any other opinion supporting the judgment in the cause, but less than a majority. The term "lead" is used when there is no majority opinion and at least two other opinions in the cause have the same number of signatories. The lead opinion is the one designated by the court to state the court's judgment in the cause.

When a separate opinion is cited in its entirety, provide the inception pages for both the separate opinion and the opinion as a whole. If a point page citation is made to a separate opinion, omit the inception page of that opinion.

The result in *California Regents v. Bakke, supra,* 438 U.S. 265 at pages 319–320 (lead opn. of Powell, J.) suggests that . . . .
(*Price Waterhouse v. Hopkins* (1989) 490 U.S. 228, 240 [109 S.Ct. 1775, 1785, 104 L.Ed.2d 268] (plur. opn. of Brennan, J.).)
(See *Asgari v. City of Los Angeles* (1997) 15 Cal.4th 744, 762 [63 Cal.Rptr. 842, 937 P.2d 273] (dis. opn. of Mosk, J.).)
(See *People v. Harris* (1994) 9 Cal.4th 407, 455–456 [37 Cal.Rptr.2d 200, 886 P.2d 1193] (conc. & dis. opn. of Kennard, J.).)

To cite point pages in a majority opinion *and* a separate opinion in the same case, cite to the majority opinion first (either with or without "maj. opn. of ___" in parentheses), insert a semicolon, then use "*id.*" for the citation to the separate opinion.

(*Davis v. City of Berkeley, supra,* 51 Cal.3d at p. 243 (maj. opn. of
Kennard, J.); see *id.* at pp. 244–245 (dis. opn. of Mosk, J.).)

(*Ehrlich v. City of Culver City* (1996) 12 Cal.4th 854, 863 [50 Cal.Rptr.2d
242, 911 P.2d 429]; see *id.* at p. 912 (conc. & dis. opn. of Werdegar,
J.).)

(*Thing v. La Chusa, supra,* 48 Cal.3d at p. 651 (maj. opn.); see *id.* at p. 669
(conc. opn. of Kaufman, J.); *id.* at p. 682 (dis. opn. of Broussard, J.).)

§ 1:11   Noting subsequent history of cited case

[A] Citation styles

Citations should note an opinion's prior or subsequent history only
if it is significant on the point for which the opinion is cited. Citing a denial
of certiorari by the United States Supreme Court, or denial of a petition for
review by the California Supreme Court, to suggest *approval* by the higher
court is disfavored, particularly for denial of review by the California
Supreme Court. (See Advisory Com. com., Cal. Rules of Court, rule 28.)

The following examples emphasize different procedural aspects of a
cited case's subsequent history.

Grant or denial of review or certiorari

(*Employment Div., Ore. Dept. of Human Res. v. Smith* (1990) 494 U.S.
872, rehg. den. (1990) 496 U.S. 913 [110 S.Ct. 2605, 110 L.Ed.2d
285].)

(*Aydin Corp. v. First State Ins. Co.* (1998) 18 Cal.4th 1183 [77 Cal.Rptr.2d
537, 959 P.2d 1213], rehg. den. Oct. 14, 1998.)

(*Steiner v. Showboat Operating Co.* (9th Cir. 1994) 25 F.3d 1459, 1464,
cert. den. (1995) 513 U.S. 1082 [115 S.Ct. 733, 130 L.Ed.2d 636].)

(*Copeland v. MBNA America, N.A.* (Colo.Ct.App. 1994) 883 P.2d 564,
565–566, cert. granted (Colo. 1994) 883 P.2d 564.)

(*Lewis v. Sacramento County* (9th Cir. 1996) 98 F.3d 434, cert. granted
June 2, 1997, ___U.S. ___ [117 S.Ct. 2406, 138 L.Ed.2d 173].)

(*Harmon v. Thornburgh* (D.C. Cir. 1989) 878 F.2d 484, 489 [278 App.D.C.
382], cert. den. *sub nom. Bell v. Thornburgh* (1990) 493 U.S. 1056 [110
S.Ct. 865, 107 L.Ed.2d 949].)

(*Matter of Care and Treatment of Hendricks* (1996) 259 Kan. 246 [912
P.2d 129], cert. granted *sub nom. Kansas v. Hendricks* (1996) ___ U.S.
___ [116 S.Ct. 1540, 134 L.Ed.2d 643].)

(*Raulerson v. State* (Fla.Dist.Ct.App. 1997) 699 So.2d 339, review granted
Mar. 5, 1998, No. 91611, 709 So.2d 537 [table].)

Modification or subsequent opinion

(*American Economy Ins. Co. v. Reboans, Inc.* (N.D.Cal. 1994) 852 F.Supp.
875, sub. opn. (N.D.Cal. 1994) 900 F.Supp. 1246.)

(*Jones v. McKenzie* (D.C.Cir. 1987) 833 F.2d 335, 339 [266 App.D.C. 85],
opn. mod. 878 F.2d 1476, 1477.)

(*People v. Ramos* (1982) 30 Cal.3d 553, 575 [180 Cal.Rptr. 266, 639 P.2d
908], judg. vacated and cause remanded *sub nom. California v. Ramos*

(1983) 463 U.S. 992 [103 S.Ct. 3446, 77 L.Ed.2d 1171], sub. opn. *People v. Ramos* (1984) 37 Cal.3d 136 [207 Cal.Rptr. 800, 689 P.2d 430].)

Disapproval, vacation, or remand

(*People v. Gamez* (1991) 235 Cal.App.3d 957, 966–969 [286 Cal.Rptr. 894], disapproved on another ground in *People v. Gardeley* (1996) 14 Cal.4th 605, 624, fn. 10 [59 Cal.Rptr.2d 356, 927 P.2d 713].)

(*Resolution Trust Corp. v. Diamond* (2d Cir. 1994) 18 F.3d 111, 113, judg. vacated and cause remanded for further consideration in light of *O'Melveny & Meyers v. FDIC* (1994) 512 U.S. 79 [114 S.Ct. 2048, 129 L.Ed.2d 67].)

(*People v. Bacigalupo* (1991) 1 Cal.4th 103, 127 [2 Cal.Rptr.2d 335, 820 P.2d 559], judg. vacated and cause remanded (1992) 506 U.S. 802 [113 S.Ct. 32, 121 L.Ed.2d 5], reaffd. (1993) 6 Cal.4th 457 [24 Cal.Rptr.2d 808, 862 P.2d 808].)

Affirmance or reversal

(*U.S. v. Gaudin* (9th Cir. 1994) 28 F.3d 943, 951 (in bank), affd. (1995) 515 U.S. 506 [115 S.Ct. 2310, 132 L.Ed.2d 444].)

(*Smiley v. Citibank* (1995) 11 Cal.4th 138 [44 Cal.Rptr.2d 441, 900 P.2d 690], affd. (1996) 517 U.S. 735 [116 S.Ct. 1730, 135 L.Ed.2d 25].)

(*Melley v. Gillette Corp.* (1985) 19 Mass.App.Ct. 511 [475 N.E.2d 1227], affd. (1986) 397 Mass. 1004 [491 N.E.2d 252].)

(*American Home Prod. v. Liberty Mut. Ins. Co.* (S.D.N.Y. 1983) 565 F.Supp. 1485, affd. as mod. (2d Cir. 1984) 748 F.2d 760.)

(*Ashmus v. Calderon* (9th Cir. 1997) 123 F.3d 1199, revd. on jurisdictional grounds *sub nom. Calderon v. Ashmus* (1998) ___ U.S. ___ [118 S.Ct. 1694, 140 L.Ed.2d 970].)

(*Malone v. City of Silverhill* (Ala.Crim.App. 1989) 575 So.2d 101, revd. on other grounds (Ala. 1990) 575 So.2d 106.)

(*Texas Utilities Elec. v. Gold Kist* (Tex.Ct.App. 1991) 817 S.W.2d 749, revd. on other grounds (Tex. 1992) 830 S.W.2d 91.)

(*New Castle County v. Continental Cas. Co. (CNA)* (D.Del. 1989) 725 F.Supp. 800, affd. in part & revd. in part (3d Cir. 1991) 933 F.2d 1162.)

For citing subsequent and related history in California opinions, and the effect of the publication rules on citability, see sections 1:17, 1:25–1:27.

[B] Frequently used abbreviations for subsequent history

affirmed. . . . . affd.
affirmed by memorandum opinion. . . . . . . affd. mem.
affirmed under the name of . . . . affd. *sub nom.*
affirming . . . . affg.
appeal dismissed . . . . app. dism.
appeal pending . . . . app. pending
certiorari . . . . cert.
certiorari denied . . . . cert. den.

certiorari granted . . . . cert. granted
denied. . . . . den.
dismissed . . . . dism.
judgment . . . . judg.
modified . . . . mod.
opinion . . . . opn.
petition . . . . petn.
rehearing denied . . . . rehg. den.
rehearing granted . . . . rehg. granted
reversed. revd.
reversing . . . . revg.
review denied. . . . . review den.
review dismissed . . . . review dism.
review granted . . . . review granted
subsequent opinion. . . . . sub. opn.
under the name of . . . . *sub nom.*

B. CALIFORNIA OPINIONS

1. Basic citation styles

§ 1:12 Official Reports and parallel citations

California opinions are published in paper-based and computer-based versions of the Official Reports, which provide the most authoritative report of California opinions. Unofficial versions of California opinions are also available in the paper-based California Reporter, and Supreme Court opinions are included in the Pacific Reporter. Both the California Reporter and Pacific Reporter are parts of the National Reporter System. Computer-based versions of California opinions are available from multiple sources, including official versions on CD-ROM and Westlaw. Note that not all unofficial versions of California opinions contain clerical corrections to text or citational corrections and enhancements made during the Official Reports editing process.

In addition to providing citations to the Official Reports, the better practice is to also provide a parallel citation to one or both paper-based unofficial reporters. Opinions, however, are customarily filed without parallel citations, particularly for California opinions, but those citations are added as enhancements for Official Reports publication. The style used in the Official Reports is to provide the official citation followed by *all* parallel citations for the first reference to the case. Point pages for parallel citations are not provided unless the authoring justice's staff does so. Parallel citations are not included for subsequent references.

For parallel citations generally, see section 1:1[F].

§ 1:13 California Supreme Court opinions

California Reports, the official reporter for opinions of the California Supreme Court, is now in the fourth series. The series are cited as Cal.4th, Cal.3d, Cal.2d, and Cal.

> *People v. Superior Court (Romero)* (1996) 13 Cal.4th 497
> *People v. Noab* (1971) 5 Cal.3d 469
> *Linsk v. Linsk* (1969) 70 Cal.2d 272
> *Arnold v. Hopkins* (1928) 203 Cal. 553

The most widely used unofficial reporters for Supreme Court opinions are the California Reporter and Pacific Reporter. Give the parallel citation in brackets after the Official Reports citation.

> *Waller v. Truck Ins. Exchange Co.* (1995) 11 Cal.4th 1 [44 Cal.Rptr.2d 370, 900 P.2d 619]
> *Gray v. Zurich Insurance Co.* (1966) 65 Cal.2d 263 [54 Cal.Rptr. 104, 416 P.2d 801]

§ 1:14 California Court of Appeal opinions

California Appellate Reports, the official reporter for published opinions of the California Courts of Appeal, is now in its fourth series. The series are cited as Cal.App.4th, Cal.App.3d, Cal.App.2d, and Cal.App.

> *People v. White* (1995) 32 Cal.App.4th 638
> *Carlisle v. Kanaywer* (1972) 24 Cal.App.3d 587
> *Redsted v. Weiss* (1945) 71 Cal.App.2d 660
> *People v. Barbera* (1926) 78 Cal.App. 277

The most widely used unofficial reporter for Court of Appeal opinions is the California Reporter, which is now in its second series (Cal.Rptr.2d). Until 1960, the unofficial reporter for Court of Appeal opinions was the Pacific Reporter. Give the parallel citation in brackets after the Official Reports citation.

> *Estate of Anderson* (1997) 56 Cal.App.4th 235, 237 [65 Cal.Rptr.2d 307]
> (*People v. Brew* (1991) 2 Cal.App.4th 99 [2 Cal.Rptr.2d 851].)
> *Board of Supervisors v. Superior Court* (1989) 207 Cal.App.3d 552, 557 [254 Cal.Rptr. 905]
> *Dynamic Ind. Co. v. City of Long Beach* (1958) 159 Cal.App.2d 294, 298–299 [323 P.2d 768]

§ 1:15 Superior court appellate division opinions

The published opinions of superior court appellate divisions are reported in volumes of the California Appellate Reports, in a separate section, or "Supplement," after the Court of Appeal opinions. For an appellate division citation, always insert "Supp." before the page number. The unofficial California Reporter also publishes opinions of appellate divisions.

> *(People v. Trapane* (1991) 1 Cal.App.4th Supp. 10, 12.) . . . *(People v.*
> *Trapane, supra,* 1 Cal.App.4th at p. Supp. 13.)
> *People v. Foretich* (1970) 14 Cal.App.3d Supp. 6, 10
> *Helgeson v. Farmers Ins. Exchange* (1953) 116 Cal.App.2d Supp. 925
> *People v. Cardas* (1933) 137 Cal.App.Supp. 788

§ 1:16 Trial court case references

Titles of California trial court cases are italicized, including the "*v.*" In parentheses following the case title, provide court information, the year of judgment, and the docket number. If the text identifies the trial court, that information may be excluded from the citation.

> *(People v. Hood* (Super. Ct. Santa Cruz County, 1986, No. 1234).)
> *(Owens v. Harding* (Super. Ct. S.F. City and County, 1991, No. 5678).)
> *(Richards v. Davis* (Mun. Ct., Downey Judicial Dist., L.A. County, 1986, No.
> 1234).)
> *(People v. Green* (Super. Ct. Merced County, 1985, No. 543).)

§ 1:17 Cases pending on appeal; related subsequent history

[A] Citation styles

To note the procedural posture of a case pending but undecided in a California appellate court, include the docket number and other material information in the citation.

Caution: Rule 977 of the California Rules of Court prohibits citing or relying on superseded Court of Appeal opinions. The grant of review by the Supreme Court renders the Court of Appeal opinion superseded and makes it noncitable (see Cal. Rules of Court, rule 976; see also § 1:25). Merely noting that cases are pending in the Supreme Court, however, is generally not read as a violation of rule 977. To refer to such cases, provide the Official Reports volume and page designation for the Court of Appeal opinion.

If a Court of Appeal opinion is ordered published pending, or upon, disposition of review by the Supreme Court, any citation to the Court of Appeal opinion should include reference to the grant of review, the Supreme Court's publication order, and any subsequent action by the Supreme Court (see Cal. Rules of Court, rule 977(d)). Once the Supreme Court disposes of the review, the Court of Appeal opinion is no longer pending on appeal. Thereafter, the citation rules and styles for nonpublished opinions apply, unless the Supreme Court's disposition directs the opinion to be, or remain, published.

> An identical question is presently pending before our Supreme Court in
> *Jones v. Smith,* review granted June 10, 1998, S012345.

(*Smith v. Lewis,* review granted June 12, 1998, S012345.)
in *Fireman's Fund Ins. Co. v. Superior Court* (1997) 65 Cal.App.4th 1205, review granted December 23, 1997, S065447, ordered published August 10, 1998, review dismissed as improvidently granted October 14, 1998.
(*In re Marriage of Nguyen* (E012345, rehg. granted July 18, 1998).)
(*Chang v. Smith* (B012345, app. pending).)
(*Howard v. Flint* (A012345, app. pending, argued May 11, 1998).)
(*Grace v. Larsen* (1992) 100 Cal.App.4th 200, petn. for review pending, petn. filed June 1, 1998, time for grant or denial of review extended to Aug. 30, 1998.)
In re Allen (order to show cause issued Oct. 11, 1998, F012345).
People v. Birkett (1997) 54 Cal.App.4th 1438, review granted September 3, 1997, S062379.

In the following example, opinions identified by case names without citations were not published by the Court of Appeal; those with Official Reports citations were published until superseded by the Supreme Court's grant of review (see Cal. Rules of Court, rule 977):

> The California Supreme Court has granted review of several appellate decisions addressing this issue. (*People v. Allen,* review granted Oct. 29, 1997, S054125; *People v. Superior Court (Branham),* review granted Oct. 29, 1997, S063653; *People v. Gainey,* review granted Oct. 29, 1997, S064917; *People v. Rizo* (1998) 61 Cal.App.4th 573, review granted May 13, 1998, S068729; *People v. Maupin* (1998) 62 Cal.App.4th 290, review granted June 17, 1998, S069616.)

[B] Docket numbers

The docket numbers of California appellate cases are six-digit numbers preceded by a letter that indicates the appellate district. No distinction is made between civil and criminal cases. The Fourth Appellate District's divisions have separate letters, D, E, and G.

S123456	Supreme Court
A123456	First Appellate District (San Francisco)
B123456	Second Appellate District (Los Angeles)
C123456	Third Appellate District (Sacramento)
D123456	Fourth Appellate District, Division One (San Diego)
E123456	Fourth Appellate District, Division Two (Riverside)
G123456	Fourth Appellate District, Division Three (Santa Ana)
F123456	Fifth Appellate District (Fresno)
H123456	Sixth Appellate District (San Jose)

§ 1:18 Citing recently filed California opinions

Official Reports citations must be provided if available, but these citations may not be available for several weeks after an opinion is filed. As-filed versions of Supreme Court and published Court of Appeal opinions are generally first available to the public from the judicial branch's Internet Web site at <http://www.courtinfo.ca.gov/opinions>, and soon thereafter from various commercial sources. Pending availability of an Official Reports citation, follow the styles provided in this section. It is helpful, but not necessary, to provide a citation to the California Daily Opinion Service (C.D.O.S.), Daily Appellate Report (D.A.R.), Westlaw, Lexis, or a similar source (e.g., the Internet URL). For citing recently filed opinions generally, see section 1:3.

If necessary, shorten the opinion title (see § 1:1[A]). This is followed by a parenthetical for the date of filing and docket number. Leave blanks for volume and page designations for the appropriate reporter, i.e., Cal.4th or Cal.App.4th.

> *People v. Franklin* (May 3, 1999, S068112) ___ Cal.4th ___
> *(People v. Massie* (Nov. 30, 1998, S010775) ___Cal.4th___ [98 D.A.R. 12109].)
> *(Taggares v. Superior Court (Mitchell)* (Mar. 13, 1998, D027874) ___ Cal.App.4th ___ [98 C.D.O.S. 1878].)
> *(People v. Weiss* (Sept. 10, 1998, A078098) ___ Cal.App.4th ___ [1998 WL 598556].)
> *Smith v. Jones* (Mar. 17, 1998, A495005) ___ Cal.App.4th ___ [1998 Cal.App. Lexis 4567]
> *Silva v. Lucky Stores, Inc.* (June 29, 1998, F026156) ___ Cal.App.4th ___ <http://www.courtinfo.ca.gov/opinions>
> *Silva v. Lucky Stores, Inc.* (June 29, 1998, F026156) ___ Cal.App.4th ___ <http://www.callaw.com>

Where the citation involves a point page reference in addition to the inception page, a reference to the point page or pages is necessary to assist the reader in accurately identifying the material cited. The reference is made in brackets; providing page numbers only (see first example) signals reference to the pagination of the court's filed opinion, but the source of page references must otherwise be specified (see second and third examples).

> *(A v. B* (May 19, 1997, S012345) ___ Cal.4th ___ [pp. 8–12].)
> *(People v. Valentine* (Mar. 25, 1999, B119774) ___ Cal.App.4th ___ [99 D.A.R. 2801, 2802–2803].)
> *(See People v. Valentine, supra,* ___ Cal.App.4th ___ [99 D.A.R. 2801, 2802–2803].)

§ 1:19 Advance pamphlet citations

Opinions reported in the advance pamphlets of the Official Reports are subject to becoming superseded and noncitable. (See Cal. Rules of

Court, rules 976 & 977; see also §§ 1:25–1:27.) Before citing an advance pamphlet opinion, check the Cumulative Subsequent History Table in the back of the most recent advance pamphlet to ensure that a rehearing or modification was not ordered or that the Supreme Court did not grant review or expressly direct that the opinion should not be published. The unofficial California Reporter has a similar table. Commercial services (e.g., Westlaw and Lexis) may also be consulted to determine citability.

The Official Reports advance pamphlets carry the pagination that will appear in the later-published bound volumes. Thus, once an opinion appears in the advance pamphlet, that page and volume information can generally be used for the permanent citation. The advance pamphlet appellate division opinions are paginated differently from the Court of Appeal opinions; this pagination is noted on the front cover of the advance pamphlets. For citing appellate division opinions, see section 1:15.

§ 1:20 Citation to opinion modifications in advance pamphlets

If a court modifies an opinion after filing, the modification is incorporated into the initial advance pamphlet report of the opinion if there is time to do so. When a modification cannot be incorporated in the initial report, the modification order is published at the back of the next available advance pamphlet on "a," "b," "c," etc. pages. The modification is later incorporated into the bound volume report of the opinion. Pending the bound volume report of the opinion in this circumstance, the modification should be noted as follows:

> (*Rodney F. v. Karen M.* (1998) 61 Cal.App.4th 233 [72 Cal.Rptr.2d 399], mod. 61 Cal.App.4th 1311d.)

Sometimes, modifications add extensively to an opinion. If there was not time to incorporate the modification into the initial advance pamphlet report, and the opinion as modified will not fit into the original range of pages, the opinion is reprinted in its entirety, as modified, in a later pamphlet with a new citation. The initial opinion and citation are deleted; refer only to the subsequent citation in the later advance pamphlet. Modifications not incorporated in the initial advance pamphlet report are noted in the Cumulative Subsequent History Table that appears toward the end of each Official Reports advance pamphlet.

§ 1:21 California Unreported Cases and other early reports

Early opinions that were omitted from the Official Reports were subsequently published in a compilation called California Unreported Cases (Cal.Unrep.). Although characterized as "unreported," these opinions are not within the ambit of California Rules of Court, rule 977, and may be cited and relied on (see § 1:25).

Hughes v. Mendocino County (1884) 2 Cal.Unrep. 333

The form of citation for other early California reports is as follows:

Coffey's Probate Decisions: *Estate of Emeric* (1890) 5 Coffey's Prob. Dec. 286

Labatt's District Court Reports: *People v. Whithurst* (1858) 2 Labatt 178

Myrick's Probate Court Reports: *Estate of Hite* (1879) Myrick's Prob. Rep. 232

Also, be aware that there were two different printings of California Reports, first series, and the pagination differs very slightly between the original and Robert Desty's reprinted version. This can, in some instances, cause a variance in point pages, but not in the inception page. The computer versions of the Official Reports were derived from the original printing and pagination, and citations in published opinions are reconciled to the original printing during the Official Reports editing process.

§ 1:22 California administrative adjudications

[A] In general

Some California agencies issue official compilations of administrative decisions. Provide citations to official compilations if available. If no official compilation is available, cite to a topical reporter (i.e., ongoing compilations of opinions, administrative decisions, and other materials focused on selected areas of law, such as labor or tax law) or a computer-based source, if available. If citing to an official compilation, a topical reporter citation may also be provided as a parallel citation in brackets. A citation to a topical service should identify the agency unless it is otherwise clear from the title of the topical reporter.

Some state agencies make decisions available shortly after filing on the agency's Web site. Many agency decisions are also available very shortly after filing through other computer-based sources, including Westlaw and Lexis. A citation to computer-based material should include the names of the parties or the proceeding, the full date (month, day, year), the issuing agency, the docket or decision number, and the Internet URL or a Westlaw or Lexis cite (see § 1:3).

Follow the citation forms provided below for specific California agency decisions; for citing federal administrative decisions, see sections 1:35, 2:44, and 2:45; for regulatory reporters and services, see section 2:16; for topical reporters and services generally, see section 3:9.

[B] California workers' compensation cases

Opinions of the California Workers' Compensation Appeals Board are reported in California Compensation Cases (Cal.Comp.Cases); those of its predecessor, the Industrial Accident Commission of California (1911 to 1935) are reported in the Decisions of the Industrial Accident Commission (I.A.C.). Cite these decisions as follows:

> *Czarnecki v. Golden Eagle Insurance Company* (1998) 63 Cal.Comp.Cases 742
> *Rabin v. Metzger* (1934) 20 I.A.C. 20

For workers' compensation cases that do not appear in California Compensation Cases, cite to the unofficial California Workers' Compensation Reporter (Cal. Workers' Comp. Rptr.). Provide the title, year, docket number, volume and page.

> *Smith v. ESIS, Inc.* (1996) SBA 74576, 74580, 24 Cal. Workers' Comp. Rptr. 139
> *Waldman v. Safeway Stores, Inc.* (1983) OAK 85358, 11 Cal. Workers' Comp. Rptr. 201

[C] Taxation decisions

Cite opinions of the State Board of Equalization (SBE) and legal rulings of the California Franchise Tax Board to the California Tax Reporter (Commerce Clearing House). Include title, date, reporter abbreviation, publisher in parentheses, and paragraph number. The page number is optional.

> *(Appeal of Harvey* (1992) 5 SBE 57 [Cal. Tax Rptr. (CCH) ¶ 402-272].)
> *(Appeal of DPF, Inc.* (Oct. 28, 1980) [1978–1981 Transfer Binder] Cal.Tax Rptr. (CCH) ¶ 206-430, p. 14,965-36.)
> *(In re Appeal of Doric Foods Corporation* (Dec. 5, 1990) Cal.Tax Rptr. (CCH) ¶ 401-688.)
> (Cal. Franchise Tax Bd., Legal Ruling No. 402 (Jan. 27, 1977) [1971–1978 Transfer Binder] Cal.Tax Rptr. (CCH) ¶ 89-526, pp. 8624–8625.) [*Note: Title is not italicized for nonadjudicatory proceedings contained in orders, rulings, and notices.*]

[D] Public Utilities Commission decisions

The California Public Utilities Commission (Cal.P.U.C.) was originally called the California Railroad Commission (C.R.C.). Thus, volumes 1 through 46 of this commission's decisions are cited as C.R.C. Volume 47 and following are cited as Cal.P.U.C. and Cal.P.U.C.2d.

> *Matter of Truck Owners' Association* (1938) 41 C.R.C. 184
> *Packard v. P.T. & T. Co.* (1970) 71 Cal. P.U.C. 469, 471
> *SoCal Gas Co.* (1983) 10 Cal.P.U.C.2d 773, 785

Cal.P.U.C., Ruling No. 9812015 (Dec. 17, 1998)
<http://www.cpuc.ca.gov>
(*In re Pacific Gas and Electric Co.* (Cal.P.U.C., Apr. 22, 1999) No. A
95-10-024, 99-04-068 [1999 WL 589171].) [*Cite does not otherwise
show agency; agency name is therefore provided.*]
(*In re Pacific Gas and Electric Co.* (Cal.P.U.C., 1999) 194 Pub.Utl.Rep.4th
(West) 1.) [*Cite is to national topical service; agency name is therefore
provided.*]

The citation style for the commission's unpublished opinions
includes the name, the year, and a reference to the decision number.

Southern California Edison Co. (1983) Cal. P.U.C. Dec. No. 83-09-007

[E] Agricultural Labor Relations Board

Decisions of the Agricultural Labor Relations Board (ALRB) are
numbered serially each year. Because the bound volumes are not consecutively paginated, the point pages refer to the filed decision. Insert the name,
date in parentheses, the volume number and abbreviation, decision number, and any point page.

(*Gallo Vineyards, Inc.* (1995) 21 ALRB No. 3.)
(*Tepusquet Vineyards* (1984) 10 ALRB No. 29, pp. 7–8.)

[F] Public Employment Relations Board

Decisions of the Public Employment Relations Board (PERB) are
issued individually, then compiled in the unofficial Public Employee
Reporter for California (PERC), which, because of its wide distribution, is
used as a parallel citation. After the title, which is often the respondent's
name, insert the year, the PERB decision number, and a parallel cite to the
PERC volume and paragraph number where the decision appears, with any
point page number.

(*California State Employees Association (Carrillo)* (1997) PERB Dec. No.
1199-S [21 PERC ¶ 28099, p. 330].)
(*Redwoods Community College District* (1996) PERB Dec. No. 1141 [20
PERC ¶ 27048].)

[G] Fair Employment and Housing Commission

The decisions of the Fair Employment and Housing Commission
(FEHC) are published by California Continuing Education of the Bar. The
compilation is entitled FEHC Precedential Decisions and is made up of
two-year binders. The citation contains the case title, year, case number,
name of the compilation, years of the binder (noted on the spine), the
abbreviation CEB and the decision number, and any page number.

(*Dept. Fair Empl. & Hous. v. Silver Arrow Express* (Nov. 5,1997) No. 97-12, FEHC Precedential Decs. ____, CEB __, p. ___.) [*Style when citation to reporter is not yet known.*]

(*Dept. Fair Empl. & Hous. v. Madera County* (1990) No. 90-03, FEHC Precedential Decs. 1990–1991, CEB 1, p. 26.)

(*Dept. Fair Empl. & Hous. v. Davis Realty Co.* (1987) No. 87-02, FEHC Precedential Decs. 1986–1987, CEB 5, p. 1.)

§ 1:23 Attorney General opinions

Cite opinions of the Attorney General by volume, page, and year (not by opinion number). Note: the year is placed in parentheses *following* the page reference. Advance sheets carry the same pagination as the bound volume. Some opinions have titles, but not all do.

(80 Ops.Cal.Atty.Gen. 203 (1997).)
(*Revocation of Parole,* 66 Ops.Cal.Atty.Gen. 239, 240 (1983).)
(*Open Meeting Requirements,* 66 Ops.Cal.Atty.Gen. 252, 253 (1983).)

Cite opinions of the Attorney General, prior to publication in the advance sheets, using a full date, as follows:

(___ Ops.Cal.Atty.Gen. ___(Sept. 4, 1996).)
(*Issuing of Bench Warrant,* ___ Ops.Cal.Atty.Gen. ___, ___ (Sept. 4,1996) [filed opn. p. 4].)

Indexed advice letters to the Attorney General's clients are occasionally cited. After 1980, the Attorney General discontinued the indexed letter classification system, although many post-1980 letters are now published as Attorney General opinions and are so cited. The style for citation of pre-1980 letters is as follows:

(Cal. Atty. Gen., Indexed Letter, No. IL 76-133 (July 21, 1976).) [*Indexed letters are not italicized.*]

§ 1:24 State Bar Court opinions

Cite State Bar Court opinions as follows:

In the Matter of Layton (Review Dept. 1993) 2 Cal. State Bar Ct. Rptr. 366

2. Effect of California publication rules

§ 1:25 Overview

Citability of California appellate opinions is governed by California Rules of Court, rules 976, 976.1, and 977. Only published opinions, or the published portions of partially published opinions, may be cited or relied on by courts or parties. All opinions of the Supreme Court are published; Court of Appeal opinions are published if they are ordered published by the court rendering the opinion or by the Supreme Court. The Court of Appeal may order publication only while it has jurisdiction over the cause, which typically lapses 30 days after the opinion is filed. When the Court of Appeal orders publication, either at the time of filing or later, the term "certified for publication" is commonly used. Opinions are immediately citable if filed with certification for publication, or immediately upon the later filing of an order for publication. These requirements are similarly applicable to opinions of superior court appellate divisions.

Published opinions that become superseded are no longer citable. Opinions become superseded by an order for rehearing by the court rendering the opinion or by a grant of review by the Supreme Court. (Cal. Rules of Court, rules 976(d), 977(a).) In addition, the Supreme Court has plenary authority to order that opinions other than its own not be published. (Cal. Rules of Court, rules 976(c), 979.)

Conversely, the Supreme Court also has plenary authority to order opinions published at any time, including upon or after the grant of review, which otherwise renders an opinion superseded. (Cal. Rules of Court, rules 976(c) & (d), 977(d), 978.)

An opinion that is not considered published may be cited or relied on only when it is relevant under the law of the case, res judicata, or collateral estoppel, or when the opinion is relevant to a criminal or disciplinary proceeding because it states the reasons for a decision affecting the same party in another such proceeding. When citing an opinion pursuant to this exception, a copy of the opinion must be provided to the court and all parties. (Cal. Rules of Court, rule 977(b) & (c).)

Although California Rules of Court, rules 976, 976.1, and 977 do not affect citability of opinions from other jurisdictions, rule 977(c) does require that copies be provided to the court and all parties for cited opinions available only from a computer-based source (e.g., Westlaw, Lexis, or the Internet).

Because published appellate court opinions are, for up to six months or so after filing, particularly susceptible to becoming superseded or ordered not published by the Supreme Court, check for citability in the Cumulative Subsequent History Table in each Official Reports advance pamphlet or a similar source of subsequent history information.

§ 1:26   Citation styles for exceptions

[A] Nonpublished opinions

When it is appropriate to cite a nonpublished California appellate opinion under one of the exceptions stated in California Rules of Court, rule 977(b) (see § 1:25), provide the title and, in parentheses, the filing date and docket number. Unless the text notes that the opinion is nonpublished, parenthetically note that fact. Also use this style when it is appropriate to cite an opinion ordered not published by the Supreme Court following an initial certification for publication by the court filing the opinion. For an opinion ordered not published, do not provide the former Official Reports citation, and do not provide a citation to an unofficial reporter in which the opinion may remain reported. Providing the date and docket number for the Supreme Court's order to not publish the opinion is helpful, but it is not required.

> (*Jackson v. Kinney* (Jan. 20, 1997, A012345) [nonpub. opn.].)
> *Subsequent reference:* (*Jackson v. Kinney, supra,* A012345.)
> (*People v. Harrison* (Dec. 18, 1997) D024993, opn. ordered nonpub. Apr. 1, 1998.)
> (*Salazar v. Honig* (May 10, 1988, B026629) review den. and opn. ordered nonpub. Sept. 1, 1988, S006146.)
> we draw the operative facts, as did the Court of Appeal, from the complaint and from the record in an appeal (*Drever Partners, Inc. v. Stephenson* (Aug. 12, 1996, A071120, A071148) [nonpub. opn.]) in a related action.
> reversed the trial court's order in a nonpublished opinion. (*Garfield Medical Center v. Belshé* (Mar. 25, 1997, B093645).)

[B] Supreme Court's grant of review

Do not cite or rely on a Court of Appeal opinion that is the subject of a grant of review that is pending in the Supreme Court unless one of the exceptions stated in California Rules of Court, rule 977(b) applies, or the Supreme Court has expressly ordered the opinion published. The citation must include reference to the grant of review and any subsequent action by the Supreme Court. (Cal. Rules of Court, rules 976(d), 977; see also § 1:25.) After disposition of the review by the Supreme Court, absent an express publication order, a Court of Appeal opinion is considered unpublished. This is so even if the Supreme Court dismisses review as improvidently granted. A citation, if appropriate, follows the style for unpublished opinions, except that reference to the grant of review and subsequent action by the Supreme Court is made.

To permit tracking pending review, review granted Court of Appeal opinions remain available within the Official Reports in the Review Granted Opinions Pamphlets, which are issued twice yearly. The opinions also remain available, with appropriate notation, in computer versions of the Official Reports during the pendency of review. If citing a review granted opinion is appropriate, provide the citation from the initial reporting of the opinion (i.e., the citation in the Review Granted Opinions Pamphlet). Also include information as to the grant of review and any subsequent action by the

Supreme Court. If, on disposition of the review by the Supreme Court, an opinion is ordered published, or ordered to remain published, the opinion is re-reported in the Official Reports with explanatory history, and the original citation from the initial report of the opinion is superseded.

> (*Green v. Rodriguez* (1998) 56 Cal.App.4th 557 [65 Cal.Rptr.2d 679], review granted May 16, 1998, S012345.)
>
> (*Green v. Rodriguez* (1998) 56 Cal.App.4th 557 [65 Cal.Rptr.2d 679], review granted on specified issues May 16, 1998, S012345.)
>
> (. . . review granted on statute of frauds issue May 16, 1998, S012345, cause ordered at large on all issues June 13, 1998.)
>
> (. . . review granted May 16, 1998, S012345, argument limited to issue of novation of contract June 13, 1998.)
>
> (*People v. Sovereign* (1993) 27 Cal.App.4th 317 [20 Cal.Rptr.2d 413], review granted Sept. 16, 1993, S033934, opn. ordered pub. pending review Oct. 13, 1994.)
>
> (*Fireman's Fund Ins. Co. v. Superior Court* (1997) 65 Cal.App.4th 1205 [78 Cal.Rptr.2d 418], review granted Dec. 23, 1997, S065447, ordered pub. Aug. 12, 1998.)
>
> (*People v. Barillas* (1996) 45 Cal.App.4th 1233, 1239–1241 [53 Cal.Rptr.2d 418], review dism. as improvidently granted and opn. ordered pub. Oct. 24, 1996.)
>
> (*People v. Harbolt* (1997) 61 Cal.App.4th 123 [71 Cal.Rptr. 2d 459], review granted Oct. 15, 1997, S063658, opn. ordered par. pub. Feb. 11, 1998.)
>
> review was granted October 11, 1990, S016988, the opinion was ordered published December 11, 1991, and review was dismissed as improvidently granted on February 13, 1992, with directions that the opinion remain published.
>
> *Anderson v. Owens-Illinois, Inc.*, review granted Oct. 19, 1995, S047602, briefing deferred pursuant to rule 29.3, Cal. Rules of Court.)

§ 1:27 Conforming references to superseded opinions; Reporter's Notes

If an appellate court inadvertently cites an opinion that has been superseded under rule 976(d), California Rues of Court, or if a cited opinion becomes superseded after the court files its opinion, the court should, when possible, remedy the citation by modification or grant of rehearing. When modification or rehearing is not possible, a Reporter's Note is often employed to achieve conformity with rule 977's prohibition on citing superseded opinions. Reporter's Notes are also sometimes used to provide subsequent history information. Reporter's Notes are used only as expressly directed by the Reporter of Decisions Office.

> **Superseded by grant of rehearing**
> (*Smith v. Jones** (Cal.App.).)

---

*Reporter's Note: Rehearing granted June 1, 1997, A012345.

(*Smith v. Jones** (Cal.App.).)

---

*Reporter's Note: Rehearing granted June 1, 1997. For the subsequent opinion, see 300 Cal.App.4th 207 [350 Cal.Rptr.2d 482].

(*Smith v. Jones** (Cal.App.).)

---

*Reporter's Note: Rehearing granted June 1, 1997, A012345. The subsequent opinion was filed September 5, 1997, but was not certified for publication.

Superseded by Supreme Court order to not publish
(*Smith v. Jones** (Cal.App.).)

---

*Reporter's Note: Opinion A012345 deleted upon direction of Supreme Court by order dated June 1, 1997.

Superseded by Supreme Court grant of review
(*People v. Nelson** (Cal.App.).)

---

*Reporter's Note: Review granted on May 29, 1996, S053008. On September 2, 1998, the cause was transferred to Court of Appeal, Second Appellate District, Division Five, with directions. Opinion was filed January 7, 1999, not for publication.

*People v. Bierman** (Cal.App.)

---

*Reporter's Note: Review granted on November 12, 1997, S064007, and cause transferred to Court of Appeal, Second Appellate District, Division Seven, with directions.

Foster-Gardner, Inc. v. National Union Fire Ins. Co. * (Cal.App.)

---

*Reporter's Note: Review granted October 15, 1997, S063425. For Supreme Court opinion, see 18 Cal.4th 857 [77 Cal.Rptr.2d 107, 959 P.2d 265].

C. CASES FROM OTHER STATES

§ 1:28 Official reporters and regional reporters; universal citations

The opinions of other jurisdictions are usually available from several paper-based and computer-based sources. Provide the National Reporter System (e.g., Atlantic Reporter, North Western Reports, and New York Supplement) citation for opinions reported therein. A citation to a state's official reports, if any, may be provided, if available, for the initial citation, with the National Reporter System citation set forth in brackets as a parallel citation. For subsequent citations to that opinion, however, cite only to the National Reporter System. (As to citation styles in general for the opinions of other states, see §§ 1:29, 1:31.)

> *(Batavia Lodge No. 196 v. N.Y. State Div. of Human Rights* (1974) 35
> N.Y.2d 143 [359 N.Y.S.2d 25, 316 N.E.2d 318].) . . . *(Batavia Lodge No.
> 196 v. N.Y. State Div. of Human Rights, supra,* 316 N.E.2d at p. 320.)
> *(Roberts v. Automobile Club of Michigan* (1984) 138 Mich.App. 488 [360
> N.W.2d 224, 227–228].) . . . *(Roberts, supra,* 360 N.W.2d at p. 228.)
> *(Enlund v. Buske* (1971) 160 Conn. 327 [278 A.2d 815].)
> *Or: (Enlund v. Buske* (Conn. 1971) 278 A.2d 815.)
> *(Hawkins v. Kane* (1998) 7 Neb.Ct.App. 220 [582 N.W.2d 620].)
> *Or: (Hawkins v. Kane* (Neb.Ct.App. 1998) 582 N.W.2d 620.)
> *(Martin v. Allianz Life Ins. Co.,* 1998 N.D. 8 [573 N.W.2d 823].) *[Note: 8 is
> the opinion number under North Dakota's citation system, not a page
> number.]*
> *Or: (Martin v. Allianz Life Ins. Co.* (N.D. 1998) 573 N.W.2d 823.)
> *(McKibben v. Grigg,* 1998 N.D.App. 5, ¶ 18 [582 N.W.2d 669, 673].)
> *[Note: Instead of point page cites, paragraph numbers are used under
> North Dakota's citation system.]*
> *Or: (McKibben v. Grigg* (N.D.Ct.App. 1998) 582 N.W.2d 669, 673.)

The above examples for North Dakota reflect a universal citation, which is a style employed by courts in a few jurisdictions to provide a citation useful in both paper-based and computer-based reports of opinions. The universal citation consists of the year and sequentially assigned numbers for filed opinions within that year. Most universal citation styles also number the paragraphs of opinions to facilitate "pinpoint citation" by referring to numbered paragraphs.

§ 1:29 Citation styles

If available, defer to the running head title from the National Reporter System regional reporter, or the state's official reporter, if a citation to that reporter is being provided with the first citation (see § 1:28). Otherwise, shorten the opinion title (see § 1:1[A]) and italicize it in its entirety, including the "v." (see § 1:1[B]).

The title is followed by a parenthetical designating the state and year of filing (see § 1:1[D]). If the court is not the state's highest court, a court designation is added after the state. For lower court designations, use the standard abbreviations set forth in The Bluebook: A Uniform System of Citation (16th ed. 1996). If an official state reporter citation is included with the initial citation, however, the state designation is omitted. If the official state reporter designation clearly identifies the court, then the court designation is also omitted (see last example below). The citation is completed with the volume number, reporter designation, and page number(s).

> *(LSP Ass'n v. Town of Gilford* (N.H. 1997) 702 A.2d 795.)
> *(State v. Stouffer* (Ohio Ct.App. 1971) 276 N.E.2d 651.)
> *(State Department of Highways v. Johns* (Alaska 1967) 422 P.2d 855.)
> *(Mutual Finance Co. v. Martin* (Fla. 1953) 63 So.2d 649.)

(*Stewart v. Hechinger* (Md.Ct.App. 1997) 702 A.2d 946.)
(*English v. State* (Okla.Crim.App. 1969) 462 P.2d 275.)
(*Ivey v. State* (Fla.Dist.Ct.App. 1975) 308 So.2d 565.)
(*Jaynes v. State* (Ind.Ct.App. 1982) 437 N.E.2d 137.)
(*First Interstate Bank v. Bland* (Tex.Ct.App. 1991) 810 S.W.2d 277.)
(*Ransom v. Ransom* (1985) 235 Ga. 656 [324 S.E.2d 437].)
(*Roberts v. Automobile Club of Michigan* (1984) 138 Mich.App. 488 [360 N.W.2d 224].)

§ 1:30 State and reporter abbreviations

[A] State abbreviations

For citations, use the following abbreviations for states or territories within parentheses. Abbreviations are not used for Alaska, Hawaii, Idaho, Iowa, Ohio, and Utah.

Ala.	Fla.	Md.	Nev.	Or.	Vt.
Ariz.	Ga.	Mass.	N.C.	Pa.	Va.
Ark.	Ill.	Mich.	N.D.	P.R.	Wash.
Cal.	Ind.	Minn.	N.H.	R.I.	W.Va.
Colo.	Kan.	Miss.	N.J.	S.C.	Wis.
Conn.	Ky.	Mo.	N.M.	S.D.	Wyo.
Del.	La.	Mont.	N.Y.	Tenn.	
D.C.	Me.	Neb.	Okla.	Tex.	

[B] Abbreviations for regional reporters

Atlantic Reporter	A.
Atlantic Reporter, Second Series	A.2d
New York Supplement	N.Y.S.
New York Supplement, Second Series	N.Y.S.2d
North Eastern Reporter	N.E.
North Eastern Reporter, Second Series	N.E.2d
North Western Reporter	N.W.
North Western Reporter, Second Series	N.W.2d
Pacific Reporter	P.
Pacific Reporter, Second Series	P.2d
South Eastern Reporter	S.E.
South Eastern Reporter, Second Series	S.E.2d
Southern Reporter	So.
Southern Reporter, Second Series	So.2d
South Western Reporter	S.W.
South Western Reporter, Second Series	S.W.2d

See The Bluebook: A Uniform System of Citation (16th ed. 1996) table T.1, page 165 et seq. for additional abbreviations for opinion reporters.

§ 1:31 Early, renumbered, and reprinted state reports

Many early American state reports bore the name of the person who reported the series, with succeeding reporters naming and numbering the particular volumes they reported. Most jurisdictions have renumbered their reports or reprinted them sequentially. For practicality, cite the renumbered or reprinted reports alone. When citing an opinion that has not been renumbered or reprinted, give the case name, year, jurisdiction, reporter designation, and page. If the court cited is not of last resort, note the authoring court within parentheses.

> (*Dale v. M'Evers* (N.Y. 1823) 2 Cowen 118.)
> (*Hawkins v. Johnson* (Ind. 1832) 3 Blackford 46.)

For citing to early United States Supreme Court reports, see section 1:32[D].

D. FEDERAL CASES

§ 1:32 United States Supreme Court opinions

[A] In general; opinion title

For the opinion title, follow the running head title from the official United States Supreme Court Reports, which is abbreviated as U.S. The title is printed in italics. If the United States Supreme Court Reports title is unavailable, use the running head title in one of the two paper-based unofficial reporters, the Supreme Court Reporter, which is abbreviated as S.Ct., or the Supreme Court Reports, Lawyer's Edition, which is abbreviated as L.Ed. and L.Ed.2d for the second series. Otherwise (e.g., for very recently filed opinions or when a computer-based version is relied upon), shorten the title if necessary (see § 1:1[A]). The year of filing is given in parentheses, and the citation is completed with the volume number, reporter abbreviation, and page number(s). (For citing recently filed Supreme Court opinions, see § 1:3.)

[B] Official reports and parallel citations

Provide official United States Supreme Court Reports citations whenever possible, but particularly for the first citation to the opinion in the document. Also provide, in brackets, a parallel citation to an unofficial reporter, if possible, with the first citation to the opinion. For subsequent references to the same opinion, official citations are preferred, but citations to an unofficial reporter are acceptable.

If the official citation is not yet available, use blanks with the first citation to signal omitted volume and page information and provide a parallel citation to an unofficial reporter. For subsequent references to the same opinion, cite only to the unofficial reporter, or continue using blanks for omitted information from the official citation and citing to an unofficial reporter in brackets.

> (*Norman v. Reed* (1992) 502 U.S. 279, 286 [112 S.Ct. 698, 116 L.Ed.2d
> 711].) . . . (*Norman v. Reed, supra,* 502 U.S. at p. 288.)
> (*Old Chief v. United States* (1997) 519 U.S. ___ [117 S.Ct. 644, 649].) . . .
> (*Old Chief v. United States, supra,* 117 S.Ct. at p. 649.)
> (*Old Chief v. United States* (1997) 519 U.S. ___ [136 L.Ed.2d 524, 527].) . . .
> (*Old Chief v. United States, supra,* 136 L.Ed.2d at p. 527.)
> *Roberts v. Galen of Virginia, Inc.* (1999) ___ U.S. ___, ___ [119 S.Ct. 685,
> 687, ___ L.Ed.2d ___] . . . (See *Roberts v. Galen of Virginia, Inc., supra,*
> ___ U.S. at p. ___ [119 S.Ct. at p. 687.)
> (see *Knowles v. Iowa* (1998) 525 U.S. ___, ___ [119 S.Ct. 484, 487–488,
> 142 L.Ed.2d 492]) . . . (*Knowles v. Iowa, supra,* 525 U.S. at p. ___ [119
> S.Ct. at pp. 487–488].)

Note that for opinions, the Official Reports publisher adds parallel citations to the unofficial reporters throughout as necessary. The publisher also adds citations to the official reporter, if available, if the opinion cites only to an unofficial reporter.

[C] Cases pending before the Supreme Court

To note that a matter is pending before the Supreme Court, provide a citation to the lower court opinion, followed by the date certiorari was granted, and the United States Supreme Court Reports and parallel unofficial citations for the grant of certiorari. Adding the Supreme Court's docket number after the date certiorari was granted is helpful but not mandatory. If the official citation is unavailable, use blanks for the page and volume numbers.

> (*Lewis v. Sacramento County* (9th Cir. 1996) 98 F.3d 434, 442, cert.
> granted June 2, 1997, ___ U.S. ___ [117 S.Ct. 2406, 138 L.Ed.2d 173].)
> (*Matter of Care and Treatment of Hendricks* (1996) 259 Kan. 246 [912
> P.2d 129], cert. granted *sub nom. Kansas v. Hendricks* (1996) ___ U.S.
> ___ [116 S.Ct. 1540, 134 L.Ed.2d 643].)
> *Pro-Choice Network of Western New York v. Schenck* (2d Cir. 1995) 67
> F.3d 377, cert. granted Mar. 18, 1996, No. 95-1065, ___ U.S. ___ [116
> S.Ct. 1260, 134 L.Ed.2d 209].
> (*People v. Tuilaepa* (1992) 4 Cal.4th 569, 595 [15 Cal.Rptr.2d 382, 842
> P.2d 1142], cert. granted Dec. 6, 1993, No. 93-5131, ___ U.S. ___
> [114 S.Ct. 598, 126 L.Ed.2d 563].)

> (*Thompson v. Keohane* (9th Cir. 1994) 34 F.3d 1073, cert. granted Jan. 23, 1995, ___ U.S. ___ [115 S.Ct. 933, 130 L.Ed.2d 879].)

See also section 1:11 for noting subsequent history, and section 1:17 for noting matters pending on appeal in California courts.

[D] Early United States Reports

Reporters' names are often used in the citation of the United States Supreme Court Reports for volumes 1 through 90 of United States Reports. This parallel reference to the reporter is optional.

> (*Buchanan v. Alexander* (1846) 45 U.S. (4 How.) 20 [11 L.Ed. 857].)   *or*
> (*Buchanan v. Alexander* (1846) 45 U.S. 20 [11 L.Ed. 857].)

See section 1:31 as to early, renumbered state reports.

§ 1:33 Intermediate federal appellate opinions

[A] United States Courts of Appeals

Except for the Supreme Court, there is no official reporter for the federal courts. United States Courts of Appeals opinions are unofficially reported in the Federal Reporter. Abbreviations for the Federal Reporter (Fed., F.2d, F.3d) do not indicate the court of decision, thus that information follows the opinion title (see § 1:1[A]) in a parenthetical with the year of decision. The Bluebook: A Uniform System of Citation (16th ed. 1996) abbreviations are used for the courts.

Opinions not reported in the Federal Reporter are often available from a computer-based source (e.g., Westlaw, Lexis, and Internet services). When citing an opinion apparently available only via a computer-based source, provide the complete date of the decision (i.e., month, day, and year) and the docket number. Use blanks in conjunction with a reporter designation only if it is certain that the opinion will be published therein. (See also § 1:3.)

> (*Scott v. Ross* (9th Cir. 1998) 151 F.3d 1247.)
> (*Cybor Corp. v. FAS Techs., Inc.* (Fed.Cir. 1998) 138 F.3d 1448.)
> (*United States v. Johnson* (7th Cir. 1994) 32 F.3d 265.)
> (*Alomar v. Dwyer* (2d Cir. 1971) 447 F.2d 482.)
> (*McLaughlin v. Cheshire* (D.C. Cir. 1982) 676 F.2d 855.)
> (*Stewart v. Wright* (8th Cir. 1906) 147 Fed. 321.)
> (*Craft v. Campbell Soup* (9th Cir. Dec. 2, 1998, No. 98-15060) ___F.3d ___ [1998 WL 828105].)
> (*Ghana v. Pierce* (9th Cir. Nov. 5, 1998, No. 97-35588) 1998 WL 790346.)

[B] Specialized federal appellate courts

Reports of certain specialized federal appellate courts, before those courts were merged into the United States Courts of Appeals for the Federal Circuit in 1982, and other appellate courts, were indexed separately in the Federal Reports. The citation, therefore, is similar to other federal appellate citations except that the court's abbreviation (not Fed.Cir.) appears in the date parenthetical. The first page of the opinion provides the proper court name; use The Bluebook abbreviations, but without spaces, for these courts.

Temporary Emergency Court of Appeals
(Pacific Coast Meat Job. Ass'n, Inc. v. Cost of Living Coun.
    (Temp.Emer.Ct.App. 1973) 481 F.2d 1388.)

United States Court of Claims
(Tibbals v. United States (Ct.Cl. 1966) 362 F.2d 266, 269.)

United States Court of Customs and Patent Appeals
(Application of Winslow (C.C.P.A. 1966) 365 F.2d 1017.)

[C] Early circuit court decisions

Decisions from the old circuit courts, abolished January 1, 1912, use C.C., abbreviating circuit court, and the appropriate district and state. States with only one district use D. after C.C., before the state abbreviation.

(Barthet v. City of New Orleans (C.C.E.D.La. 1885) 24 Fed. 563.)
(United States v. Iron Silver Mine Co. (C.C.D.Colo. 1885) 24 Fed. 568.)
United States v. Hand (C.C.D.Pa. 1810) 26 F.Cas. 103 (No. 15, 297).

§ 1:34 Federal trial court opinions

[A] Federal Supplement; computer-based sources and topical reporters

Federal trial court decisions are unofficially reported in the Federal Supplement, which includes cases determined in the United States District Courts; the Special Court, Regional Rail Reorganization Act; the United States Court of International Trade; and rulings of the Judicial Panel on Multidistrict Litigation. Until 1980, the Federal Supplement also contained decisions of the United States Customs Court. Cites to the Federal Supplement (F.Supp.) must, following the opinion title (see § 1:1[A]), specify the court of decision in a parenthetical with the year of decision. The Bluebook: A Uniform System of Citation (16th ed. 1996) abbreviations are used for the courts, but spaces are not used following periods in the abbreviations.

Federal trial court opinions are also available from computer-based sources (e.g., Westlaw, Lexis, and Internet services), and are also often available in topical reporters (i.e., ongoing compilations focusing on selected areas of the law, such as labor or tax law, and often including full-text judicial opinions).

When citing an opinion from a computer-based source, provide the complete date of the decision (i.e., month, day, and year) and the docket number (see also § 1:3). Judicial opinions from topical reporters are cited in the same style as federal administrative adjudications (see § 1:35). Examples are included below.

United States District Courts

(*Jackson v. East Bay Hosp.* (N.D.Cal. 1997) 980 F.Supp. 1341.)

(*Clajon Production Corp. v. Petera* (D.Wyo. 1994) 854 F.Supp. 843.)

(*U.S. v. Baez-Ortega* (D.P.R. 1995) 906 F.Supp. 740.)

(*Williams v. Dark* (E.D.Pa. 1993) 844 F.Supp. 210.)

(*Hinkfuss v. Shawano County* (E.D.Wis. 1991) 772 F.Supp. 1104.)

(*American Airlines v. Austin* (D.D.C. 1991) 778 F.Supp. 72.) [*Note: This is the District of Columbia district court.*]

United States v. Nieves (S.D.N.Y. 1985) 608 F.Supp. 1147, 1149–1150.

(*Pascutoi v. Washburn-McReavy Mortuary* (D.Minn. 1975) 11 Fair Empl.Prac.Cas. (BNA) 1325.)

(*In re Healthcare Services Group, Inc. Securities Litigation* (E.D.Pa. 1993) Fed. Sec. L. Rep. (CCH) ¶ 97,374, pp. 95,978–95,979.)

Cytryn v. Cook (N.D.Cal. 1990) [1990 Transfer Binder] Fed. Sec. L. Rep. (CCH) ¶ 95,409

(*Washington Metropolitan Transit Authority v. One Parcel of Land* (D.Md. Nov. 23, 1993, Civ. A. No. HAR-88-618) 1993 U.S.Dist. Lexis 18485.)

(*F.T.C. v. Solomon Trading Co.* (D. Ariz. 1994) 1994-1 Trade Cas. (CCH) ¶ 70,267.)

United States Court of International Trade

(*Cultivos v. Miramonte S.A. v. U.S.* (Ct.Internat.Trade 1997) 980 F.Supp. 1269.)

United States Customs Court

(*General Instrument Corporation v. United States* (Cust.Ct. 1973) 359 F.Supp. 1390.)

Judicial Panel on Multidistrict Litigation

(*In re Rio Hair Naturalizer Products Liability Lit.* (J.P.M.L. 1995) 904 F.Supp. 1407.)

[B] Federal Rules Decisions (F.R.D.)

Federal Rules Decisions is an unofficial reporter for opinions, decisions, and rulings involving the Federal Rules of Civil Procedure and the Federal Rules of Criminal Procedure. Follow the general citation style set forth in [A].

(*Harrison v. Edison Brothers Apparel Stores, Inc.* (M.D.N.C. 1993) 146 F.R.D. 142.)

Roberts v. Homelite Div. of Textron, Inc. (N.D.Ind. 1986) 109 F.R.D. 664, 668.

Federal Rules Decisions also contains some monographs relevant to federal civil procedure. They are cited in the same manner as law review articles (see § 3:8):

> *Service of Process Abroad: A Nuts and Bolts Guide* (1988) 122 F.R.D. 63.
> (Kaufman, *Appellate Advocacy in the Federal Courts* (1977) 79 F.R.D. 165, 171.)

[C] Federal Claims Reporter (Fed.Cl.)

The Federal Claims Reporter unofficially reports cases decided in the United States Court of Federal Claims since 1992 and claims appeals decided by the Federal Circuit and the United States Supreme Court. Follow the general citation style set forth in [A].

> (*American Airlines, Inc. v. U.S.* (Fed.Cl. 1998) 40 Fed.Cl. 712.) [*trial court*]
> (*Stanley v. U.S.* (Fed.Cir. 1998) 40 Fed.Cl. 1023.) [*appellate court*]

[D] Federal bankruptcy, tax, and other decisions

There are various other specialized topical reporters for federal opinions, including the Bankruptcy Reporter (B.R.), Tax Court Memorandum Decisions (T.C.M.) and the Reports of the United States Tax Court (T.C.). Follow the general citation style set forth in [A], except that since Tax Court Memorandum Decisions and Reports of the United States Tax Court specifies the court, that information is not included with the date.

> *In re CFLC, Inc.* (Bankr. 9th Cir. 1997) 209 B.R. 508, 513.
> (*In re County of Orange* (Bankr. C.D.Cal. 1997) 219 B.R. 543, 551.)
> *Siewart v. C.I.R.* (1979) 72 T.C. 326, 332–333.
> *Kong v. Commissioner* (1990) 60 T.C.M. (CCH) 696
> (*Gamma Farms v. United States* (N.D.Cal. 1990) 90-2 U.S.Tax Cas. (CCH)
>   ¶ 50,378, pp. 85,165–85,166.)

§ 1:35 Federal agency adjudications

As with California administrative agencies (see § 1:22), some federal agencies issue official compilations of administrative decisions. Cite to official compilations if available. If no official compilation is available, cite to a topical reporter or a computer-based source, if available (e.g., Westlaw, Lexis, or the Internet, including Web sites for particular agencies). If no such source is available, provide relevant identifying information (i.e., the names of the parties or the proceeding, the full date of the decision, the issuing agency, and the docket number or its equivalent). If citing to an official compilation, a topical reporter citation may also be provided as a parallel citation in brackets. A citation to a topical service should identify the agency unless it is otherwise clear from the title of the topical reporter.

When citing administrative decisions, set forth the title (see § 1:1[A]), a parenthetical for the adjudicating agency (if necessary) and year of decision, the volume number, reporter abbreviation, and publisher parenthetical (e.g., Commerce Clearing House (CCH) or Bureau of National Affairs, Inc. (BNA)), and paragraph, section, or page number. The adjudicating agency does not have to be identified in the date parenthetical if the reporter abbreviation identifies the adjudicating agency. Follow The Bluebook: A Uniform System of Citation (16th ed. 1996) rules for names and abbreviations for both official and unofficial publications and services. A citation to computer-based material should include the names of the parties or the proceeding, the full date (month, day, year), the issuing agency, the docket or decision number, and the Internet URL or a Westlaw or Lexis cite (see also § 1:3).

> (*Elite Limousine Plus* (1997) 324 NLRB 992.) [*Note: The Decisions and Orders of the National Labor Relations Board, which is abbreviated NLRB, is an official reporter for the board, and NLRB identifies the source of the opinion.*]
> (*Frontier Hotel* (Nov. 8, 1982) 265 NLRB No. 46, p. 1.) [*Note: This example is to the advance pamphlet version of a decision.*]
> (*Roe v. Kidder Peabody & Co.* (S.D.N.Y. 1990) 52 Fair Empl.Prac.Cas. (BNA) 1865.)
> (*City of Pasadena* (1990) 96 Lab.Arb.Rep. (BNA) 26, 29.)

E. INTERNATIONAL CASES

§ 1:36 English decisions

[A] Opinions up to 1864

Early English decisions were reported in numerous series, usually designated by the name of the individual who served as reporter. Most of these early opinions were then collected and reprinted in a series called English Reports—Full Reprint (Eng.Rep.), consisting of 176 volumes with a two-volume table of cases. Because the early reporter series are not generally available, no practical purpose is usually served by citing to them—a citation to the English Reports is sufficient. Include the year in parentheses, then the volume and page numbers with the reporter abbreviation. If the deciding court is provided, include the abbreviation in the date parenthetical.

> (*M'Naghten's Case* (1843) 8 Eng.Rep. 718.)
> (*Tulk v. Moxhay* (Ch. 1848) 41 Eng.Rep. 1143.)
> (*Armory v. Delamirie* (K.B. 1722) 93 Eng.Rep. 664.)

If an opinion was not reprinted in the English Reports, cite to the particular reporter series that published the decision, using the same citation format as above. Standard law dictionaries such as Black's Law Dictionary and Ballentine's Law Dictionary contain tables of abbreviations for these reporters. Use a calendar year for the citation, not a court term or regnal year.

[B] Opinions after 1864

Most opinions reported after 1864 appear in a series called Law Reports, which is divided according to the deciding court and the year. For citing to other examples, see The Bluebook: A Uniform System of Citation (16th ed. 1996) table T.2, page 276 et seq. The general format is as follows:

(*Board of Education v. Rice* (1911) App.Cas. 179.)

§ 1:37 Other nations' court decisions

When referring to reports from another country, cite to the official or primary source and, where available, parallel publications. Give the date in parentheses, along with the jurisdiction's abbreviation. Citations from computer-based sources of opinions are also acceptable. For further information, consult The Bluebook: A Uniform System of Citation (16th ed. 1996) table T.2, page 276 et seq.

(*Bouley v. Rochambeau* (Fr. 1963) D. Jur. 555.)
Dominelli Service Stations v. Petro-Canada, Inc. (1992) Ont. Lexis 199,
    200 [construing Landlord and Tenant Act].

CHAPTER 1
—Notes—

CONSTITUTIONS, STATUTES, RULES, AND RELATED MATERIALS

A. CONSTITUTIONS

§ 2:1   General considerations; abbreviations

Use roman numerals to designate articles of both the United States and California Constitutions. Use arabic numbers for sections, clauses, and amendments. Do not use abbreviations outside of parentheses, but within parentheses use abbreviation styles shown in sections 2:2 and 2:3. For capitalization rules, see section 4:10[A].

§ 2:2   United States Constitution and amendments

References to the United States Constitution should include the descriptive words "federal," "United States," or similar designation, unless the federal document is clearly understood from the context. Within parentheses, the abbreviation "U.S." is always before the abbreviation "Const."

> The due process clause of the United States Constitution forbids enforcement.
> The Fourteenth Amendment to the United States Constitution . . . .
> Article IV, sections 3 and 8 of the United States Constitution vest jurisdiction in the federal government.
> (U.S. Const., art. I, § 5, cl. 3.)
> (U.S. Const., art. VI.)
> (U.S. Const., 6th Amend.)
> (U.S. Const., 4th & 5th Amends.)

§ 2:3   California Constitution

References to the California Constitution may omit the descriptive words "state" and "California" if no confusion will result, but within parentheses, the abbreviation "Cal." is always used before the abbreviation "Const."

> (Cal. Const., art. VI, § 10.)
> (Cal. Const., arts. IV, V & VI.)
> (Cal. Const., art. VI, § 1; *id.*, art. III, § 1.)
> (Cal. Const., art. XIII, § 28, subd. (f), par. (3).)
> Article XXII, section 22 of the state Constitution provides that . . . .
> but article I, section 24 of the California Constitution provides . . . .
> as the Constitution provides (art. IV, § 21, subd. (b)), . . .
> the Constitution's court unification provisions (art. VI, § 23, subds. (a)–(c)) require that . . . .
> (Cal. Const., art. IX, § 9, subd. (b), 2d par.) . . . .

For citing proposed constitutional amendments, see section 2:27.

§ 2:4 New, former, amended, or redesignated provisions

The text or a footnote should clearly signal that a citation is to a provision that was recently added, repealed, amended, or renumbered. References to the former 1849 California Constitution in its entirety should also be signalled.

(Cal. Const., art. VI, § 10, former art. VI, § 5.)

(See former art. XXIV, § 4, now art. VII, § 4.)

(Cal. Const., art. I, § 31, added by initiative, Gen. Elec. (Nov. 5, 1996), commonly known as Prop. 209.)

(Cal. Const. of 1849, art. IV, § 37.)

Prior to its amendment in 1974, former article VI, section 19 of the California Constitution provided: . . .

The double jeopardy clause first appeared in the California Constitution of 1849, article I, section 8, where the language tracked the federal guaranty. The provision was moved essentially unchanged to article I, section 13 of the California Constitution of 1879, and finally came to rest in article I, section 15.

Browne, Report of the Debates in the Convention of California on the Formation of the State Constitution (1850) (hereafter Browne) . . .

(Browne, Rep. of Debates in Convention of Cal. on Formation of State Const. (1850) pp. 225–231.)

2 Willis and Stockton, Debates and Proceedings, California Constitutional Convention 1878–1879, pages 924–981 (hereafter Debates)

(2 Willis & Stockton Debates and Proceedings, Cal. Const. Convention 1878–1879, pp. 1038–1039, 1478–1481.)

(Cal. Const. Revision Com., Proposed Revision (1966) p. 63.)

Former article I, section 18 read: "Neither slavery, nor involuntary servitude, unless for the punishment of crime, shall ever be tolerated in this State."

and section 17, subdivision (a) of article XVI (former art. XIII, § 42) . . . .

former article XX, section 22 (now art. XV, § 1) . . . .

Article XIII C, section 2[1] requires majority voter approval.

Article VI, section 16,[2] addresses judicial elections.

article II, section 10,[3] provides . . . .

Pursuant to article I, section 16 of the California Constitution[4] . . . .

(See Cal. Const., art. XIII, § 1, as adopted Nov. 5, 1974.)[5]

---

1. Added by initiative measure adopted by the California voters in the November 5, 1996, General Election.

2. Amendment adopted June 2, 1998.

3. New section adopted June 8, 1976. The provisions of this section were transferred from article IV, former section 24.

4. At the time this case was argued the appropriate constitutional provision was article I, section 7. Its number was changed by vote of the people on November 5, 1974.

5. Former article XIII, section 1, was substantially consistent in the parts pertinent to this appeal.

B. CALIFORNIA CODES, STATUTES, REGULATIONS, ORDINANCES, AND CHARTERS

§ 2:5   General guidelines

The following sections provide general guidance on citation styles for statutes, rules, regulations, and related materials most often relied on in legal writing. For sources not specifically covered here, the information provided should be inversely proportional to the availability of the source (i.e., provide more information for obscure material). For capitalization rules, see section 4:10[B].

[A] Official version of codes

There is no designated official version of California's codes, but the Legislative Counsel maintains all California codes on the Internet at <http://www.leginfo.ca.gov>. Commercial versions of the California codes (e.g., West's Annotated California Codes and Deering's California Codes) have been enhanced with publishers' headings, enactment notes, and other addenda that are not part of the actual enactments. The most authoritative version of each enactment is that set forth in the Statutes and Amendments to the Codes (see § 2:11).

For example, the heading "Libel, what is" appears in many published versions of Civil Code section 45. That heading was added by publishers and is not part of the official text of the statute, nor is a note after the section reading "Enacted 1872." The section numbers and subdivision designations are those of the statutes themselves, however, and may be included in a quote.

[B] Short forms for code citations

To avoid repetitive references to a single code or set of rules, the code name may be omitted after the initial citation if a footnote or parenthetical reference explains that all undesignated section references will be to that code. Only one code designation, however, may be omitted in this manner in each document (e.g., opinion or brief). When the code name has been omitted, subsequent references simply refer to section numbers, but watch for clarity if an undesignated code section is juxtaposed in the same sentence or paragraph with citations designating different codes. In this context, all code citations in the sentence or paragraph should be designated, notwithstanding a parenthetical or footnote to the contrary.

Code of Civil Procedure section 631[1] provides that a jury trial may be waived by written consent filed with the clerk. Section 631 also provides, however, that the court may allow a jury trial even after a party has waived a jury. (§ 631, subd. (d).)

---

1. All further statutory references are to the Code of Civil Procedure unless otherwise indicated.

Where the author does not employ a parenthetical or footnote to omit a code designation throughout, the code designation may nonetheless be omitted for subsequent references to the same section within a paragraph, provided the first reference in the paragraph designates the code. Omitting code designations in this manner is only suggested for facilitating the flow of text and readability; thus code designations should generally not be omitted for parenthetical citations. Within parentheses, a code designation is preferred, but *id.* may be used instead of the code designation provided the designation was given earlier in the paragraph, there are no intervening citations, and there is some change from the prior cite. When there is no change and no intervening citations, *ibid.* may be used. (Note: *supra* is never used with code cites.)

[C] Order of authority

The order of citations is not governed by rigid rules. Citation sequence is arranged to best support the proposition stated, generally with the most pertinent authority cited first. When *quoting* from a statute or rule, always list it first. Constitutional and statutory citations generally are given priority over case cites. When a constitutional provision or statute is cited together with cases construing it, the statutory cite should precede the cases. References to secondary authorities should follow citations of constitutions, statutes, and cases.

When several equally relevant statutory authorities from the same code are cited, cite them in numerical order. When citing out-of-state statutes or rules, list them in alphabetical order by state.

§ 2:6   California code sections

Outside parentheses, use unabbreviated code names and spell out "section" before the code section number. For subdivisions, insert a comma after the code section number and spell out "subdivision." Commas are generally used following the subdivision designations within sentences. Use the singular with "et seq."

Civil Code section 51
Civil Code sections 51 and 51.2

Civil Code section 1000 et seq.
Civil Code sections 1006 et seq., and 1013 et seq.
Section 844 of the Penal Code
Section 1203.1b of the Penal Code
Probate Code section 233, subdivision (b), provides. . .
The Tahoe Regional Planning Compact, Government Code section 66801,
    article VII, subdivision (a), requires . . . .
Elections Code, division 15, chapter 1 (§ 15000 et seq.)

Within parentheses, use code abbreviations followed by a comma and the section symbol (§) before the code section number. For subdivisions, insert another comma after the code section number and use the abbreviation "subd." Use a double section symbol (§§) for citing more than one section, but only one section symbol when using "et seq." (If a section symbol is unavailable, use the abbreviations "sec." or "secs." as appropriate.) Use a comma or ampersand (&) to separate multiple subdivisions of the same code. Citations to multiple codes, or code cites combined with other authority, in the same parenthetical are separated by semicolons.

(Bus. & Prof. Code, § 16700 et seq.)
(Code Civ. Proc., § 564, subd. (a).)
(Pen. Code, § 1203.1ab.)
(Civ. Code, §§ 1810.2–1812.12.)
(Pen. Code, §§ 118, 118a, 126.)
(Prob. Code, §§ 610 et seq., 670 et seq.)
(Evid. Code, § 700; see Pen. Code, § 1321.)
(Pen. Code, § 1016; Evid. Code, § 1300; *Teitlebaum Furs, Inc. v. Dominion Ins. Co. Ltd.* (1962) 58 Cal.2d 601, 605–606 [25 Cal.Rptr. 559, 375 P.2d 439].)

Parenthetical statutory citations embedded within a sentence are not punctuated with a period. If, however, the parenthetical citation stands alone after the end of a full sentence, it is completed with a period.

Because defendant could not satisfy the second prong (Code Civ. Proc., §§ 391.1, 391.2), his motion was denied.
A "health care provider" includes clinics licensed pursuant to the Health and Safety Code (Health & Saf. Code, § 1200) and individuals licensed pursuant to the Business and Professions Code (Bus. & Prof. Code, § 657, subd. (b)). (See also Bus. & Prof. Code, § 2060.)

§ 2:7   California code subdivisions and other enumerations

Outside parentheses, insert a comma after the code section number and spell out "subdivision." There is no comma following the subdivision designation unless the grammatical context requires it. For parenthetical citations, insert a comma after the code section number and use the abbreviation "subd." Sometimes, repeated use of "subdivision" in text and "subd." in connection with oft-repeated citations is unwieldy. For not more than a few oft-repeated citations, a short-cite form omitting "subdivision" (or "subd.") for each citation may be expressly adopted. For example: "Penal Code section 243, subdivision (f) (hereafter Penal Code section 243(f))."

As a general rule, do not use additional terms to designate subparts of subdivisions. To refer to multiple subparts of a single subdivision, use the singular form, "subdivision": e.g., Probate Code section 1951, subdivision (b)(1) and (3). Within parentheses, use a comma or ampersand (&) to separate multiple subdivisions of the same code (e.g., "Code Civ. Proc., § 437c, subds. (a) & (b)"; *or* "Code Civ. Proc., § 437c, subds. (a), (b)").

A potential for citational imprecision results from the various styles used over the years in numbering or designating code sections and subdivisions. Subdivisions are generally designated alphabetically by lowercase letters in parentheses, but numerical designations are sometimes used, and some designations may use words rather than figures for numbers. Likewise, the Legislature has not always used parentheses in designating subdivisions. And not all alphabetically or numerically designated enumerations within sections are characterized as subdivisions. For example, enumerations of material encompassing only a portion of the substantive content are not subdivisions (see, e.g., Civ. Code, § 47, subd. (b)).

As a result, be exact in citing California code sections. Subdivisions should be specified as such, and a statute's precise terminology, if any, should be used to describe enumerations of material that are not subdivisions. Within subdivisions, likewise track a statute's precise terminology for enumerations of material. If a section or subdivision has several unnumbered or unlettered paragraphs, specific paragraphs should be referenced (e.g., second paragraph outside parentheses; 2d par. within parentheses).

Code of Civil Procedure section 526, which has subdivisions (a) and (b), is followed by separate sections designated as 526a and 526b. If a citation reads "section 526(a)," precisely what is the author citing?

Welfare and Institutions Code section 707 has various enumerations, several described as "criteria," as portions of different subdivisions. (Cite these criteria as, e.g., Welf. & Inst. Code, § 707, subd. (e), criteria (A) & (C).) Similarly, Penal Code section 190.3 has no subdivisions, but a portion of the section consists of alphabetically designated "factors" that must be described as such (e.g., Pen. Code, § 190.3, factor (g).)

Additional examples:
Civil Code section 1782, subdivision (a)(1).
and subdivision (b)(2) of section 2019 of the Code of Civil Procedure . . . .

Penal Code section 1170.12, subdivisions (b)(1)(A) and (B), and (c)(2)(A)(i)
(Civ. Code, § 48.9, subds. (c)(1) & (d).)
(Civ. Code, § 48.9, subd. (c)(1), (2).)
(Civ. Code, § 48a, subd. 4(a), (c).)
(Code Civ. Proc., § 262.8, subd. (b).)
(Gov. Code, § 66801, art. V, subd. (b).)
(Pen. Code, § 261, subd. (a)(1), (2) & (4).)
(Code Civ. Proc., § 437c, subds. (a)–(c).)
(Pen. Code, § 243, subd. (f)(1)–(6).)
(Pen. Code, § 1203.1c, subd. (c).)
Civil Code section 48a, subdivision 2, states: . . .
under section 437c, subdivisions (*l*) and (*o*), of the Code of Civil
    Procedure . . . .
(Civ. Code, §§ 45a, 46, subds. 1, 2 & 4.)
(Code Civ. Proc., § 26, subd. Two.)
(Code Civ. Proc., § 337, subd. 3.)
(Code Civ. Proc., § 340, subd. (1).)
(Code Civ. Proc., § 2025, subds. (*l*), (n) & (*o*).)
(Pen. Code, § 26, par. One.)
(Pen. Code, § 190.3, factors (a), (b) & (d).)
(Welf. & Inst. Code, § 707, subd. (e), criteria (A) & (C).)
(Pen. Code, § 1389, art. III, subd. (a).)
Section 596 of the Penal Code, second paragraph, provides . . . .
This section does not apply to control of predatory animals. (Pen. Code,
    § 596, 2d par.)
in former section 526, second subdivision 4 of the Code of Civil
    Procedure . . . .
(Former Code Civ. Proc., § 526, 2d subd. 4.)

§ 2:8   Code abbreviations

These are the abbreviations for California codes:

Business and Professions Code	Bus. & Prof. Code
California Code of Regulations (see § 2:16)	Cal. Code Regs.
California Uniform Commercial Code*	Cal. U. Com. Code
Civil Code	Civ. Code
Code of Civil Procedure	Code Civ. Proc.
Corporations Code	Corp. Code
Education Code	Ed. Code

---

* Section 1101 of California's Uniform Commercial Code states that the code may be cited as the Uniform Commercial Code, but clarity requires adding "California" in citations to California's version to distinguish it from the national Uniform Commercial Code. (See *Bank of America v. Lallana* (1998) 19 Cal.4th 203, 206, fn. 1.)

Elections Code	Elec. Code
Evidence Code	Evid. Code
Family Code	Fam. Code
Financial Code	Fin. Code
Fish and Game Code	Fish & G. Code
Food and Agricultural Code	Food & Agr. Code
Government Code	Gov. Code
Harbors and Navigation Code	Harb. & Nav. Code
Health and Safety Code	Health & Saf. Code
Insurance Code	Ins. Code
Labor Code	Lab. Code
Military and Veterans Code	Mil. & Vet. Code
Penal Code	Pen. Code
Probate Code	Prob. Code
Public Contract Code	Pub. Contract Code
Public Resources Code	Pub. Resources Code
Public Utilities Code	Pub. Util. Code
Revenue and Taxation Code	Rev. & Tax. Code
Streets and Highways Code	Sts. & Hy. Code
Unemployment Insurance Code	Unemp. Ins. Code
Uniform Commercial Code	Cal. U. Com. Code
	or U. Com. Code
Vehicle Code	Veh. Code
Water Code	Wat. Code
Welfare and Institutions Code	Welf. & Inst. Code

Abbreviations frequently used in the parenthetical citation of the codes include:

and following	et seq.	pages	pp.
article	art.	paragraph	par.
articles	arts.	paragraphs	pars.
chapter	ch.	part	pt.
chapters	chs.	parts	pts.
clause	cl.	section	§
clauses	cls.	sections	§§
division	div.	subdivision	subd.
divisions	divs.	subdivisions	subds.
following	foll.	title	tit.
page	p.	titles	tits.

For capitalization rules pertaining to code citations, see section 4:10[D].

§ 2:9 Annotated codes

To cite to publisher-added materials from annotated codes, describe the material, note the volume number (if any), the publisher and code, year of the volume's publication (or supplement), provision to which the material refers, and page. West's code volumes are numbered; Deering's are not. Subsequent citations to publisher-added material are treated in the same manner as citations to other books (see § 3:1).

> (See Historical and Statutory Notes, 26B West's Ann. Ed. Code (1994 ed.) foll. § 24600, p. 536.)
> (Cal. Law Revision Com. com., 32 West's Ann. Gov. Code (1995 ed.) foll. § 845, p. 452.)
> (Sen. Com. on Judiciary, com. on Assem. Bill No. 3212 (1965 Reg. Sess.) reprinted at 29B pt. 4 West's Ann. Evid. Code (1995 ed.) foll. § 1200, pp. 3–4.)
> (Cal. Law Revision Com. com., 53 West's Ann. Prob. Code (1997 supp.) foll. § 6454, p. 181.)
> (Legis. Com. com., Deering's Ann. Code Civ. Proc., § 1710.45 (1998 supp.) p. 147.)
> (See cases collected in Deering's Ann. Code Civ. Proc. (1981 ed.) foll. § 1263.320 under heading Comparable Sales, pp. 281–283.)
> The Legislature's intent is evident from an examination of the selected language. (See Legis. Com. com., Deering's Ann. Corp. Code (1977 ed.) foll. § 110, p. 24.)
> The official code comment on section 9207, prepared by the American Law Institute and National Conference of Commissioners on Uniform State Laws, is in agreement. (See Official Comments on U. Com. Code, Deering's Ann. Cal. U. Com. Code (1986 ed.) foll. § 9207, p. 448.)
> (Cal. Law Revision Com. com., reprinted at 29B pt. 1 West's Ann. Evid. Code, *supra*, foll. § 210 at p. 23.)
> (Code commrs., note foll., Ann. Pen. Code, § 484 (1st ed. 1872, Haymond & Burch, commrs. annotators) pp. 188–190.)
> (See Code commrs. note foll. 1 Ann. Civ. Code, § 26 (1st ed. 1872, Haymond & Burch, Commrs.-annotators) p. 3 (hereafter Haymond & Burch).

§ 2:10 Recent enactments; advance legislative services

When the effect of recent enactments or amendments is relevant, include citational information for such changes. Refer to the session year, chapter, and section numbers enacting the change. A complete citation to the Statutes and Amendments to the Codes (i.e., with a page number) will generally not be possible for several years after enactment due to the lag in issuing this publication (see § 2:11).

> Civil Code section 1366.3 (added by Stats. 1996, ch. 1101, § 3) provides in pertinent part: . . .
>
> Penal Code section 190.6, as amended by Statutes 1996, chapter 1086, section 1, provides: . . .
>
> (Prob. Code, § 1460, as amended by Stats. 1996, ch. 863, § 5.)
>
> (Code Civ. Proc., § 403, added by Stats. 1996, ch. 713, § 1.)
>
> (Gov. Code, § 8686, subd. (b), as amended by Stats. 1997, 1st Ex. Sess., ch. 4X.)

In addition to providing a citation to the session year, chapter, and section number, a parallel citation to an advance legislative service (e.g., Deering's California Advance Legislative Service *or* West Group's California Legislative Service) may be of temporary assistance. In citing to an advance legislative service, include the pamphlet number, publisher and title, and page of the pamphlet on which the enactment is located. (The advance legislative services are not designed or intended to be permanent publications; thus the citations are customarily deleted from the bound volumes of the Official Reports.)

> (Pen. Code, § 502.8, as amended by Stats. 1997, ch. 554, § 1, No. 5 Deering's Adv. Legis. Service, p. 2781.)
>
> (Health & Saf. Code, § 25208.16, as amended by Stats. 1997, ch. 330, § 1, No. 6 West's Cal. Legis. Service, p. 1946.)

§ 2:11　Statutes and Amendments to the Codes; session laws

The session laws or chaptered laws enacted in each legislative session are published in the permanent bound volumes known as the Statutes and Amendments to the Codes. The California Legislature convenes in regular two-year sessions on the first Monday in December of each even-numbered year and adjourns on November 30 of the following even-numbered year (for example, the 1997–1998 Regular Session ran from December 2, 1996, through November 30, 1998). The Governor may also at various times cause the Legislature to assemble in an extraordinary session (e.g., to enact various flood relief measures). (Cal. Const., art. IV, § 3.)

When a bill is enacted, it is assigned a chapter number by the Secretary of State. (Gov. Code, § 9510.) Although a regular legislative session spans two years, each year's enacted bills are separately numbered. Thus, for example, the Statutes of 1999 are the bills enacted from December 1998 until December 31, 1999; the Statutes of 2000 are the bills enacted after December 31, 1999, until the end of the session. (Gov. Code, § 9510.5.)

The effective date of a statute is sometimes specified in the bill itself. Measures with an urgency designation are usually effective immediately upon enactment. Otherwise, statutes become effective as provided in

Government Code section 9600 (generally on the January 1 that follows 90 days after enactment).

Unlike codes, which arrange statutes by subject matter, the Statutes and Amendments to the Codes arrange the statutes in chronological order. Laws enacted in extraordinary session are usually published in the following year's Statutes. Citations to Statutes are treated in the same manner as citations to code sections (see § 2:5). Page numbers for the Statutes and Amendments to the Codes are not available for several years after each session. If page numbers are unavailable, a reference only to the chapter suffices.

> (Stats. 1949, ch. 456, § 1, p. 799.)
> (Stats. 1996, ch. 162, § 3.20(a).)
> (Stats. 1957, 1st Ex. Sess. 1956, ch. 10, § 1, p. 298.)
> Section 1042 was enacted by Statutes 1919, chapter 178, section 7, pages 267–268.

§ 2:12 Uncodified initiative acts

The texts of all initiative measures adopted by the electorate within the previous year must eventually be published at the beginning of the Statutes and Amendments to the Codes volumes for that year. (See Gov. Code, § 9766, subds. (d), (e).) To cite an uncodified original initiative act, give the Statutes reference and year, the page number, and the initiative section, if any. For example, section 2 of the Usury Law, as first enacted, is cited as (Stats. 1919, p. lxxxiii, § 2). There have been periods, however, when this has not been the case. In that case, cite to one of the annotated codes that include initiative measures.

In citing initiative measures in the annotated codes, do not include publishers' unofficial section numbers. To illustrate: the Chiropractic Act, as amended, is published in West's Annotated Business and Professions Code volumes as "sections 1000-1 to 1000-19." But that is merely the publisher's classification as a finding aid; the act has never formally been made part of the Business and Professions Code and should not be cited as such. Instead, give the name of the act and the provision number, then add a citation in the style of a cite to publisher-added material. (See § 2:9.)

> Section 10, subdivision (b) of the Chiropractic Act lists causes for suspension of a practitioner's license. (3A West's Ann. Bus. & Prof. Code (1990 ed.) p. 225.) or (Deering's Ann. Bus. & Prof. Code (1998 supp.) appen. I, foll. § 25761, p. 91.)
> Defendant argues that under the Usury Law, section 3, he is not so restricted. (Deering's Ann. Uncod. Measures 1919-1 (1973 ed.) p. 78.) or (10 West's Ann. Civ. Code (1985 ed.) foll. § 1916.12, p. 178.)

Similarly, cite a legislative amendment to an uncodified initiative measure by naming the act and the provision, followed by a cite to an annotated code. Because uncodified initiative measures are sometimes difficult to locate and identify, an explanatory footnote is often useful; see, for example, *Cartwright v. Board of Chiropractic Examiners* (1976) 16 Cal.3d 762, 764, fn. 1 [129 Cal.Rptr. 462]:

> Following disciplinary proceedings under section 10 of the Chiropractic Act,[1] . . .

---

1. The Chiropractic Act is an initiative measure appearing in West's Annotated Business and Professions Code following section 1000 and in the appendix to Deering's Business and Professions Code.

If the uncodified act is very recent, cite to the ballot pamphlet or to an advance legislative service. See section 2:10 for advance legislative services; section 2:34 for ballot pamphlets.

§ 2:13 Uncodified statutes

Some statutes have never been codified. A number of these statutes have been collected and appear in such works as Deering's Water— Uncodified Acts and Deering's Uncodified Initiative Measures and Statutes, and have been assigned chapter numbers or other sequential designations by publishers. The appropriate citation style includes a reference to both the session laws and the independent collection.

> (Stats. 1992, ch. 776, § 1, p. 3727, West's Ann. Wat.—Appen. (1995 ed.) ch. 134, p. 938.) *or*
> (Stats. 1992, ch. 776, § 1, p. 3727, Deering's Ann. Wat.—Uncod. Acts (1997 supp.) Act 6915, p. 275.)

§ 2:14 Repeals, reenactments, and amendments

Use "former" when citing a statute that has been repealed. Similarly, note "former" if there has been an intervening substantive change in the statute. If, following amendment, the subdivisions within a section have been redesignated, the prior version should be referred to as "section 246, former subdivision (c)(1)," or "section 12, former subdivision 2, now subdivision (b)." The "former" signal is given each time the provision is cited, unless the author, by footnote or parenthetical, declares in some way that all references are *either* to an earlier version *or* to the present identical but renumbered version. When dealing with repeals, or repeals and reenactments, it is helpful to track the language and history of former versions by including citations to the Statutes and Amendments to the Codes with the inception cite.

That sentence was added to former Government Code section 31461 in
1993 (Stats. 1993, ch. 396, § 3, p. 2238) in a subdivision that was
repealed by the 1995 amendment (Stats. 1995, ch. 558, § 1).
Former Code of Civil Procedure section 1032, enacted in 1933, was
repealed in 1986 and replaced by a new Code of Civil Procedure section
1032 addressing the same subject matter. (Stats. 1986, ch. 377, §§ 5–6,
pp. 1578–1579.)
Former Civil Code section 34.5, as amended (Stats. 1987, ch. 1237, § 2, p.
4396, repealed by Stats. 1993, ch. 219, § 2, p. 1578) read in full: . . .
(Former Civ. Code, § 2975, added by Stats. 1959, ch. 528, § 2, p. 2496
and repealed by Stats. 1963, ch. 819, § 2, p. 1997, eff. Jan. 1, 1965.)
Former Civil Code section 4700, subdivision (a), was repealed and
reenacted as section 4009 of the Family Code without substantive
change. (Stats. 1992, ch. 162, § 3, p. 464 [repealing Civ. Code
provision]; Stats. 1992, ch. 162, § 10, p. 582 [enacting Fam. Code
§ 4009].)
The dismissal statutes were repealed and reenacted as Code of Civil
Procedure section 583.110 et seq. in 1984 without substantive change.
(Stats. 1984, ch. 1705, § 4, p. 6176 [repealed]; Stats. 1984, ch. 1705,
§ 5, pp. 6176–6181 [reenacted].)
In 1970, Insurance Code section 11580.1, former subdivision (d) was
repealed (Stats. 1970, ch. 300, § 3, p. 573), but similar language was
added to section 11580.1 as subdivision (b)(4) the same year (Stats.
1970, ch. 300, § 4, p. 573).

§ 2:15 Statutory titles and headings

[A] Titles

A comprehensive legislative scheme encompassing several consecutive sections of a particular code may be cited by its popular title, with a section reference to the code:

The Cartwright Act, contained in division 7 of the Business and Professions
Code (§ 16700 et seq.), limits . . . The Unruh Civil Rights Act (Civ. Code,
§ 51 et seq.).
The Davis-Stirling Common Interest Development Act (Civ. Code, § 1350
et seq.) addresses . . .
and the Consumers Legal Remedies Act (Civ. Code, § 1750 et seq.) applies
to . . . .
in the Enforcement of Judgments Law (Code Civ. Proc., § 680.010 et
seq.) . . . .
in the Agricultural Labor Relations Act of 1975 (Lab. Code, div. 2, pt. 3.5,
ch. 1, § 1140 et seq.).

If the legislative scheme involves several codes or numerous
nonconsecutive sections from a single code, cite the title of the act and the
relevant year and chapter for the statute or statutes.

> The Determinate Sentencing Act (Stats. 1976, ch. 1139, p. 5061) as
> amended (Stats. 1977, ch. 165, p. 639) requires . . . .
> For additional examples of popular titles of statutes, see section 4:10[B].

[B] Headings

Legislative enactments often contain headings introducing code sections, articles, chapters, and divisions. Exercise caution in relying on these headings as some expression of legislative intent. Some enactments specify that the headings are to be disregarded (e.g., Prob. Code, § 4), and some headings are added by a publisher, not by the Legislature (see § 2:5[A]). A publisher's headings are not an indication of legislative intent.

§ 2:16 Regulatory material

[A] California Code of Regulations; Office of Administrative Law

The California Code of Regulations is the official compilation of all state agency regulations. It includes material covered by the Administrative Procedure Act (Gov. Code, § 11340 et seq.), including agency guidelines, bulletins, manuals, instructions, orders, standards, and rules. Currently, the code contains 27 titles. Twenty-six of the titles (titles 1–23 and 25–27) are published in looseleaf binders. Those titles are also available on the Internet through the Office of Administrative Law at <http://ccr.oal.ca.gov>, on CD-ROM, through online legal research services (e.g., Westlaw and Lexis), and on microfiche. Title 24 (Building Standards) is published separately. Information on its availability can be obtained through the Building Standards Commission at <http://www.bsc.ca.gov>. The California Code of Regulations was called the California Administrative Code until January 1, 1988.

Cite a regulation by its title number and section number. For new or recently amended regulations, it is advisable to provide the register year, register issue number, and date relating to that action. New regulations are published in weekly updates in the California Regulatory Code Supplement. Each week's update is identified by register year and issue number. Citations to regulations are treated in the same manner as citations to codes (see § 2:5).

> (Cal. Code Regs., tit. 14, § 925.4.)
> (Cal. Code Regs., tit. 22, § 100170, subd. (a)(6).)
> Industrial Welfare Commission wage order No. 4-89 regulates employee
> overtime. (Cal. Code Regs., tit. 8, § 11040, subd. 3(A)(1), (2).)
> under California Code of Regulations, title 14, section 925.4, . . .
> emergency regulations affecting steelhead fishing (Cal. Code Regs., tit. 14,
> §§ 7.00, 7.50, Register 98, No. 7 (Feb. 6, 1998) pp. 14–24.8) . . . .

the fee schedule for the Bureau of Private Postsecondary and Vocational
Education (Cal. Code Regs., tit. 5, § 74015, Register 98, No. 2 (Jan. 9,
1998) p. 402.21).
The Guidelines for the Implementation of the California Environmental
Quality Act (Cal. Code Regs., tit. 14, § 15000 et seq.; hereafter
Guidelines). . . .

[B] Other regulatory material

Notices of proposed regulatory changes and summaries of new regulations promulgated by California state agencies are published by the Office
of Administrative Law in the California Regulatory Notice Register (known
familiarly as the notice register or Z register). The notice register contains
notices and summaries, not text of regulations. Citations should give the
notice register year and issue number, and the page on which the item is
located.

(Cal. Reg. Notice Register 98, No. 24-Z, p. 1595.)

Regulatory material not subject to inclusion in the California Code
of Regulations (e.g., advice letters or case-specific interpretations) is dis-
seminated by the issuing agency, often via the agency's Web site. A citation
to such material should include the issuing agency, item, date, and page.

(Cal. Dept. of Justice, Div. of Law Enforcement, Information Bull. No.
92-22-BCID, July 29, 1992.)
(Consumer Product Safety Com., Off. of Gen. Counsel, Advisory Opn.
No. 312 (Mar. 6, 1991) p. 3.)

[C] Topical services

For areas of the law subject to close government regulation, various
topical services provide compilations of administrative and regulatory
material (e.g., regulations, rules, notices, orders, letters, reports, memo-
randa, and administrative adjudications). Citations to these topical services, when available, are helpful. Include as much of the following
information as is practical in the sequence suggested: (1) A description of
the item cited; (2) in parentheses, the date of adoption, filing, or issuance, if
applicable; (3) volume, if applicable; (4) publication title; (5) a parenthetical identifying the publisher; and, (6) paragraph, section, or page designations. (The term "transfer binder" in some publications is used to designate
the volume that holds materials pending hardcover binding.) Subsequent
citations can use *supra* in place of the date.

(Cal. Franchise Tax Bd., Notice No. 97-4 (June 2, 1997) Cal. Tax Reports
(CCH) ¶ 402-923.)

(Cal. Franchise Tax Bd., Legal Ruling No. 402 (Jan. 27, 1977) [1971–1978
    Transfer Binder] Cal. Tax Reports (CCH) ¶ 89-526, pp. 8624–8625.)
California Department of Health Care Services, All County Welfare
    Directors Letter No. 89-54 (July 24, 1989) [1988–1991 Transfer Binder]
    Medi-Cal Guide (CCH) paragraph 7108, pages 2915–2916 . . .
(Legal Ruling No. 348, Cal. Tax Reports (CCH) ¶ 204-903, *supra*, at
    p. 14,417.)
(Opn. Letter No. 1575, *supra*, Lab. L. Reports (CCH) ¶ 31,440 at
    p. 43,760.)

The following are examples for citing administrative adjudications
(see also ch. 1):

Appeal of Union Carbide Corporation (Apr. 5, 1984) Cal. Tax Reports
    (CCH) paragraph 400-813, page 23,211 . . .
(*Appeal of Hagen* (Apr. 9, 1986) 4 SBE 587, Cal. Tax Reports (CCH) ¶
    401-312.)
(*Appeal of DPF, Inc.* (Oct. 28, 1980) [1978–1981 Transfer Binder] Cal. Tax
    Reports (CCH) ¶ 206-430, p. 14,965-36.)
Furnish v. Merlo, supra, 128 Lab. Cas. (CCH) ¶ 57 at page 755 . . .

Topical services may also include pertinent judicial opinions
reviewing administrative adjudications and other regulatory action. A citation to a topical service may be included when these judicial opinions are
cited. For California Court of Appeal opinions, however, be sure the opinion is citable under rule 977, California Rules of Court. For citing judicial
opinions generally, including those in topical services, see chapter 1; for citing analytical material in topical services, see chapter 3.

§ 2:17 Local ordinances, codes, and charters

Identify the ordinance, code, or chapter, then the section or ordinance number. Use the exact designations (numbers, letters, symbols) of
the local enactments. Within parentheses, use the abbreviations in section
2:8, above. Always abbreviate "number" (No.). When the enactment cited is
not in force at the time of citation, specify the pertinent dates. The words
"charter," "ordinance," "resolution," and the like are capitalized only when
used with the name of the political subdivision or entity or when there is a
short cite. These citations are treated in the same manner as citations to
codes and regulations (see §§ 2:5, 2:16[A]). *Supra* is not used with subsequent citations.

[A] Ordinances

San Jose Ordinance No. 24680 added section 17.10.600 to the San Jose
    Municipal Code.
City of Escondido Ordinance No. 91-3, section 6.5

Section 17.12.010.I of the Roseville Sign Ordinance specifically prohibits: . . .

In resolution No. 94-73, the Albany City Council submitted the issue to the voters.

(L.A. Res. No. 1234.)

(Santa Ana Ord. No. NS-2160, adding art. VIII, § 10-400 et seq. to Santa Ana Mun. Code.)

[B] Codes

Los Angeles County Code section 22.08.160 P . . .

Los Angeles Municipal Code former section 91.0303(a)5 was found unconstitutional as applied.

Subdivisions (a)(2) and (c) of section 178 of the San Francisco Planning Code require . . . .

Santa Monica Municipal Code parts 9.04.06.030 and 9.04.04.100 address zoning.

(Nevada County Land Use and Development Code, art. 29, § L-II 29.2.)

(S.F. Planning Code, § 178, subds. (a)(2) & (c).)

(Santa Monica Mun. Code, pt. 9.12.010.)

(Lafayette Mun. Code, § 8-608, subd. (9).)

(Sac. County Code, ch. 9.87, § 9.89.020.)

[C] Charters

San Diego City Charter, article IX, section 143 . . .

Santa Monica City Arts Commission Charter (hereafter Charter) . . . . Charter section II states . . . .

Section 5.101 of the Charter of the City and County of San Francisco (hereafter Charter section 5.101) . . .

(Sac. County Charter, § 71-F(h).)

(S.F. Charter, §§ 8.102, 8.103.)

C. CALIFORNIA STATE AND LOCAL COURT RULES; STATE BAR RULES

§ 2:18 California Rules of Court

Give the title of the rules, followed by a comma, the word "rule," and the number. Do not use the designation "subdivision" (or "subd." in parentheses) when citing to California Rules of Court, State Bar rules and standards, appellate court local rules, trial court local rules, or Judicial Council sources. Citations to West's or Deering's Annotated Rules of Court, including State Bar rules, follow the style for citations to annotated codes (see § 2:9). An authoritative version of the Rules of Court, including recent amendments, is available on the Internet through the California Judicial Council at <http://www.courtinfo.ca.gov/judicialcouncil/>.

California Rules of Court, rule 224.

under California Rules of Court, rule 421(a)(1), (b)(2) . . . .
California Rules of Court, rules 4 and 5.
according to the Advisory Committee comment, California Rules of Court,
rule 28(e)(2) . . . .
(Cal. Rules of Court, rule 976.)
(Cal. Rules of Court, rules 106, 107(b), 976(c).)
(Cal. Rules of Court, rule 416(a), (b) & (d).)
(Cal. Rules of Court, rule 423(a)(2), (3) & (b)(5), (6).)
(Advisory Com. com., 23 pt. 2 West's Ann. Codes, Rules (1996 ed.) foll. rule
435, p. 66.)
(Advisory Com. com, Deering's Ann. Codes, Rules (1988 ed.) foll. rule 435,
p. 168.)

For capitalization of rules material, see section 4:10[C].

§ 2:19 Local appellate court rules, policies, and practices

Give the court of origin (including the division, if applicable), the name of the provisions cited, and the specific provision being cited. Include the provision's descriptive heading if the author's context for the cite does not make that redundant. Appellate court rules and related material are available from various commercial sources and also on the Internet at the judicial branch's Web site at <http://www.courtinfo.ca.gov.>

(Cal. Supreme Ct., Internal Operating Practices and Proc., VII A,
Submission.)
(Cal. Supreme Ct., Policies Regarding Cases Arising from Judgments of
Death, policy 2-6.)
(Ct. App., First Dist., Local Rules of Ct., rule 2(a), Docketing statements.)
(For requirements for augmentation of record on appeal, see Ct. App., First
Dist., Internal Operating Practices and Proc., III A, Procedures for
processing cases, Appeals, § 25(c).)
(Ct. App., First Dist., Policy Statement A, Assignment of writ petitions.)
(Ct. App., Second Dist., Local Rules, rule 2(a), Augmentation of record.)
(Ct. App., Second Dist., Div. Four, Internal Practices, IV, Oral argument.)
(Ct. App., Third Dist., Internal Practices, VI, Regular appeals; Oral
argument.)
(Ct. App., Third Dist., Internal Practices, appen. A-2, Augmentation of
record.)
(Ct. App., Fourth Dist., Local Rules, rule 1, Service of writ petitions.)
(Ct. App., Fourth Dist., Div. One, Internal Practices and Proc., VI A,
Screening and Processing of Cases.)
(Ct. App., Fifth Dist., Internal Practices, III C, Writs.)
(Ct. App., Sixth Dist., Internal Practices, II F, Settlement.)

§ 2:20 Local trial court rules

Local court rules are available from commercial sources and also directly from many courts via the Internet. The judicial branch's Web site at

<http://www.courtinfo.ca.gov> provides links to Web sites for local courts, including rules. In citing local court rules, give the court of origin, the name of the provisions cited (rules of court, internal practices, standards, etc.), and the particular provision and number.

> The Superior Court of Alameda County, Local Rules, rule 5.1 so provides.
> (Super. Ct. Alameda County, Local Rules, rule 5.1.)
> (Super. Ct. Contra Costa County, Stds. of Prof. Courtesy, std. IV.)
> (Super. Ct. L.A. County, Local Rules, rule 10.16.)
> (Super. Ct. L.A. County, Local Rules, rule 13.1.)
> (Super. Ct. Kern County, Rules for Admin. Civil Litigation, rule 10.)
> (Super. Ct. Alameda County, Local Rules, rule 13.1, Briefs.)
> (Super. Ct. L.A. County, Local Rules, rule 11.0 (c), Writ jurisdiction.)

§ 2:21 Standards of Judicial Administration, Code of Judicial Conduct, and Commission on Judicial Performance policies and rules

Judicial responsibilities and conduct are defined by the Standards of Judicial Administration Recommended by the Judicial Council and the California Code of Judicial Ethics, which are divisions I and II, respectively of the Appendix to California Rules of Court. Judicial conduct is also regulated by the Policy Declarations of the Commission on Judicial Performance and the Rules of the Commission on Judicial Performance. For citation purposes, give the name of the provisions and the provision number.

> (Cal. Stds. Jud. Admin., § 8.5.)
> (Cal. Code Jud. Ethics, canon 5A(3).)
> canon 3B(7)(a) of the California Code of Judicial Ethics, as
>   amended, . . .
> Section 9, California Standards of Judicial Administration, addresses
>   continuances.
> Rules of the Commission on Judicial Performance, rule 126 . . .
> rule 126 of the Rules of the Commission on Judicial Performance . . .
> (Rules of Com. on Jud. Performance, rule 126.)
> Policy Declarations of the Commission on Judicial Performance,
>   policy 1.1 . . .
> (Policy Declarations of Com. on Jud. Performance, policy 1.1.)

§ 2:22 Judicial Council reports and comments

The Judicial Council is charged with recommending procedures and adopting rules for improving the administration of justice and the courts. (Cal. Const., art. VI, § 6.) Many reports and recommendations, including those by committees and advisory committees, are available on the Internet through the California Judicial Council at <http://www.courtinfo.ca.gov/judicialcouncil/>.

(Judicial Council of Cal., Ann. Rep. (1994) p. xiii [total number of authorized judicial positions as of June 30, 1993].)

(Judicial Council of Cal., Rep. on Sen. Bill No. 1668 and Assem. Bill No. 3139 (1985–1986 Reg. Sess.) Mar. 21, 1986, p. 2.)

(Judicial Council of Cal., Advisory Com. Rep., Achieving Equal Justice for Women and Men in the California Courts (1996) p. 318.)

(Jud. Council of Cal., Admin. Off. of Cts., Rep. on Court Statistics (1997) Fiscal Year 1995–1996 Data and Statewide Trends for California Appellate and Trial Courts, p. 21.)

(Judicial Council of Cal., com., reprinted at 14 West's Ann. Code Civ. Proc. (1973 ed.) foll. § 415.50, p. 561.)

(Judicial Council of Cal., com., reprinted at Deering's Ann. Code Civ. Proc. (1991 ed.) foll. § 415.50, p. 676.)

(See Rules on Appeal, adopted by Judicial Council of Cal. Mar. 30, 1943, eff. July 1, 1943, printed at 22 Cal.2d 1, 28.)

(Judicial Council Forms, form AB-110.)

§ 2:23 State Bar rules and standards

The rules and procedures of the State Bar of California are often included in commercial compilations of rules (e.g., annual desktop editions of California rules by various publishers). Provide the name of the provisions and the provision number. If the author's context does not indicate the source of the rule (i.e., the State Bar), then the cite should include an appropriate reference.

(Rules and Regs. of State Bar, art. I, § 2.)

(Rules Regulating Admission to Practice Law, rules II, § 1 & X, § 6.)

(Rules Prof. Conduct, rule 1-100(D)(2).)

(Rules Proc. of State Bar, rule 51(c)(4).)

(Rules Proc. of State Bar, tit. IV, Stds. for Atty. Sanctions for Prof. Misconduct, std. 1.7.)

(State Bar Ct. Rules of Prac., rule 1110(a).)

(State Bar Stds. Certif. Crim. L., § 5.1.4.) [*Also*, Certif. Fam. L.; Certif. Tax L.; Certif. Workers' Comp. L.; Certif. Immig. and Nat. L.; Certif. Estate Planning, Trust and Prob. L.]

article I, section 2 of the Rules and Regulations of the State Bar.

the State Bar Rules Regulating Admission to Practice Law, rule 5, section 4 provides . . . .

Rule 3-110(A) of the Rules of Professional Conduct . . .

Rule 7-106(A) of the State Bar Rules of Professional Conduct . . .

rule 201(a) of the Rules of Procedure of the State Bar . . .

Rules of Procedure of the State Bar, title IV, Standards for Attorney Sanctions for Professional Misconduct, standard 1.2(b)(iii) (all further references to standards are to this source). . . . As stated in standard 1.2(b)(ii), . . . (See std. 1.2(b)(iv).)

rule 1110(a) of the State Bar Court Rules of Practice sets forth . . . .

Section 3.1.1 of the State Bar Standards for Certification in Criminal Law . . .

D. CALIFORNIA LEGISLATIVE HISTORY AND GOVERNMENTAL MATERIALS

§ 2:24 General guidelines

In recent years legislative and governmental materials have become more readily accessible for interpreting statutory provisions. For a description of these sources, see Henke's California Law Guide (3d ed. 1995) chapters 4, Legislative Intent, and 11, Law Libraries and Legal Databases, and also appendix A, Publishers/Vendors of California Legal Information. Also, Web sites for some law school libraries provide guides on conducting a legislative history search, with descriptions of legislative source material. In addition, some opinions have mentioned the Legislative Intent Service, which is a commercial service providing legislative history documents and analyses in a report format for particular enactments.

While citation style is fairly standardized for frequently cited materials (see §§ 2:25–2:29), formulaic styles cannot, as a practical matter, be provided for the diversity of items now readily available. As to items for which a specific style and example is not given, provide as much of the following information as possible in the order listed:

1. Name of the item's author or the issuing entity (not to be confused with a bill's author, who is not usually included in legislative history citations);

2. Name or description of the document;

3. Legislative bill to which the document applies;

4. Legislative session;

5. Date of the document or action taken;

6. Volume and name of the publication in which the document is contained; and

7. Section number or page number where the document can be found.

§ 2:25 Bills and subsequent legislative action

[A] Senate and Assembly bills

Each two-year legislative session convenes on the first Monday in December of even-numbered years and adjourns on November 30 of the following even-numbered year. Bills introduced into the Legislature have a life until the session ends and are numbered consecutively for the two-year period. Designate the house of introduction, number assigned, legislative session, and any section number. (See also § 2:11.)

(Sen. Bill No. 123 (1993–1994 Reg. Sess.) § 1.)

(Assem. Bill No. 123 (1995–1996 Reg. Sess.) § 1.)
(Assem. Bill No. 971 (1993–1994 Reg. Sess.) as introduced Mar. 3, 1993.)
(Sen. Bill No. 11X (1997–1998 1st Ex. Sess.).)

[B] Subsequent legislative action on bills

References to legislative action following a bill's introduction should specify (in addition to house of introduction, number, and legislative session) the acting entity, the action taken, and the date of action. The examples below include two cites with cross-references to the house's final history for that session.

It is noteworthy that Senate Bill No. 18 (1991–1992 Reg. Sess.) was amended by the Assembly on May 25, 1992.
(Assem. Amend. to Sen. Bill No. 18 (1991–1992 Reg. Sess.) May 25, 1992.)
(Sen. Amend. to Assem. Bill No. 1 (1995–1996 Reg. Sess.) June 12, 1995.)
(Conf. Amend. to Sen. Bill. No. 1989 (1979–1980 Reg. Sess.) Aug. 27, 1980.)
(Sen. Bill No. 958, approved by Governor, Sept. 30, 1991, Sen. Final Hist. (1991–1992 Reg. Sess.) p. 598.)
(Assem. Bill No. 770, 3d reading June 25, 1987, 1 Assem. Final Hist. (1987–1988 Reg. Sess.) p. 575.)

For citing legislative committee analyses and reports, see section 2:28.

[C] Pre-1973 bills

Until 1973, a regular legislative session lasted only one year. Bills introduced during extraordinary sessions were numbered independently of the regular session. Designate the house of introduction, number assigned, legislative session, and any section number.

(Sen. Bill No. 176 (1972 Reg. Sess.) § 1.)
(Assem. Bill No. 20 (1971 1st Ex. Sess.) § 4.)

§ 2:26 Senate and Assembly resolutions

Cite legislative resolutions in the same manner as bills. Designate house of introduction, resolution number, and legislative session.

(Sen. Res. No. 1 (1991–1992 Reg. Sess.).)
(Assem. Res. No. 1 (1995–1996 Reg. Sess.).)

Adopted concurrent resolutions (relating to business of the Legislature) and joint resolutions (relating to the federal government) are assigned resolution chapter numbers. They are published in Statutes and Amendments to the Codes, and that source should be cited once a citation is available. The session parenthetical is inserted after the Stats. year designation.

(Sen. Conc. Res. No. 1, Stats. 1991 (1991–1992 Reg. Sess.) res. ch. 126, par. 8.5, p. 6171.)

(Assem. Conc. Res. No. 162, Stats. 1990 (1989–1990 Reg. Sess.) res. ch. 165, pp. 8383-8384.)

(Assem. Joint Res. No. 21, Stats. 1988 (1987–1988 Reg. Sess.) res. ch. 3, pp. 6051–6052.)

Senate Joint Resolution No. 10 (1995–1996 Reg. Sess.) resolution chapter 70, relative to the federal government's role in state transportation projects . . . .

§ 2:27 Constitutional amendments

Cite proposed amendments in the same manner as bills (see § 2:24). When the proposed constitutional amendment is *not adopted* by the Legislature, simply designate the house of introduction, number assigned, and legislative session. For amendments proposed by other bodies, do not include a session designation.

(Sen. Const. Amend. No. 1 (1997–1998 Reg. Sess.).)

(Assem. Const. Amend. No. 1 (1997–1998 Reg. Sess.).)

(Cal. Const. Revision Com., Proposed Revision (1966) p. 63.)

(Cal. Const. Revision Com., Final Rep. and Recommendations to Governor and Legis. (1996) pt. III, Changing K-12 Education, item No. 23.)

Constitutional amendments *adopted* by the Legislature are assigned consecutive chapter numbers. They appear in Statutes and Amendments to the Codes and should be cited to that source. Give the house of introduction and number, the legislative session, the "Stats." year, the resolution chapter number, and the page number.

(Sen. Const. Amend. No. 6, Stats. 1988 (1987–1988 Reg. Sess.) res. ch. 67, pp. 6115–6116.)

(Assem. Const. Amend. No. 4, Stats. 1978 (1977–1978 Reg. Sess.) res. ch. 77, pp. 4819–4820.)

For citing repealed, new, recently amended, or transferred sections of the California Constitution, see section 2:4.

§ 2:28 Legislative committee reports and analyses

[A] Reports on specific legislation

Provide the committee name, the document cited (analysis, comment, report, etc.), the bill to which it applies, the legislative session, a date identifying the version of the legislation (if material) and the page at which the cited matter is located.

(Sen. Rules Com., Off. of Sen. Floor Analyses, 3d reading analysis of Sen. Bill No. 1324 (1993–1994 Reg. Sess.) as amended May 27, 1995, par. 6.)

(Sen. Com. on Judiciary, Analysis of Sen. Bill No. 1827 (1993–1994 Reg. Sess.) as amended Mar. 26, 1994.)

(Assem. Com. on Transportation, Rep. on Sen. Bill No. 1209 (1993–1994 Reg. Sess.) as amended July 14, 1993, p. 3.)

(Sen. Rules Com., Off. of Sen. Floor Analyses, Rep. on Sen. Bill No. 1531 (1993–1994 Reg. Sess.) May 10, 1994, p. 2.)

(Assem. Com. on Consumer Protection, Governmental Efficiency and Economic Development, Rep. on Assem. Bill No. 1382 (1991–1992 Reg. Sess.) May 8, 1991 [proposed amendment].)

(Sen. Com. on Judiciary, com. on Assem. Bill No. 3212 (1965 Reg. Sess.) reprinted at 29B pt. 4 West's Ann. Evid. Code (1995 ed.) foll. § 1200, pp. 3–4.)

(Cal. Dept. Corrections, Estimates and Statistical Analysis Section, Analysis of Sen. Bill No. 1857 (1983–1984 Reg. Sess.) Apr. 9, 1984, attachment A.) [*Note: Date is the date of the analysis.*]

as stated at pages 1–2 of the report by the Senate Committee on the Judiciary on Assembly Bill No. 162 (1989–1990 Reg. Sess) as introduced.

[B] Reports not related to specific legislation

Name the committee, the title and date of the report or hearing, and the page on which the cited material appears. If the volume's contents are not consecutively numbered (e.g., the Appendix to the Senate Journal), relocate the page number designation to avoid confusion (see Sen. J. examples below).

(Sen. Select Com. on Children and Youth, Rep. on Child Abuse Reporting Laws, Juvenile Court Dependency Statutes, and Child Welfare Services (Jan. 1988) p. i.)

(Assem. Select Com. on Cal. Wine Production and Economy, Interim Hearing on Wine and Grape Research and its Impact on Cal. Wine Industry (Oct. 16, 1991), testimony of Linda Bisson, p. 78.)

(Assem. Com. on Elections, Reapportionment and Const. Amends, hg. on redistricting, identification of communities of interest in the Mid and Lower San Joaquin Valley areas (June 20, 1991), letter of Roberto G. Romandia, p. 130.)

as noted in the Senate Permanent Factfinding Committee Report on Natural Resources, Geothermal Resources, section 1, page 9, Appendix to Senate Journal (1967 Reg. Sess.).

For citing individual documents not collected in a volume, see section 2:35.

§ 2:29 Legislative Counsel opinions, reports, and digests

The Legislative Counsel drafts legislation, renders legal opinions, provides legal counsel to legislative committees and state agencies, and summarizes bills. If the document cited concerns a bill, identify the bill and the legislative session.

[A] Opinions and reports

Include the opinion number and date. Citations to an opinion published in a legislative journal should include that cross-reference.

> (Ops. Cal. Legis. Counsel, No. 22732 (Sept. 26, 1986) School Facilities Fees: Special School Taxes, p. 4.)
>
> (Ops. Cal. Legis. Counsel, No. 18082 (July 9, 1986) p. 11.)
>
> The opinion of the Legislative Counsel of California, No. 32596, filed December 17, 1993, entitled California Marketing Act of 1937: Issuance of Marketing Orders, at page 2, states . . . .
>
> (See Ops. Cal. Legis. Counsel, No. 15616 (June 30, 1982) Mobilehome Residency Law (Assem. Bill No. 2429) 10 Assem. J. (1981–1982 Reg. Sess.) pp. 17855–17856.)
>
> (Legis. Counsel, Rep. on Sen. Bill No. 1140 (1961 Reg. Sess.) p. 1.)

[B] Digests

Identify the document and note the legislative session. If the digest appears in the Summary Digest section of Statutes and Amendments to the Codes, follow the examples below:

> (Legis. Counsel's Dig., Sen. Conc. Amends. to Assem. Bill No. 888 (1995–1996 Reg. Sess.).)
>
> (Legis. Counsel's Dig., Sen. Conc. Res. No. 4 (1985–1986 1st Ex. Sess.).)
>
> (See Legis. Counsel's Dig., Sen. Bill No. 1870, 6 Stats. 1982 (1981–1982 Reg. Sess.) Summary Dig., p. 430.)
>
> (Legis. Counsel's Dig., Assem. Bill No. 162 (1989–1990 Reg. Sess.) 4 Stats. 1989, Summary Dig., p. 121.)
>
> as the Legislative Counsel's Digest of Assembly Bill No. 307 (3 Stats. 1971 (Reg. Sess.) Summary Dig., p. 11) notes . . . .

§ 2:30 Other legislative sources

Other offices in the Capitol are regularly involved in providing research and analysis of legislation (e.g., under the Joint Legislative Budget Committee, the Legislative Analyst's Office provides fiscal and policy analyses of legislation, including ballot initiatives). Identify the author or agency, the document, bill, legislative session, document date, if available, and page.

> (Legis. Analyst, analysis of Assem. Bill No. 3833 (1983–1984 Reg. Sess.) p. 1.)

(Legis. Analyst, Rep. to Joint Legis. Budget Com., analysis of 1974–1975
Budget Bill, Sen. Bill No. 1525 (1973–1974 Reg. Sess.) p. 626.)
(Sen. Democratic Caucus, analysis of Assem. Bill No. 493 (1983–1984 Reg.
Sess.) as amended Sept. 7, 1983, p. 2.)
(Sen. Republican Caucus, analysis of Assem. Bill No. 3833 (1983–1984 Reg.
Sess.) p. 2.)
(Off. of Sen. Floor Analyses, 3d reading analysis of Sen. Bill No. 2079
(1989–1990 Reg. Sess.) June 7, 1990, p. 1.)
(Assem. Off. of Research, 3d reading analysis of Assem. Bill No. 114
(1989–1990 Reg. Sess.) June 30, 1989, p. 2.)

For Legislative Analyst's ballot summaries, see section 2:34; for legislative committee reports, see section 2:28.

§ 2:31 Legislative journals, Governor's messages, and executive orders

The Assembly Journal and Senate Journal volumes contain the daily minutes of the legislative proceedings of each house. These volumes also contain some committee reports, Governor's messages on legislation signed or vetoed, records of votes, and other material. Identify the author and the item, and provide the volume designation, legislative session, and page.

[A] Legislative journals

(Sen. Com. on Judiciary, Rep. on Assem. Bills Nos. 25 & 68 (1983–1984
Reg. Sess.) 3 Sen. J. (1983–1984 Reg. Sess.) p. 4882.)
as the vote record showed. (4 Assem. J. (1993–1994 Reg. Sess.) p. 6464.)
as the vote record showed. (3 Sen. J. (1983–1984 Reg. Sess.) p. 4882.)

[B] Governor's messages and executive orders

(Governor's veto message to Assem. on Assem. Bill No. 2414 (Sept. 30,
1994) 6 Assem. J. (1993–1994 Reg. Sess.) p. 9470.)
(Governor's veto message to Assem. on Assem. Bill No. 3476 (Sept. 20,
1992) Recess J. No. 24 (1991–1992 Reg. Sess.) p. 10271.)
(Governor's veto message to Sen. on Sen. Bill No. 937 (1991–1992 Reg.
Sess.) Sen. Daily File (Sept. 26, 1992) p. 68.)
(Governor's budget message to Leg. (Nov. 9, 1981) 10 Assem. J. (1981 1st
Ex. Sess.) p. 3.)
(Governor's Exec. Order No. W-15-91 (July 17, 1991).)
(Governor's Objections to Budget Act of 1991, Stats. 1991, ch. 118, pp.
791–810.)

§ 2:32 Government reports from departments and agencies

Give the author or agency, name of the report (for specific legislation, legislative session information is parenthetically included with the name), date of the report, and any chapter, table, section, and page.

[A] Reports on specific legislation

(Cal. Youth and Adult Correctional Agency, analysis of Sen. Bill No. 2079 (1989–1990 Reg. Sess.) Aug. 31, 1990, p. 1.)

(Cal. Dept. of Industrial Relations, Enrolled Bill Rep. on Assem. Bill No. 276 (1989–1990 Reg. Sess.) prepared for Governor Deukmejian (Sept. 19, 1989) pp. 1, 4.)

(Cal. Highway Patrol, Enrolled Bill Rep. on Assem. Bill No. 766 (1987–1988 Reg. Sess.) Sept. 18, 1987.)

(Dept. Consumer Affairs, Enrolled Bill Rep. on Assem. Bill No. 3374 (1977–1978 Reg. Sess.) Aug. 30, 1978, p. 3.)

[B] Reports not related to specific legislation

(Cal. Dept. of Corrections, Cal. Prisoners and Parolees, 1993 and 1994 (1996) Behavior of Inmates in CDC Institutions, p. 67.)

(Cal. Highway Patrol, Statewide Integrated Traffic Records System (SWITRS), Ann. Rep. of Fatal and Injury Motor Vehicle Traffic Accidents (1990) table 6C: Fatal and Injury Truck Accidents by County, 1986–1990, p. 39.)

(Cal. P.U.C. and Cal. Dept. Health Services, Rep. to Legis., Potential Health Effects of Electric and Magnetic Fields from Electric Power Facilities (1989) p. C-20.)

(Com. on Cal. State Government Organization and Economy, The Bureaucracy of Care (1983) pp. 128–129 (hereafter Bureaucracy of Care).)

(Cal. Dept. of Housing and Community Development, A Survey of Second Unit Ordinances in Cal., An Approach to Increasing the Housing Supply (Nov. 1982) pp. 25–26, 42, 44.)

§ 2:33 Law Revision Commission reports, recommendations, and comments

The Law Revision Commission is a statutory body charged with making recommendations and reports on updating California law. Note from the examples that citation forms differ depending on whether the source cited is the California Law Revision Commission Reports or one of the annotated codes, which sometimes include material from the commission as editorial enhancements. When using the print version of an annotated code rather than the original source, include the date of publication for the code volume and the section to which the commission's report or comment pertains (see also § 2:9). California Law Revision Commission materials are available on the commission's Web site at <http://www.clrc.ca.gov/>.

(Recommendation: Inheritance by Foster Child or Stepchild (Oct. 1997) 27 Cal. Law Revision Com. Rep. (1997) p. x6 [preprint copy].)

Recommendation on Unfair Competition Litigation (Nov. 1996) 26
California Law Revision Commission Report (1996) page 232 . . .
(Recommendation Relating to Uniform Durable Power of Attorney Act
(Dec. 1980) 15 Cal. Law Revision Com. Rep. (1980) p. 357.)
(Cal. Law Revision Com. com., 29B West's Ann. Evid. Code (1995 ed.) foll.
§ 351, p. 180.)
(See Cal. Law Revision Com. com., Deering's Ann. Fam. Code (1994 ed.)
foll. § 3021, p. 226.)
(7 Cal. Law Revision Com. Rep. (1965) p. 1, reprinted in Deering's Ann.
Evid. Code (1986 ed.) foll. § 1502, p. 518].)

§ 2:34 Ballot pamphlets

[A] Citation to pamphlet

Ballot pamphlets for state elections, issued by the Secretary of State,
contain arguments, analyses, and texts of measures submitted to the electorate. For citation purposes, ballot pamphlets are identified by date and
type of election. State elections are designated as primary or general or special. (Elec. Code, § 9081; see Elec. Code, § 9084 [contents].) Other elections are local (municipal, district, school district, etc.), consolidated (with
a state election), emergency, or recall. (See Elec. Code, § 10000 et seq.)
Voter pamphlets are prepared by local elections officials. (Elec. Code, §
13307; see Elec. Code, §§ 13308, 13312.)

(Ballot Pamp., Primary Elec. (June 2, 1998) argument in favor of Prop. 220,
p. 10.)
(Ballot Pamp., Primary Elec. (June 2, 1998) text of Prop. 220, p. 65 et seq.)
(See Ballot Pamp., Gen. Elec. (Nov. 7, 1972), argument in favor of Prop. 11,
pp. 26–27; *id.*, rebuttal to argument against Prop. 11, p. 28.)
(Santa Clara County Sample Ballot and Voter Information Pamp., Gen. Elec.
(Nov. 5, 1996) analysis of Measure A by county counsel, p. 20)
(hereafter Pamphlet).) . . . (Pamphlet, *supra*, text of Measure A, pp.
020–021.)
(S.F. Voter Information Pamp. (Nov. 6, 1990) pp. 126, 142, 152.)
according to the analysis of Proposition 32 by the Legislative Analyst,
printed in the ballot pamphlet for the General Election of November 6,
1994.

[B] Name of measure

If the name used is the measure's official name (e.g., Measure A,
Proposition 13) capitalize the name throughout. Voter measures also often
become known by a popular name (e.g., the "Victims' Bill of Rights," the
"Three Strikes" law). Authors may adopt such popular names for use in the
opinion, brief, or other document by enclosing the adopted name with quotation marks for the first use, then using the name thereafter without

quotation marks, or by parenthetically adopting the name without quotation marks after the first citation to the official cite. Adopted popular names are capitalized at the discretion of the author.

> Article I, section 1 of the California Constitution (the Privacy Initiative) was added in 1972. (Ballot Pamp., Gen. Elec. (Nov. 7, 1972), argument in favor of Prop. 11, pp. 26–27; *id.,* rebuttal to argument against Prop. 11, p. 28.)
>
> The Fair Responsibility Act of 1986 (Civ. Code, §§ 1431–1431.5), known as Proposition 51, begins with a statement of "Findings and Declaration of Purpose" (Civ. Code, § 1431.1).
>
> Penal Code section 1170.12 is the codification of the initiative version of the "Three Strikes" law (Prop. 184, as approved by voters, Gen. Elec. (Nov. 8, 1994)).
>
> In June 1978, California voters approved Proposition 13, also known as the "Jarvis-Gann Property Tax Initiative," which added article XIII A to the state Constitution.
>
> The residential growth control initiative commonly known as Proposition A is found in chapter 32A of the City of Oceanside Municipal Code.

§ 2:35 Letters and memoranda

When a letter or memorandum is incorporated in a volume, such as a legislative report (see § 2:28) or a commercial publication (see § 2:16), cite to that work. When it is a stand-alone item (e.g., part of the record in the proceeding at issue) cite to it separately. Provide the author or authoring agency, a description of the document (e.g., letter or memorandum), the legislative bill and session (if applicable), the date of the document, and the volume and page number of the publication containing the document, if any. (For general guidelines on citing legislative history material, see § 2:24.)

> (Chief Counsel Richard B. Inglehart, letter to Assemblyman Bob Epple, Jan. 12, 1994.)
>
> (Lawrence E. Green, Cal. Land Title Assn., letter to Sen. Quentin Kopp, Apr. 5, 1993.)
>
> (Paul Gladfelty, Associated Gen. Contractors of Cal., mem. to Dan Friedlander, Chief of Staff to Sen. Quentin Kopp, May 3, 1993.)
>
> (PERS Asst. Exec. Officer Sandra C. Lund, mem. to PERS Chief Executive Officer Dale Hanson, Nov. 12, 1992, p. 1.) [*This example assumes the PERS acronym was previously specified by the author as an adopted name.*]
>
> (State Bd. of Equalization, letter of intent to Governor Deukmejian re Sen. Bill No. 124 (1989–1990 Reg. Sess.) June 7, 1990.)
>
> (Gen. Legis. Counsel, League of Cal. Cities, letter to Governor Edmund G. Brown, Jr. (1977–1978 Reg. Sess.) Sept. 15, 1978, Governor's chaptered bill files, ch. 1113.)

(Sen. Russell, sponsor of Sen. Bill No. 901 (1987–1988 Reg. Sess.), letter to Governor, Aug. 28, 1988.) [*Order of information is slightly modified in this example to permit clearer identification of author.*]
and State Board of Equalization Letters to County Assessors Nos. 89/34, Base-Year Value Corrections (Apr. 7, 1989), 90-/03, Proposition 58 (Jan. 10, 1990), and 91/53, Refunds Resulting From Base Year Value Corrections (July 16, 1991).
The letter from Senator Maddy to which this initial section of the statute referred appears in the Journal of the Senate (1989–1990 Reg. Sess.) volume 5, pages 8463–8465.

§ 2:36 Internet sources of legislative history information

Much legislative information is accessible via the Internet from various state offices and agencies. Many of these can be reached through links on the State of California's Web site at <http://www.ca.gov/s/>, or through direct Internet addresses (see below). Information found on state government Web sites should be cited in the manner otherwise prescribed in this manual for the information (see, for example, § 2:24, which provides guidelines for citing legislative information when no specific example is provided). In addition to the cite, it is helpful to note that the Internet was relied on as the source, particularly for material not otherwise readily available. In noting such reliance, include as much of the Uniform Resource Locator (URL) (i.e., the Internet address) information as is necessary to facilitate locating the material on the Web site. The URL information is placed in angled brackets, followed by the date the Web site was visited, signalled by the phrase "as of" in conjunction with the date, using regular brackets when the citation is in parentheses.

(Ballot Pamp., Primary Elec. (June 2, 1998) argument in favor of Prop. 220, p. 10, at <http://Primary98.ss.ca.gov/VoterGuide/Propositions/220.htm> [as of Feb. 25, 1999].)

The following is a sampling of government Internet sources for California legislative material:

State of California's Web site
<http://www.ca.gov/s/>
This site provides links to the executive, judicial, and legislative government branches, and to most state offices and agencies.

Official California Legislative Information [Legislative Counsel of California]
<http://www.leginfo.ca.gov/>
This site, maintained by the Legislative Counsel, contains a comprehensive collection of legislation information. At present, the Bill Information link allows access to all bills introduced from the 1993–1994 session forward, including bill texts, amendments, committee analyses, bill digests, votes, and status. The California Law link provides access to all 29 California

codes, the state Constitution, and uncodified statutes. The Daily Updates link allows status checks on the current legislative session, including legislation, as well as any veto messages.

California Secretary of State
<http://www.ss.ca.gov/>
The ballot pamphlets of current and recent state elections (from 1996 forward) can be found at this site, with full texts of all ballot measures, including the analyses of the Legislative Analyst, arguments, and rebuttals.

Legislative Analyst's Office
<http://www.lao.ca.gov/>
This site hosts a list of all Legislative Analyst's Office reports and publications from 1985 to the present, most of which can be accessed directly from the site.

E. FEDERAL STATUTES, RULES, AND OTHER MATERIALS

§ 2:37 United States Code

The preferable citation for codified statutes currently in force is to the United States Code (U.S.C.), but the United States Code Annotated (U.S.C.A.) and the United States Code Service (U.S.C.S.) are also acceptable. Cite the title number, the code compilation, and the section number. Neither the word "subdivision" nor the abbreviation "subd." is used with federal statutes. For codified statues, it is usually not helpful to cite the Public Law or Statutes at Large instead of providing the code cite, but a Statutes at Large reference is helpful for superseded provisions and other circumstances described in section 2:38. Rarely, language in the codified version will differ from the Public Law or Statutes at Large version; the latter controls and should be cited in such circumstances.

(7 U.S.C. § 5.) *or* (7 U.S.C.A. § 5.) *or* (7 U.S.C.S. § 5.)
(26 U.S.C. § 2056(b)(7)(B)(v).)
(42 U.S.C. §§ 2000e(b), 12111(5)(A).)
(52 Stat. 821, 15 U.S.C. § 717 et seq.)
(86 Stat. 770, as amended, 5 U.S.C. Appen. §§ 1–15.)
(50 U.S.C. Appen. § 510.)
(Fair Labor Standards Act of 1938, § 13(b)(11), 29 U.S.C § 213(b)(11).)
   [*Citation is to section 13 of the Act, which is section 213 of title 29.*]
the Age Discrimination in Employment Act (29 U.S.C. § 621 et seq.).
the Americans with Disabilities Act (42 U.S.C. § 12111 et seq.).
This definition applies to section 1983 of title 42 of the United States Code.
Title I of ERISA was codified as subchapter I of chapter 18 of title 29 of the United States Code. (See hist. notes, 29 U.S.C.A. (1999) foll. § 1002, p. 731.)
Title 42 United States Code section 2000bb-1 states: . . .

The Railroad Retirement Act of 1937, 50 Statutes at Large 309, as
amended, 45 United States Code section 228b(a)4 . . . .
under title VII of the Civil Rights Act of 1964 (42 U.S.C. § 2000e et seq.) as
amended by the Equal Employment Opportunity Act of 1972 (Pub.L.
No. 92-261, 86 Stat. 103).

§ 2:38 Public Laws and Statutes at Large

The Statutes at Large volumes contain the chronological compilation
of all enactments for each congressional session. A Statutes at Large citation
indicates the volume and the page (e.g., 100 Stat. 298). In most instances, citing to the codified version of statutes (i.e., citing to the United States Code) is
preferred, but a citation to the Statutes at Large should be made when referring to (1) a recent enactment, (2) a repealed or superseded law, (3) an
uncodified law, or (4) an enactment scattered among several titles, making a
United States Code reference impractical. A Statutes at Large citation is also
helpful when referring to a law's enactment, amendment, or repeal.

A bill is assigned a public law number immediately upon enactment
(e.g., Pub.L. No. 105-100). The number before the hyphen is the congressional session and the second number is the number of the enactment for
that session. Federal laws first appear in separate pamphlets as slip laws and
later in the bound Statutes at Large as session laws.

Cite the act name, the public law number, the section or chapter
cited, the full date, the Statutes at Large volume and page, and the reference
source, if any. If the law has no formal name, use "Act of" plus the date.

Congress has now passed the Child Support Performance and Incentive Act
of 1999 (Pub.L. No. 105-200 (July 16, 1998) 112 Stat. 645, 1998 U.S.
Code Cong. & Admin. News, No. 7). [*U.S. Code Cong. & Admin. News
reference is an optional parallel cite.*]
The AFDC program was amended by the Welfare Reform Act of 1996.
(Pub.L. No. 104-193 (Aug. 22, 1996) 110 Stat. 2105.) [*Note: This
example assumes the AFDC acronym was previously defined.*]
(Antiterrorism and Effective Death Penalty Act of 1996, Pub.L. No. 104-132
(Apr. 24, 1996) 110 Stat. 1214, 1217; see also 28 U.S.C.A. § 2244.)
(Act of Feb. 20, 1905, ch. 592, § 1-23, 33 Stat. 724.)
(Act of Aug. 27, 1958, Pub.L. No. 85-767, § 2, 72 Stat. 899.)
whereas under the Civil Rights Act of 1991 (Pub.L. No. 102-166 (Nov. 21,
1991) 105 Stat. 1071) . . . .
The federal Fair Housing Amendments Act of 1988 (Pub.L. No. 100-430,
§ 13(a) (Sept. 13, 1988), 102 Stat. 1636) has been codified in 42 United
States Code section 3601 et seq. in the Fair Housing Act.

For citing to the United States Code Congressional and Administrative News, see section 2:47.

§ 2:39 Popular names

Providing an act's popular name, if any, often assists in identification and may be helpful as an abbreviated form to avoid lengthy repetition.

> Defendant contends that the Americans with Disabilities Act of 1990 (ADA) (42 U.S.C. § 12111 et seq.) mandates an additional jury instruction. However, the ADA . . . .
>
> Respondents rely on the wording of the Wagner-O'Day Act (41 U.S.C. §§ 46–48 (1938)) (hereafter Wagner). . . . Wagner came into being as a response to . . . .
>
> Jurisdiction is covered in section 1964(c) of title 18 of the United States Code, which is part of the Racketeer Influenced and Corrupt Organizations Act (RICO); it provides that a person injured by a RICO violation may sue in any appropriate United States district court. (Pub.L. No. 91-452, tit. IX (Oct. 14, 1970) 84 Stat. 944.)

§ 2:40 Internal Revenue Code

The Internal Revenue Code, appearing under title 26 of the United States Code with identical section numbering, is sometimes cited by its own name without a parallel reference to either the United States Code or the Statutes at Large.

Several Internal Revenue Codes have been enacted. If the citation is to the current code, the date of enactment is unnecessary. If an author is comparing an earlier and a later provision, code enactment dates should be included. It is also helpful to cite to the Statutes at Large when citing a superseded or repealed code provision (see § 2:38).

> (Int.Rev. Code, § 7237(c).)
>
> Internal Revenue Code of 1986 section 1012.
>
> Section 61 of the Internal Revenue Code (26 U.S.C. § 61) defines gross income.

§ 2:41 Congressional bills and resolutions

Note the house, number, legislative session, section (if any), page, and year.

[A] Bills

> (H.R. No. 49, 105th Cong., 1st Sess., § 2, p. 1 (1997).)
>
> (Sen. No. 2301, 105th Cong., 2d Sess. (1998).)

[B] Resolutions

> (H.Res. No. 20, 105th Cong., 1st. Sess. (1997).)
>
> (Sen.Res. No. 79, 105th Cong., 1st Sess. (1997).)

After adoption, single house resolutions are cited to the Congressional Record; joint resolutions are cited to the Statutes at Large or the Congressional Record.

> (Sen.Res. No. 10, 100th Cong., 1st Sess. (1991) 100 Cong. Rec. 100.)
> (Sen.J.Res. No. 59, 86th Cong., 1st Sess. (1959) 73 Stat. 111.)
> (H.Con.Res. No. 10, 100th Cong., 2d Sess. (1991) 150 Stat. 150.)

[C] Citation abbreviations

House Bill No. 46	H.R. No. 46
Senate Bill No. 28	Sen. No. 28
House Resolution No. 5	H.Res. No. 5
Senate Resolution No. 103	Sen.Res. No. 103
House Concurrent Resolution No. 114	H.Con.Res. No. 114
Senate Concurrent Resolution No. 22	Sen.Con.Res. No. 22
House Joint Resolution No. 10	H.J.Res. No. 10
Senate Joint Resolution No. 3	Sen.J.Res. No. 3

§ 2:42 Congressional reports, documents, hearings, debates, and addresses

The reports, documents, debate transcripts, and other material generated by Congress appear in many published and computerized sources. The Congressional Record (Cong. Rec.) contains a verbatim record of all congressional debates, proceedings, and activities. It is published daily and compiled in bound form at session's end. Because it is repaginated in its compiled edition, a citation to the daily edition should so indicate.

The Journals of both the House and Senate also record daily proceedings. The United States Code Congressional and Administrative News prints bills, reports, and other documents. In addition, bills, reports, and documents of both houses are available on the Internet at <http://www.house.gov/Welcome2.html> (House of Representatives) and <http://www.senate.gov/home.html> (Senate). Congress also publishes reports and documents as separate, stand-alone items.

[A] Reports

Give the document and number, the Congress and session, and the page and year. In 1969 (91st Cong.) the number of the Congress became part of the report number.

> (H.R.Rep. No. 103-88, 1st Sess., pp. 3, 6, 7 (1993).)
> (Sen.Rep. No. 103-361, 2d Sess. (1994), reprinted in 1994 U.S. Code Cong. & Admin. News, p. 3262.)
> (Sen.Rep. No. 103-111, 1st Sess., p. 9 (1993), reprinted in 1993 U.S. Code Cong. & Admin. News, p. 1898.)

[B] Documents

Give the title, house, document number, Congress and session, year, and page.

> (Engle Central Valley Project Docs., H.R.Doc. No. 246, 85th Cong., 1st
>   Sess., pt. 2 (1957) pp. 698–702.)
> (Recommendations for Soc. Security Legislation, Sen.Doc. No. 208, 80th
>   Cong., 2d Sess. (1949) at p. 38.)

[C] Committee hearings

Give the house and committee, any subcommittee, the Congress and session, and the section and page numbers. The title of the hearings, if included, should begin the citation. If specific testimony is cited, insert the witness's name at the end of the citation.

> (Religious Freedom Restoration Act of 1990, Hearings before House Com.
>   on Judiciary, Subcom. on Civil and Constitutional Rights on H.R. No.
>   5377, 101st Cong., 2d Sess., § 99, at p. 122 (1990), written testimony
>   of Rep. Solarz.)
> (Abortion Clinic Violence, Oversight Hearings before House Com. on
>   Judiciary, Subcom. on Civil and Constitutional Rights, 99th Cong., 1st
>   and 2d Sess. (1987).)
> (Hearings before House Com. on Ways and Means on H.R. No. 5076, 96th
>   Cong., 2d Sess. (1980).)
> (Hearings before Sen. Com. on Finance on Sen. No. 1130, 74th Cong., 1st
>   Sess., at pp. 1311, 1328 (1935).)
> (Hearings before House Com. on Interior and Insular Affairs, Subcom. on
>   Indian Affairs and Public Lands, on Sen. No. 1214, 95th Cong., 2d Sess.,
>   pp. 191–192 (1978), testimony of Tribal Chief Calvin Isaac, Mississippi
>   Band of Choctaw Indians.)

[D] Debates and floor proceedings

Cite to the Congressional Record, or to the Senate Journal (Sen. J.) or House Journal (H.R.J.) if the material does not appear in the Congressional Record. Early debates are also reported in the Congressional Globe and are cited in a similar manner.

> (Remarks of Rep. Clay, Debate on H.R. No. 4280, 98th Cong., 2d Sess.
>   (1984), reprinted in ERISA: Selected Legislative History 1974–1985 (BNA
>   1986) p. 252.)
> (House Debate on H.R. No. 8442, 74th Cong., 2d Sess., 80 Cong. Rec.
>   8102 (daily ed. May 27, 1936).)
> (Remarks of Rep. Montague, 55 Cong. Rec. 4922 (1917).)
> (Remarks of Sen. Humphrey, 106 Cong. Rec. 7266 (daily ed. Apr. 8,
>   1960).)

(Remarks of Sen. Smith, Sen. J., 100th Cong., 2d Sess. (1981) p. 1234.)
(Remarks of Sen. Grimes, Cong. Globe, 38th Cong., 1st Sess. (1864)
   p. 2123.)

[E] Messages and addresses

(See Pres. Nixon, radio and television address, Aug. 15. 1971, reprinted in
   1971 U.S. Code Cong. & Admin. News, No. 7, at p. 1933.) [*Note: This*
   cite is to an advance pamphlet.]
President Nixon's Message to Congress on Revenue Sharing (117 Cong.
   Rec. 5811 (daily ed. Feb. 4, 1971)) . . . .

For citing to the United States Code Congressional and Administrative News, see section 2:47.

§ 2:43 Treaties and international agreements

Indicate title, type of document (treaty, agreement, protocol, etc.), subject of agreement, subject country, and date of signing. In most cases, the document's title will supply this information. Lengthy titles may be paraphrased. Cite to United States Treaties and Other International Agreements (U.S.T.); pre-1950 treaties and agreements are generally cited to the Statutes at Large. Parallel citations may be made to the Department of State's collection, which is in three series: Treaty Series (T.S.) 1908–1945, Executive Agreement Series (E.A.S.) 1929–1945, and Treaties and Other International Acts Series (T.I.A.S.) 1945 to date. Each document is identified by number within its series.

(Convention Between United States and United Kingdom for Avoidance of
   Double Taxation, Dec. 31, 1975, 31 U.S.T. 5670, 5677, T.I.A.S. No.
   9682.)
(Extradition Treaty Between United States of America and United Mexican
   States, Agreement of May 4, 1978, 31 U.S.T. 5059, 5065, T.I.A.S. No.
   9656.)
(Convention on the Service Abroad of Judicial and Extrajudicial Documents
   in Civil or Commercial Matters, Nov. 15, 1965, 20 U.S.T. 361, T.I.A.S.
   No. 6638 (hereafter the Hague Service Convention).)
(Treaty of Transit of Military Aircraft with Mexico, Apr. 1, 1941, par. 3, 55
   Stat. 1191, T.S. No. 971.)
(Education: Financing of Exchange Programs with the Republic of Korea,
   Agreement of Sept. 24, 1971, U.S.T. 2056, T.I.A.S. No. 7240 (eff. Nov.
   26, 1971).) [*Note: When an additional date is material (such as*
   effective date), include it in a parenthetical at the end.]

For the citation of charters, resolutions, and records of international organizations, see The Bluebook: A Uniform System of Citation (16th ed. 1996) section 20.1, p. 139 et seq.

§ 2:44 Federal administrative rules and regulations — Code of Federal Regulations

In general, when referring to administrative regulations and rules, cite to the Code of Federal Regulations (C.F.R.) or to the Federal Register (Fed.Reg.), which is the daily supplement to the regulations. (If the material is not published in C.F.R. or Fed.Reg., or is not customarily cited by referring to those publications, use the style described in § 2:45.) Federal regulations are designated as "parts" in text, even though the section symbol is used in parenthetical citations.

The Code of Federal Regulations is divided into 50 titles, and thus the C.F.R. cite is to the *title* number and *part* number. The Federal Register cite, however, is to the *volume* number and *page* number. In parentheses, insert the year of the C.F.R. edition (from the volume's spine), or the date of the Fed.Reg. edition. Providing the common name of the regulations is optional.

> (Foreign Assets Control Regs, 31 C.F.R. § 500.808 (1998).)
>
> (32 C.F.R. § 581.3(c)(5) (1997).)
>
> (Hague Internat. Child Abduction Convention, text and legal analysis, 51 Fed.Reg. 10504 (Mar. 26, 1986).)
>
> (Off. Alien Prop., vesting order No. 2506, 8 Fed.Reg. 16343 (Dec. 4, 1943).)
>
> Part 97.105 of the Federal Communication Commission regulations (47 C.F.R. (1997)) provides . . . .
>
> The appropriate HHS regulation, 45 Code of Federal Regulations part 201.3(a) (1997), provides . . . .
>
> On July 29, 1971, the USDA issued new regulations. (7 C.F.R. §§ 270–274, 36 Fed.Reg. 14102–14120, amended Apr. 19, 1972, 37 Fed.Reg. 7724.)
>
> See also Guidelines for State Courts; Indian Child Custody Proceedings (44 Fed.Reg. 67584 et seq. (Nov. 26, 1979)).

§ 2:45 Agency documents; topical services

In many instances, documents may only be obtained from the issuing agency, although many agencies make documents available on agency Web sites. A great deal of administrative material is also available in topical services. Follow the citation styles in section 2:16[C] for topical services. Cite federal agency documents by providing the name of the issuing agency, title of the document, date, and the page of the document where the cited material is found. Quite a few federal agencies have official reporters. If these are used, follow the citation style in section 2:32 for agency citations, or in section 2:36 for Internet sources.

The following examples include references to documents made available by issuing agencies and documents compiled in topical services:

(Off. of Comptroller of the Currency, interpretative letter (Feb. 17, 1995) pp. 9–11.)

(Municipal Solid Waste Task Force, U.S. Environmental Protection Agency, The Solid Waste Dilemma: An Agenda for Action (Feb. 1989) pp. 1–2.)

(Off. of Research and Statistics, Soc. Sec. Admin., Dept. of Health, Ed. and Welf., Nat. Health Ins. Proposals, as introduced in 97th Cong., 2d Sess. (May 1981) p. 4.)

(Off. of Technology Assessment, U.S. Cong., Biological Effects of Power Frequency Electric and Magnetic Fields (1989) p. 4 (hereafter OTA Report).)

(U.S. Dept. Commerce, Statistical Abstract (1996 ed.) table 799, p. 533.)

(Fed. Deposit Ins. Corp., advisory opn. FDIC No. 92-47 (July 8, 1992) [1992–1993 Transfer Binder] Fed. Bank. L. Rep. (CCH) ¶ 81,534, p. 55,731.)

(See Securities and Exchange Com., Special Study of Securities Markets, H.R.Doc. No. 95, 88th Cong., 1st Sess., pt. 2, pp. 355–356 (1963) (hereafter referred to as Special Study).)

(Fed. Trade Com., Enforcement Policy With Respect to Physician Agreements to Control Medical Prepayment Plans (1981) 1033 Antitrust Trade Reg. Rptr. (BNA) I-1, I-8.)

(Remarks of Rep. Clay, Debate on H.R. 4280, 98th Cong., 2d Sess. (1984), reprinted in ERISA: Selected Legislative History 1974–1985 (BNA 1986) p. 252.)

§ 2:46 Federal court rules

Citations to federal court rules include a reference to the relevant United States Code title (e.g., title 28 for the federal rules of evidence and civil procedure; title 18 for the federal rules of criminal procedure). The date is not generally included, but if a rule has been recently amended, provide the amendment date to avoid confusion. Give the general name of the rules, the number of the particular rule cited, and the United States Code reference.

(Fed. Rules Civ.Proc., rule 4, 28 U.S.C.)
(Fed. Rules Civ.Proc., rule 12(c), 28 U.S.C.)
(Fed. Rules Crim.Proc., rules 35, 37(a)(12), 18 U.S.C.)
(Fed. Rules App.Proc., rule 9(c), as amended Apr. 29, 1994, 28 U.S.C. [West's Cal. Rules of Court (Fed. ed. 1998 rev.) p. 24].)
(Fed. Rules Evid., rule 804(a)(4), (b)(1), 28 U.S.C.)
Rule 23 of the Federal Rules of Civil Procedure (28 U.S.C.) provides . . . .
rule 1007 of the Federal Rules of Evidence (28 U.S.C.), effective July 31, 1993, . . .

For local federal court rules and rules of the United States Supreme Court, provide the name of the rules (specifying "Civ.," "Crim.," etc., where appropriate), the particular court, and the rule number.

(U.S. Supreme Ct. Rules, rule 10.)

(U.S. Cir. Ct. Rules (9th Cir.), rule 3-1.)
(U.S. Dist. Ct., Local Civ. Rules, Northern Dist. Cal., rule 11-1(b).)
(U.S. Dist. Ct., Local Civ. Rules, Central Dist. Cal., rule 1.0 [West's Cal.
    Rules of Court (Fed. ed. 1998 rev.) p. 549].)
and rule 3-1, United States Circuit Rules (9th Cir.) [West's Cal. Rules of
    Court (Fed. ed. 1998 rev.) p. 14] in part provides . . . .

§ 2:47 United States Code Congressional and Administrative News

The United States Code Congressional and Administrative News (U.S. Code Cong. & Admin. News) publishes all laws enacted during each congressional session, legislative history, proclamations, executive orders, and reorganization plans. Each year's volumes are numbered. The advance pamphlet's pagination differs from that of the later bound volume, but the statutes printed in each volume bear only their permanent Statutes at Large references, not page numbers. (See also § 2:38.) Cite the year, publication, pamphlet number (if citation is to an advance pamphlet), and page number (if any).

(1991 U.S. Code Cong. & Admin. News, at pp. 374–375.)
(Pub.L. No. 105-124 (Dec. 1, 1997) 111 Stat. 2534, 1997 U.S. Code Cong.
    & Admin. News.)
The legislative history is described in 1998 United States Code
    Congressional and Administrative News, No. 7, at page 281. [*Note: This*
    citation is to the advance pamphlet.]
(For legis. hist., see 1997 U.S. Code Cong. & Admin. News, pp.
    1217–1224.)

§ 2:48 Executive orders and presidential proclamations

Cite to the daily Federal Register, which publishes all executive orders and presidential proclamations, or title 3 of the Code of Federal Regulations (C.F.R.), which publishes only those of general interest. Always give the date of the document. The C.F.R. cite must include the edition year as well (see § 2:44). Parallel cites, when available, are also helpful.

(Exec. Order No. 12832, 58 Fed.Reg. 5905 (Jan. 19, 1993).)
(Exec. Order No. 13090, 63 Fed.Reg. 36153 (June 29, 1998), 1998 U.S.
    Code Cong. & Admin. News, No. 7, p. B93.) [*Parallel cite to an advance*
    pamphlet.]
(Exec. Order No. 11615, 36 Fed.Reg. 15727 (Aug. 17, 1971) as amended
    by Exec. Order No. 11617, 36 Fed.Reg. 17813 (Sept. 2, 1971).)
(Pres. Proc. No. 6257, 56 Fed.Reg. 10353 (Mar. 7, 1991), 1991 U.S. Code
    Cong. & Admin. News, p. A26.)
(Pres. Proc. No. 6616 (Oct. 20, 1993), 3 C.F.R. 142 (1994).)
is found in Executive Order No. 9788, 11 Federal Register 11981 (Oct. 14,
    1946), 50 United States Code Annotated, appendix, section 6, note.

and Executive Order No. 12742, 56 Federal Register 1079 (Jan. 8, 1991), 1991
     United States Code Congressional and Administrative News, page B5, states
     that . . . .
See Executive Order No. 13067 (Nov. 3, 1997) 3 Code of Federal
     Regulations (1998) page 230, regarding trade with Sudan.

F. MODEL CODES AND STANDARDS; UNIFORM LAWS

§ 2:49 Model codes and uniform laws

When citing the text of a section, name the model code and give the
section number. When citing to the Code and Commentaries, or to the
commentaries alone, refer to the Code and Commentaries, designate the
type of reference (commentary, note, etc.), and give the section and page
numbers. A citation to an annotated uniform laws compilation should follow the style for annotated code references (see § 2:9). For citation of
Restatements, see chapter 3.

     (Model Pen. Code, § 250.3.)
     (Model Pen. Code, § 2.02, subd.(2)(b)(ii).)
     (Model Pen. Code & Commentaries, com. to § 221.1, p. 67.)
     (Model Pen. Code & Commentaries, com. 2 to § 2.02, p. 235, fn. 11.)
     in 2 American Law Institute, Principles of Corporate Governance: Analysis
         and Recommendations (1994) section 7.12, pages 164–165.
     based on the earlier Model Code of Evidence, rule 401.
     That act can be found in 9B West's Uniform Laws Annotated (1987)
         Uniform Parentage Act, page 287.
     (1 West's U. Laws Ann. (1994 supp.) U. Com. Code, com. to § 1-203,
         p. 30.)
     (7 West's U. Laws Ann. (1985) U. Arbitration Act, § 12, subd. (a).)
     (3B West's U. Laws Ann. (1992) U. Com. Code, pp. 127–129.)
     (8 West's U. Laws Ann. (1983) U. Prob. Code (1969) § 2-109, pp. 66–67.)
     (9B West's U. Laws Ann. (1987) U. Parentage Act, comrs. note, pp.
         287–290.)
     (7B West's U. Laws Ann. (1998 supp.) U. Securities Act of 1985, § 605,
         subd. (c).)

§ 2:50 American Bar Association codes, standards, and opinions

The American Bar Association has issued both a Model Code of Professional Responsibility (in 1969) and Model Rules of Professional Conduct
(in 1983). Give the volume number (if any), the name of the code, standard,
or opinion, and designate the provision and number (or letter). A citation to
standards includes a date for identification and a page reference. A citation
to an opinion includes the opinion number, date, and page.

     (ABA Model Rules Prof. Conduct, rule 1.16(a)(1).)
     (ABA Model Code Prof. Responsibility, DR 7-107(E).)

American Bar Association Model Code of Professional Responsibility, Disciplinary Rule 7-107(E).

rule 5.6 of the American Bar Association Model Rules of Professional Conduct.

and see the American Bar Association Model Code of Professional Responsibility, Ethical Considerations 7-10 and 7-37.

3 American Bar Association Standards for Criminal Justice (2d ed. 1980) standard 15-3.4, page 15.90 . . .

(See 4 ABA Stds. for Crim. Justice (2d ed. 1980) com. to std. 21-3.2, p. 21.42.)

(ABA Project on Stds. for Crim. Justice, Administration of Criminal Justice (1974), The Defense Function, p. 101 et seq.) [Published in book form.]

(ABA Stds. for Lawyers Who Represent Children in Abuse and Neglect Cases (1996) std. G-1.)

(ABA Com. on Prof. Ethics, opn. No. 91-359 (1991) p. 4.)

(2 ABA Informal Ethics Opns., informal opn. No. 917 (1985) p. 65.)

(ABA Recent Ethics Opns., informal opn. No. 1325 (Mar. 31, 1975) p. 2.)

CHAPTER 2
—Notes—

CHAPTER 3

TREATISES, TEXTBOOKS, RESTATEMENTS, PERIODICALS, AND OTHER SECONDARY SOURCES

§ 3:1 Treatises, textbooks, practice guides, and Witkin

[A] Citation to volume

Give the volume number (if any), author, title, edition (if more than one), year of publication for the particular volume cited, section or paragraph number, and page number, if available (some computer-based publications do not have page numbers; it is not necessary to reference the paper-based version merely for this information). When citing a footnote or endnote, put the note number after the number of the page on which the note begins. Chapter titles are recommended but not essential. Always use arabic numbers for volume designations.

Within parentheses, abbreviate the word "California." Also abbreviate words such as "paragraph" and "page," and use "§" for the word "section." Note that when setting forth titles of treatises, textbooks, practice guides, and the Witkin publications within parentheses, only California is abbreviated (i.e., as Cal.). No abbreviations are used outside parentheses. For citing to CD-ROM versions of publications, see section 3:15.

The order of citation is not governed by rigid rules. References to secondary authorities generally follow citations to constitutions, statutes, and cases. When quoting, always cite the quoted authority first.

> (4 Witkin, Summary of Cal. Law (9th ed. 1987) Real Property, § 800, pp. 977–978.)
> (2 Herlick, Cal. Workers' Compensation Law (5th ed. 1994) Liens, § 17.4, p. 17-10.)
> (Prosser & Keeton, Torts (5th ed. 1984) § 33, p. 201, fn. 78.)
> 1 Witkin and Epstein, California Criminal Law (2d ed. 1988) section 13, page 17.

If there are two authors, give both their names, connected by "and" (or & if in parentheses); if there are more than two, use only the first named author and et al. Use last names only.

> (2 Ehrman & Flavin, Taxing Cal. Property (3d ed. 1997) General Valuation Principles, § 17:19, pp. 44–46.)
> (Grodin et al., The Cal. State Constitution: A Reference Guide (1993) pp. 243–244.)
> (4 Levy et al., Cal. Torts (1993) Defamation Defenses and Privileges, § 45.12[4], p. 45-66.)

Use the title that appears on the volume's title page. *Exceptions*: (1) The word "on" may be omitted from titles consisting of the author's name and the subject connected by "on," such as "Couch on Insurance"; (2) Prosser and Keeton's treatise (Law of Torts) is often abbreviated as, simply, Torts.

(5 Couch on Insurance (3d ed. 1997) § 78:2, p. 78-9.) *or* (5 Couch, Insurance (3d ed. 1997) § 78:2, p. 78-9.)

(1 Nimmer on Copyright (1997) Subject Matter of Copyright, § 2.03, p. 2-28.) *or* (1 Nimmer & Nimmer, Copyright (1997) Subject Matter of Copyright, § 2.03, p. 2-28.)

(6 Powell on Real Property (1998) Real Estate Investment Trusts, § 44.01[5], p. 44-9.)

(6 Williston on Contracts (4th ed. 1995) § 13:9, p. 490.)

(Prosser & Keeton, Torts (5th ed. 1984) § 33, p. 201, fn. 78.)

Prosser and Keeton on Torts (5th ed. 1984) section 33, page 201, footnote 78, . . .

When a treatise is commonly known by the name of a revising editor, substitute the reviser's name for the number of the edition.

(8 Wigmore, Evidence (McNaughton ed. 1961) § 2286, p. 531.)

(4 Wigmore, Evidence (Chadbourn ed. 1972) § 1083, pp. 216–217.)

(6C Appleman, Insurance Law and Practice (Buckley ed. 1979) § 4463, p. 623.)

(1A Appleman, Insurance Law and Practice (rev. ed. 1981) § 311, p. 311.)

(5 Appleman on Insurance 2d (Holmes ed. 1998) § 24, p. 3.)

Looseleaf publications often update the title page when new or replacement pages are published. Use the date on the current title page as the publication year (but not the date on a separate title page for supplemental materials). When citing a specific looseleaf page, it is sometimes helpful to add the release or revision date indicated on the bottom of that page (e.g., if the material discussed has recently undergone significant change); insert the date information exactly as indicated on the page. If a looseleaf page is from the original printing, it may not have a revision date.

(4 Ballantine & Sterling, Cal. Corporation Laws (4th ed. 1998) § 484.01, p. 23-49 (rel. 72-4/99).)

(2 Wilcox, Cal. Employment Law (1998) Employee Torts, § 30.07[1], p. 30-47 (rel. 11- 3/95).)

4 Manaster and Selmi, California Environmental Law and Land Use Practice (1998) Growth Management and Development Limits, section 63.27, page 63-25 (7/97).

Additional examples of commonly cited publications:

in 10 Witkin, Summary of California Law (9th ed. 1989) Parent and Child, section 15, page 52.

7 Witkin, California Procedure (4th ed. 1997) Judgments, section 145, page 659.

(1 Witkin & Epstein, Cal. Criminal Law (2d ed. 1988) Crimes Against the Person, § 512, p. 579.)

(1 Witkin, Cal. Evidence (3d ed. 1986) Circumstantial Evidence, § 287, pp. 257–258.)

(3 Erwin et al., Cal. Criminal Defense Practice (1997) Speedy Trial, ch. 62, p. 62-15 (rel. 35- 5/96).)

(2 Miller & Starr, Cal. Real Estate (2d ed. 1989) § 3:11, p. 71.)

(1 Herlick, Cal. Workers' Compensation Law (5th ed. 1994) § 10.18, p. 10-33.)

(2 McCormick, Evidence (4th ed. 1992) Hearsay, § 251, p. 118.)

(2 Wharton's Criminal Law (15th ed. 1994) § 140, pp. 248–249.)

(2 LaFave, Search and Seizure (3d ed. 1996) § 4.9(e), p. 649.)

(4 Mallen & Smith, Legal Malpractice (4th ed. 1996) Litigation, § 32.1, p. 128.)

The Rutter Group publications are cited by author(s), title, and with expanded date parenthetical. The paragraph designations suffice for the Rutter Group publications, although the author may include page numbers if available. Because paragraph numbers include a colon and page numbers are hyphenated, use "to" when a cite includes multiple paragraphs or pages.

(Weil & Brown, Cal. Practice Guide: Civil Procedure Before Trial (The Rutter Group 1997) ¶ 10:106 et seq., p. 10-43 et seq.)

(Croskey et al., Cal. Practice Guide: Insurance Litigation (The Rutter Group 1997) ¶ 3:33, p. 3-6.)

(Eisenberg et al., Cal. Practice Guide: Civil Appeals and Writs (The Rutter Group 1997) ¶¶ 8:15 to 8:18, pp. 8-4 to 8-6 (rev. # 1, 1998).)

Hogoboom and King, California Practice Guide: Family Law (The Rutter Group 1998) paragraph 12:100, page 12-20.4.

[B] Citation to supplement

The term "supplement" generally describes any update material issued at regular intervals (e.g., every year) for a publication, including update material issued in softcover pamphlets for bound volumes or looseleaf publications (but not looseleaf pages issued to replace or add to the main text) and the update inserts for the inside back cover of bound volumes, which are sometimes called "pocket parts." When citing to a supplement or pocket part, include "supp." in the parenthetical and provide the section, paragraph, or page of the supplement. When citing to an update alone, the parent volume's edition and date are omitted.

(3A Corbin on Contracts (1998 supp.) § 654E.)

(9 Witkin, Cal. Procedure (1999 supp.) Appeal, § 11A, p. 5.)

(7 Witkin, Summary of Cal. Law (1999 supp.) Constitutional Law, § 134, p. 88.)

(2 Ehrman & Flavin, Taxing Cal. Property (1998 supp.) § 32:03, p. 130.)

8 Witkin, California Procedure (1999 supp.) Enforcement of Judgment, section 389C, pages 44–45.

[C] Citation to volume and supplement

A single citation can refer to the same section of both a volume and its supplement, as in the following examples, if the reference is intended to be a general citation to text discussion. However, a single citation to both volume and supplement cannot be used if point pages are provided; in that case, use *id.* for the supplement reference.

> (See 3 Witkin & Epstein, Cal. Criminal Law (2d ed. 1989 & 1998 supp.) Punishment for Crime, § 1418.)
> (See 5 Witkin & Epstein, Cal. Criminal Law (2d ed. 1989 & 1998 supp.) Trial, § 2590.)
> (2 Harper et al., Law of Torts (1986 & 1998 supp.) § 6.12.)
> (See 2 Witkin, Cal. Procedure (4th ed. 1996) Courts, § 342, p. 411; *id.* (1994 supp.) § 397, p. 32.)

[D] Subsequent references to publication: *ibid.*, *id.*, *supra,* and short cites

To repeat an identical reference in the same paragraph, without any intervening citation, use *ibid.* To cite the same volume and a *different* page or section, use *id.* and insert the new page or section number. *Ibid.* and *id.* are used only to refer to the immediately preceding authority cited in the same paragraph.

Use *supra* when the subsequent reference is in a different paragraph, or when the subsequent reference is in the same paragraph, but with intervening citations to other authority. A citation in a footnote appended to a paragraph is considered intervening for purposes of using *supra.*

When a subsequent reference is in a different paragraph, give the volume number (if any), the author's name, the title, the word *supra* (omitting the edition and year, to signal that it was previously cited), and the section and page number. After this information is provided once in a paragraph, subsequent *supra* references in the same paragraph may be further abbreviated. Typically, the volume number, if any, the author's name, and the section and page information will suffice: for example, 6 Witkin, *supra,* § 748 at p. 83 after an inception cite in the same paragraph to 6 Witkin, Summary of Cal. Law (9th ed. 1988) Torts, § 732, p. 60.

For multivolume works, use *supra* for subsequent references to different volumes with the same publication date as the volume first cited. When the publication year is different, the citation is treated as an initial cite.

When a particular reference work will be cited often in a document, the author may adopt an abbreviated form of citation (i.e., a short cite) for subsequent references requiring the *supra* signal. Adopting a short cite is typically done by setting forth the short cite in parentheses immediately following the initial cite, prefaced by the word "hereafter," if desired. A short cite typically allows the title to be omitted from subsequent references, but it may not be used to omit information deemed necessary for identifying and locating cited material.

> the court concluded that the point was valid. (See 2 Koch, Administrative Law and Practice (1997) § 2.23, pp. 105–107.) The next contention is based on the same legal theory (*ibid.*) and can be so considered. (*Note: Both cites to same volume and page.*)
>
> the court based its holding on that theory (2 Corbin, Contracts (1995) § 5.28, p. 142). A possible exception to that theory (*id.* at p. 147) is raised by appellants. (*Note: Two cites to same volume, different pages.*)
>
> For a discussion of defendant's contention, see Fleming on Torts (3d ed. 1965) pages 491 to 492. This view is also held by other authorities (see, e.g., Prosser on Torts (3d ed. 1964) p. 865), but in light of the facts of this case a better solution is available to us (Fleming, *supra,* at p. 493). (*Note: Initial reference and subsequent reference in same paragraph with intervening citation.*)
>
> The crime of conspiracy calls for several distinctions, both in connection with double jeopardy and with double punishment. (3 Witkin & Epstein, Cal. Criminal Law (2d ed. 1989) Punishment, § 1413, p. 1673.)
>
> A conspiracy is a distinct offense from the substantive crime for purposes of double jeopardy. (3 Witkin & Epstein, Cal. Criminal Law, *supra,* § 1413, p. 1674.) (*Note: Initial reference followed by a subsequent reference in a new paragraph.*)
>
> (2 Witkin, Cal. Procedure (4th ed. 1996) Courts, § 40, p. 67.) . . . (3 Witkin, *supra,* Actions, § 161, p. 231.) (*Note: Both volumes published in 1996, thus permitting "supra" for the subsequent cite.*)
>
> *But:* (1 Witkin, Cal. Procedure (4th ed. 1996) Attorneys, § 47, p. 77.) . . . (9 Witkin, Cal. Procedure (4th ed. 1997) Appeal, § 827, p. 853.) (*Note: Volumes published in different years, thus precluding use of supra.*)
>
> discussed in 5 Witkin and Epstein, California Criminal Law (2d ed. 1988) Trial, section 2905, page 3555 (hereafter Witkin & Epstein).
>
> "An attack on the defendant's attorney can be seriously prejudicial as an attack on the defendant himself, and, in view of the accepted doctrines of legal ethics and decorum [citation], it is never excusable." (5 Witkin & Epstein, *supra,* Trial, § 2914, p. 3570.) (*Note: Initial reference adopting a short cite with a subsequent reference in a different paragraph.*)
>
> (*People v. Slack* (1989) 210 Cal.App.3d 937, 940 [258 Cal.Rptr. 702]; 1 LaFave & Scott, Substantive Criminal Law (1986) Justification and Excuse, § 5.4, pp. 627–640 (hereafter LaFave); 1 Wharton's Criminal Law (15th ed. 1993) Defenses, § 90, pp. 614–628 (hereafter Wharton); Perkins & Boyce, Criminal Law (3d ed. 1982) Impelled Perpetration, § 2, pp. 1064–1072 (hereafter Perkins).) "However, the 'modern cases have tended to blur the distinction between duress and necessity.'" (LaFave, *supra,* at p. 628; see also Perkins, *supra,* at pp. 1064–1065.)

(Note: Adoption of multiple short cites with subsequent references in a different paragraph.)

For use of *ibid.*, *id.*, and *supra* with citations to opinions, see chapter 1; for use with annotated codes and compilations of legislative materials, see chapter 2.

§ 3:2 Continuing Education of the Bar and Center for Judicial Education and Research publications

The publications of the California Continuing Education of the Bar (Cont.Ed.Bar) and the California Center for Judicial Education and Research (CJER) are cited by volume number (if any), author, title, parenthetical with publisher and publication year, and section and page number (if any). The author of an individual chapter is not given, but the use of chapter titles is encouraged. If the publication is a second or later edition, the style is "(Cont.Ed.Bar 2d ed. [*year*])" or "(CJER 2d ed. [*year*])." If the section number is given, the page number is needed only if it assists the reader in quickly locating the material.

> (Cal. Criminal Law: Procedure and Practice (Cont.Ed.Bar 4th ed. 1998)
> §§ 39.4, 42.7, pp. 1060, 1149.)
> (Cal. Tort Guide (Cont.Ed.Bar 3d ed. 1996) Animals, § 3.2, p. 67.)
> (Employment Law Compliance for New Businesses (Cont.Ed.Bar 1997)
> Employment Agreements, § 3.22, p. 3-10.)
> (Bernhardt, Cal. Mortgage and Deed of Trust Practice (Cont.Ed.Bar 2d ed.
> 1990) § 1.3, p. 5.)
> (1 Cal. Liability Insurance Practice: Claims and Litigation (Cont.Ed.Bar 1994)
> § 1.28, pp. 1–21 to 1-22.)
> (1 Jefferson, Cal. Evidence Benchbook (Cont.Ed.Bar 3d ed. 1997) Hearsay
> and Nonhearsay Evidence, § 1.45, p. 31.)
> (1 Kostka & Zischke, Practice Under the Cal. Environmental Quality Act
> (Cont.Ed.Bar 1997) §§ 12.3–12.6, pp. 459–466.)
> As explained in 2 California Conservatorships and Guardianships
> (Cont.Ed.Bar 1990) sections 15.88–15.89, pages 872–875, . . .
> (Heafey, Cal. Trial Objections (Cont.Ed.Bar 6th ed. 1998) Unduly
> Inflammatory, § 30.2, p. 342.)
> (Cal. Judges Benchbook: Civil Proceedings Before Trial (CJER 1995) Law
> and Motion, § 6.81, p. 276.)
> (CJER Felony Sentencing Handbook (CJER 1997) p. 11.)
> in CJER Mandatory Criminal Jury Instructions Handbook (CJER 1997)
> Selected Common Instructional Errors, section 3.13.

When citing a supplement to a Continuing Education of the Bar or CJER volume, add "supp." to the expanded parenthetical, as follows:

> (Bernhardt, Cal. Mortgage and Deed of Trust Practice (Cont.Ed.Bar 1997
> supp.) § 1.14.)

California Attorney's Damages Guide (Cont.Ed.Bar 1998 supp.) section
  2.33A, page 91, . . .
(Cal. Judges Benchbook: Civil Trials (CJER 1995 supp.) Witnesses, § 8.90.)

For citing to an updated looseleaf or topical reporter published by
Continuing Education of the Bar, see section 3:9. For citing to CD-ROM
versions of Continuing Education of the Bar materials, see section 3:15.

§ 3:3 Legal encyclopedias, Blackstone's Commentaries

[A] Legal encyclopedias, generally

Citations to legal encyclopedias should include the volume number,
encyclopedia title, the volume's publication year, the subject, section number, footnote number (if citing to footnote), and page number. If the citation is simply a general reference, the page number may be omitted. If the
citation is outside of parentheses, the encyclopedia title and words such as
"page" and "section" are spelled out; if within parentheses, they are
abbreviated.

(5 C.J.S. (1993) Appeal and Error, § 641 & fn. 41, p. 65.)
(7 Cal.Jur.3d (1989) Attorneys at Law, § 43.)
(47 Am.Jur.2d (1995) Judgments, § 717, p. 185.)
That issue is covered in 55 American Jurisprudence Second (1996)
  Mortgages, section 366, page 99. It is discussed further in 55 American
  Jurisprudence Second, *supra*, Mortgages, section 367.

[B] Abbreviations for legal encyclopedias

American Jurisprudence	Am.Jur.
American Jurisprudence Second	Am.Jur.2d
California Jurisprudence	Cal.Jur.
California Jurisprudence Second	Cal.Jur.2d
California Jurisprudence Third	Cal.Jur.3d
Corpus Juris	C.J.
Corpus Juris Secundum	C.J.S.

[C] Blackstone's Commentaries

Several editors have republished Blackstone's Commentaries on the
Laws of England, with annotations. These editions note the original page
number with an asterisk (the star paging system). When citing the Commentaries directly from these annotated reprints, omit the date and edition,
and use the original page numbers. However, when citing to an annotation,
note the editor, publication date, edition, and annotation page number.

2 Blackstone's Commentaries 296 *or*
2 Blackstone, Commentaries 296

(2 Jones's Blackstone (1916) pp. 2387, 2390.)
1 Cooley's Blackstone (4th ed. 1899) page 142, footnote 4.

§ 3:4 Dictionaries

Citations to dictionaries should include the volume number (if any), title (from the title page), edition, publication year of volume (from the copyright page), and page number. Noting the column number is optional. If the citation is in parentheses, use abbreviations for "page" and "column," and use "Dict."

(American Heritage Dict. (2d college ed. 1982) p. 476.)
(See Black's Law Dict. (6th ed. 1990) p. 810, col. 2.)
(See Black's Law Dict. (7th ed. 1999) p. 810, col. 2.)
(5 Oxford English Dict. (2d ed. 1989) p. 556.)
(Oxford English Dict. (2d ed. CD-ROM 1994).)
(Webster's 3d New Internat. Dict. (1981) p. 1206.)
(Webster's New World Dict. (3d college ed. 1991) p. 450.)
(Webster's 9th New Collegiate Dict. (1989) pp. 28–29.)
(Bander, Law Dict. of Practical Definitions (1966) p. 4.)
(Garner, Dict. of Modern Legal Usage (2d ed. 1995) p. 842.)
(17A Words and Phrases (1958) p. 63.)
in 16 Words and Phrases (1997 supp.) at page 7, column 2.
from Webster's New International Dictionary (2d ed. 1941) page 18 . . .
defined by Webster's Third New International Dictionary (1981) at page 786.
In Webster's Ninth New Collegiate Dictionary (1989) page 105 . . .
found in Webster's College Dictionary (1991) at page 32.
Ballentine's Law Dictionary (3d ed. 1969) at page 489 states: . . .
5 Oxford English Dictionary (2d ed. 1989) page 556.
in 1 Schmidt, Attorney's Dictionary of Medicine (1998) page A-111.
in the American Heritage Dictionary, *supra*, at page 489.

§ 3:5 Jury instructions: CALJIC and BAJI

California Jury Instructions, Civil, Book of Approved Jury Instructions, is cited as BAJI, and California Jury Instructions, Criminal, is cited as CALJIC. Both sets are prepared by the Committee on Standard Jury Instructions of the Superior Court of Los Angeles County. Each set is generally updated once or twice a year; the updates are cumulative for new or revised versions of instructions still in force.

Use the abbreviations BAJI and CALJIC both in the body of a sentence and within parentheses, and always use the abbreviation "No." for "number." Whenever a jury instruction given or requested at trial is quoted or described in detail, or when identification of the jury instruction is merely for background of context (i.e., the instruction is not an issue on appeal), only the title and number are given. For example:

> BAJI No. 6.20 was not given.
>
> As given at defendant's trial, CALJIC No. 2.21.2 states: "A witness who is willfully false in one material part of his or her testimony is to be distrusted in others. You may reject the whole testimony of a witness who willfully has testified falsely as to a material point, unless, from all the evidence, you believe the probability of truth favors his or her testimony in other particulars."
>
> In the present case, as to the issue of malice, the trial court instructed the jury (pursuant to a modified version of BAJI No. 7.05) that the qualified privilege "is lost . . . if the person making the statement was: [¶] 1. Motivated by hatred or ill-will toward the plaintiff which induced the publication; or [¶] 2. Without a good-faith belief in the truth of the statement."
>
> The guilt and penalty juries received standard instructions identifying a wide range of factors bearing on credibility (CALJIC No. 2.20), and explaining that discrepancies within or between witness accounts could be the product of innocent misrecollection or honest differences in perception and do not necessarily mean such testimony should be discredited (CALJIC No. 2.21.1). With the approval of both parties, the trial court also gave the standard instruction concerning false testimony at each phase of trial (CALJIC No. 2.21.2).

If the historical development of an instruction is relevant, provide the edition and date, in addition to the instruction number, the first time the instruction is cited. For new or revised instructions printed only in the annual supplement or pocket part, include the year the instruction was added or revised, its status as new, revised, or re-revised, and the bound volume edition that the instruction updates. These guidelines also apply when referring to use notes or comments following CALJIC or BAJI instructions. For subsequent citations, *supra* may be used to signal the prior citation and substitute for parenthetical volume and date information (see also § 3:1[D]).

> BAJI No. 2.60 (7th ed. 1986) previously required . . .
> and former CALJIC No. 9.44 (5th ed. 1988), which . . .
> (CALJIC No. 2.27 (6th ed. 1997).)
> (BAJI No. 2.21 (8th ed. 1994).)
> (BAJI No. 7.70 (1992 re-rev.) (7th ed. 1986).)
> (BAJI No. 7.91 (1995 new) (8th ed. 1994).)
> was based on BAJI No. 9.00.7 (1997 rev.) (8th ed. 1994).
> and CALJIC No. 3.02 (1994 rev.) (5th ed. 1988) previously stated . . .
> (Com. to CALJIC No. 2.50.01 (6th ed. 1996) p. 362.)
> (Use Note to BAJI No. 2.02 (8th ed. 1994) p. 142.)
> Use Note to BAJI No. 3.60 (1997 rev.) (8th ed. 1994) page 220 points out . . . .

and the Comment to BAJI No. 6.00.2 (8th ed. 1994) at page 242 states
that . . . .

§ 3:6 Restatements

Cite Restatements by title and section number. If the citation is
within parentheses, use abbreviations for "comment," "illustration,"
"appendix," "subdivision," and "page," and "§" for "section." The date of
the Restatement is optional. When citing a comment or illustration, give the
page number. (When citing an original Restatement in parentheses, a
comma is inserted for clarity between "Rest." and the title.)

> section 100 of the Restatement Second of Trusts.
> the Restatement Second of Agency, section 433.
> the Restatement Second of Torts, section 868, comment c, page 275 . . .
> the Restatement Second of Trusts (§ 96, com. d, illus. 1, p. 245).
> (Rest., Conf. of Laws, § 22.)
> (Rest., Contracts, § 342, com. a, p. 561.)
> (Rest., Contracts, § 479, com. a, illus. 1, p. 915.)
> (Rest., Property, Future Interests (1936) § 157.)
> (Rest.2d Agency, §§ 39, 76, com. c, p. 196.)
> (Rest.2d Agency, § 39, com. b, p. 130.)
> (Rest.2d Torts, §§ 302, 302A, 431.)
> (Rest.2d Trusts, § 108, com. f, p. 239.)
> (See Rest.2d Agency (appen.) § 164, reporter's notes, pp. 249–252.)

When citing a draft version of a Restatement that has not been
approved and promulgated, or when citing a proposed final draft, use the
following forms:

> the Restatement Second of Judgments, section 68.1 (Tent. Draft No. 3,
>   1976), denying preclusive effect to an unreviewable judgment.
> (Rest.3d Torts, Products Liability (Tent. Draft No. 2, Mar. 13, 1995) § 8.)
> (Rest.3d Property, Servitudes (Tent. Draft No. 1, Apr. 5, 1989) § 2.1, com.
>   c., p. 7.)
> (Rest., Law Governing Lawyers (Tent. Draft No. 4, *supra*) § 209, subd. (2).)
> (Rest., Torts (Proposed Final Draft No. 2) § 91.)

§ 3:7 Annotated reporters

[A] General guidelines

A citation to an annotation in a selective reporter consists of the word
"Annotation" (or "Annot." if the cite is within parentheses), the annotation
title (recommended but not required), the volume's publication date, the volume number, the name of the reporter, and the inception page. Provide the
section or footnote number. Include the point page if quoting or if otherwise
necessary to assist the reader in locating the cited material. As with law

reviews (see § 3:8), the word "page" or abbreviation "p." is not used in the initial reference to an annotation. Always abbreviate the title of the reporter (see below for abbreviations). The author's name is never given.

When giving the annotation title, use the title's original hyphenation and other punctuation. Do not use italics. In some volumes, annotation titles are published in all capital letters; when citing these, only use initial capital letters. Use initial capital letters for all words except articles ("a," "an," "the"), coordinating conjunctions ("or," "and," etc.), and prepositions of four letters or fewer ("into," "from," "of," "for," "to," etc.).

Annotation, Minor's Entry into Home of Parent as Sufficient to Sustain Burglary Charge (1994) 17 A.L.R.5th 111, 116, section 2 . . . .

Annotation, Determination of Materiality of Allegedly Perjurious Testimony in Prosecution Under 18 USCS §§ 1621, 1622 (1975) 22 A.L.R.Fed. 379.

Annotation (1983) 20 A.L.R.4th 23, and cases cited, . . .

Cases from other jurisdictions on this general subject are collected in Annotation (1981) 7 A.L.R.4th 1146.

(Annot., Exclusion of Public During Criminal Trial (1956) 48 A.L.R.2d 1436.)

(Cases collected in Annot., 92 A.L.R.Fed. 893.)

(Annot., Recovery of Damages for Expense of Medical Monitoring to Detect or Prevent Future Disease or Condition (1994) 17 A.L.R.5th 327, 340.)

(Annot. (1994) 19 A.L.R.5th 439 [collecting cases].)

(Cf. Annot., What Constitutes Single Accident or Occurrence Within Liability Policy Limiting Insurer's Liability to a Specified Amount Per Accident or Occurrence (1988) 64 A.L.R.4th 668.)

(See Annot., Event Triggering Liability Insurance Coverage as Occurring Within Period of Time Covered by Liability Insurance Policy Where Injury or Damage Is Delayed—Modern Cases (1993) 14 A.L.R.5th 695, 729, § 6, and cases cited.)

(Annot., Mistake of Law as Ground for Annulment of Compromise, 1916D Am. & Eng.Ann.Cas. 347, 349.)

[B] Citation to supplement

(See Annot., Liability of Property Owner for Damages from Spread of Accidental Fire Originating on Property (1994) 17 A.L.R.5th 547, 620, § 9, and later cases (1997 supp.) p. 18.)

(See Annot., Propriety of Lesser-Included-Offense Charge to Jury in Federal Homicide Prosecution (1991) 101 A.L.R.Fed. 615, and later cases (1997 supp.) p. 26.)

(See generally Annot., Admissibility of Hearsay Evidence in Probation Revocation Hearings (1982) 11 A.L.R.4th 999 (1993 supp.) § 4 and cases cited.)

Annotation, Award of Custody of Child Where Contest Is Between Child's
   Grandparent and One Other Than Child's Parent (1970) 30 A.L.R.3d
   290, 316, section 14, and later cases (*id.* (1998 supp.)).
See generally Annotation, Admissibility of Hearsay Evidence in Probation
   Revocation Hearings (1982) 11 A.L.R.4th 999 (1993 supp.) section 4,
   and cases cited.

[C] Abbreviations for annotated reporters

American and English Annotated Cases	Am. & Eng.Ann.Cas.
American Annotated Cases	Ann.Cas.
American Decisions	Am.Dec.
American Law Reports	A.L.R.
American Law Reports, Second Series	A.L.R.2d
American Law Reports, Third Series	A.L.R.3d
American Law Reports, Fourth Series	A.L.R.4th
American Law Reports, Fifth Series	A.L.R.5th
American Law Reports, Federal Series	A.L.R.Fed.
Lawyers' Reports Annotated	L.R.A.
Lawyers' Reports Annotated (New Series)	L.R.A.(N.S.)

§ 3:8   Law reviews and bar journals

[A] General guidelines

In citing articles from law reviews and bar journals, list the author, the title of the article (in italics), the date, the volume number, the abbreviation of the periodical, the inception page, and any point pages. The title of the periodical is always abbreviated, whether the citation is in text or in a parenthetical citation. As with annotations (see § 3.7) the word "page" or abbreviation "p." is not used in the initial reference to a law review article. If there are two authors, give both names, connected by "and" (or "&" in parentheses); if there are more than two, use only the first named author and "et al." Use last names only. Notes and comments are cited in the same manner as articles, except that "Note" and "Comment" are used instead of the author, even when the note or comment is signed. Again, a shortened title may be used for subsequent references. Do not abbreviate "Comment" in this context within parenthetical citations.

Abbreviate "Law Review" as "L.Rev.," and "Law Journal" as "L.J." Insert a space between the abbreviation of the school or the journal and "L.Rev." or "L.J." For abbreviations of some commonly cited journals, see the list in [B] below. For abbreviations of other law reviews and journals, consult The Bluebook: A Uniform System of Citation (16th ed. 1996) abbreviations.

Do not shorten the article's title in the first reference. Follow the title's punctuation. Use quotation marks only if the original title does. In some law reviews, article titles are published in capital letters only; if so, change the capitalization to initial capital letters. (For initial capitals in annotation titles, see § 3:7[A].) For subsequent references after the first full citation, an abbreviated reference (short cite) can be used (e.g., the author's name or a shortened version of the title).

(Faigman & Wright, *The Battered Woman Syndrome in the Age of Science* (1997) 39 Ariz. L.Rev. 67 (hereafter *Battered Woman Syndrome*).)

(Sullivan, *Unconstitutional Conditions* (1989) 102 Harv. L.Rev. 1415, 1443.)

(Lessig, *The Zones of Cyberspace* (1996) 48 Stan. L.Rev. 1403.)

(Delgado, *Rodrigo's Fifteenth Chronicle: Racial Mixture, Latino-Critical Scholarship, and the Black-White Binary* (1997) 75 Tex. L.Rev. 1181 (hereafter Delgado).)

(Rubin, *Peer Sexual Harassment: Existing Harassment Doctrine and Its Application to School Children* (1997) 8 Hastings Women's L.J. 141 (hereafter Rubin).)

(Hill, *Defamation and Privacy Under the First Amendment* (1976) 76 Colum. L.Rev. 1205, 1284, fn. omitted.)

That issue was discussed in Friendly, *"Some Kind of Hearing"* (1975) 123 U.Pa. L.Rev. 1267, 1269–1270, footnote 10 (hereafter Friendly). . . . In Friendly, *supra*, at page 1270, . . .

(Note, *Hacking Through the Computer Fraud and Abuse Act* (1997) 31 U.C. Davis L.Rev. 283.)

(Comment, *The Limitations of Trademark Law in Addressing Domain Disputes* (1997) 45 UCLA L.Rev. 1487 (hereafter *Domain Disputes*).)

(See Comment, *Corporal Punishment in the Public Schools* (1971) 6 Harv.C.R.-C.L. L.Rev. 583.)

(See Note, *Should We Believe the People Who Believe the Children?: The Need for a New Sexual Abuse Tender Years Hearsay Exception Statute* (1995) 32 Harv. J. on Legis. 207, 237 (hereafter Note).) . . . (See Note, *supra*, 32 Harv. J. on Legis. at pp. 238–239.)

As explained in Note, *State Civil Service Law—Civil Service Restrictions on Contracting Out by State Agencies* (1980) 55 Wash. L.Rev. 419, 434–435, footnotes 76–84, and cases cited (hereafter *State Civil Service*) . . . (See *State Civil Service*, *supra*, 55 Wash. L.Rev. at p. 435.)

[B] Abbreviations for frequently cited law reviews and journals

A partial list of commonly cited law reviews and journals and their abbreviated forms follow. For other law reviews and journals, consult The Bluebook and the Index to Legal Periodicals.

California Law Review (UC Berkeley; Boalt Hall)	Cal. L.Rev.
California Western Law Review	Cal. Western L.Rev.
Ecology Law Quarterly	Ecology L.Q.
Harvard Civil Rights-Civil Liberties Law Review	Harv.C.R.-C.L. L.Rev.
Harvard Law Review	Harv. L.Rev.

Hastings Constitutional Law Quarterly	Hastings Const. L.Q.
Hastings Law Journal	Hastings L.J.
Loyola University of Los Angeles Law Review	Loyola L.A. L.Rev.
Pacific Law Journal	Pacific L.J.
Pepperdine Law Review	Pepperdine L.Rev.
San Diego Law Review	San Diego L.Rev.
Santa Clara Law Review	Santa Clara L.Rev.
Southern California Law Review	So.Cal. L.Rev.
Southwestern University Law Review	Sw.U. L.Rev.
Stanford Law Review	Stan. L.Rev.
U.C.L.A. Law Review	UCLA L.Rev.
U.C. Davis Law Review	U.C. Davis L.Rev.
University of San Francisco Law Review	U.S.F. L.Rev.

§ 3:9   Topical law reporters and services

Topical reporters and services are ongoing compilations of decisions, administrative materials, and analytical material focusing on selected areas of law, such as labor or tax law. Covered here are citation styles for analytical material and other secondary reference matter included in some topical reporters and services.

Some topical reporters and services equally fit the description for law reviews and journals (see § 3:8), particularly reporters or services whose content is mostly or exclusively analytical. The citation styles are thus similar. Because topical reporters and services are produced in a variety of formats, no uniform or formulaic citation style for analytical material is feasible. Include as much of the following information as is practical, in the sequence suggested, to facilitate identifying and locating cited material: (1) a description of the item cited (e.g., author and italicized title, where applicable); (2) a parenthetical for the publisher and date of publication (publisher is optional); (3) the volume (and issue) number; (4) publication title, abbreviated; and (5) page, paragraph, or section designations. Abbreviate the publication title both in parentheses and in the text. "Law Reporter" is abbreviated as "L.Rptr.," and "Law Reports" is abbreviated as "L.Rep."

> In Suarez, *From the Jaws of Defeat: Miranda After Peevy*, volume 1998, No. 7, Cal. Crim. Defense Prac. Rptr. 406, the author revisits . . . . [*Note: This cite is to a monthly pamphlet not yet integrated into its yearly binder; the date parenthetical is omitted because the volume designation provides it.*]
>
> (*Dynamic Concepts, Inc. v. Truck Ins. Exchange* (1998) 98 Cal.Tort Rptr. 107–111.) [*Note: This cite is to a summary and commentary, not a verbatim report of the opinion.*]
>
> in Fraser, *Telecommunications Competition Arrives: Is Universal Service Out of Order?* (1995) volume 15, No. 4, Cal. Reg. L.Rptr. 1, 5.

> (Fellmeth, *Unfair Competition Act Enforcement by Agencies, Prosecutors, and Private Litigants: Who's on First?* (1995) vol. 15, No. 1, Cal. Reg. L.Rptr. 1, 8.)
>
> (Chin, *Significant Developments in Real Estate Sales* (Cont.Ed.Bar 1998) 21 Real Prop. L.Rptr. 72, 73.)
>
> (See Stokes, *The SLAPP Statute: A Three-Year Retrospective on a Constitutional Experiment* (Cont.Ed.Bar 1996) 17 Civ. Litigation Rptr. 411, 415.)
>
> Eastman, *Correcting the Ten Most Common Misconceptions About CEQA* (Cont.Ed.Bar 1998) 21 Real Prop. L.Rptr. 97.
>
> In Turner, *California's Summary Adjudication Procedure* (Cont.Ed.Bar 1997) 19 Civ. Litigation Rptr. 88, Justice Turner observed that . . . .

If the text material in a looseleaf publication has undergone recent significant change, it is sometimes helpful to provide the release or revision date indicated on the bottom of the page; insert the date exactly as indicated (see also § 3:1[A]).

> (1 Cal. Trial Practice: Civil Procedure During Trial (Cont.Ed.Bar 3d ed. 1995) Handling Trials Efficiently, § 1.9, p. 13 (rev. 3/97).)

For citing judicial opinions reported in topical law reporters and services, see chapter 1; for citing administrative regulatory material, see chapter 2.

§ 3:10 Legal citation manuals

When citing legal citation manuals, list the title, edition, date of publication, and section number. The page number is optional and may be added if it assists the reader in locating the reference quickly. When the citation is in parentheses, use the abbreviations "p." for page, "§" for section, "&" for "and," and "¶" for paragraph.

> (Cal. Style Manual (4th ed. 2000) § 1:28 et seq.)
>
> pursuant to the California Style Manual, *supra,* section 1:16 et seq.
>
> (The Bluebook: A Uniform System of Citation (16th ed. 1996) §§ 14.1, 14.2, pp. 93–94.)
>
> and The Bluebook, *supra,* T-15, page 319 et seq., contains a listing of topical services.

§ 3:11 Magazines

When citing magazine articles, note the author's name (if any), title of article (in italics), date, name of publication, and page number. In general, legal magazines and other professional publications use a citation format similar to law reviews and journals and do not use "page" or "p." before the page number in a full citation. General interest magazines do use "page," "p.," or "pp." in the citation.

> (Davis et al., *Prevalence and Incidence of Vertically Acquired HIV Infection in the United States* (Sept. 20, 1995) 274 JAMA 952.)
> (Gladwell, *Do Parents Matter?* (Aug. 17, 1998) The New Yorker, at p. 57.)
> Booth, *The Bad Samaritan* (Sept. 7,1998) Time, at page 59.
> in Mann, *Who Will Own Your Next Good Idea?* (Sept. 1998) The Atlantic Monthly, pages 61–62, . . .

§ 3:12 Newspapers

When citing newspaper articles, note author's name (if any), title of article (in italics), name of publication, date (in parentheses: month, day, year), page, and column number (optional). In citing newspapers that number each section separately, include the section designation with the page number (e.g., p. A22). "Page" and "column" are spelled out when the reference is not in parentheses. Always abbreviate the month.

> (Budnick, *Muzzling the Campaign Watchdog*, S.F. Recorder (Apr. 7, 1998) p. 1.)
> (Carrizosa, *Unwed Father Can't Try to Prove Paternity*, S.F. Daily J. (Apr. 7, 1998) p. 1.)
> (Silberfeld, *Scientific Law of Unintended Consequences*, Nat.L.J. (Jan. 19, 1998) p. A22.)
> (Smith, *Now as Then*, S.F. Chronicle (Mar. 7, 1989) p. 2, col. 4 (hereafter Smith).) . . . (Smith, *supra*, p. 3, col. 1.)
> in Frantz, *Sweepstakes Could Face Restrictions*, N.Y. Times (Sept. 2, 1998) page A18, column 6, . . .
> (Wall Street Journal (Aug. 21, 1998) p. 1, col. 6.)

§ 3:13 Books, essays, pamphlets, reference works, and interviews

[A] General rule

When citing books, essays, pamphlets, reference works, or interviews, list author, title (not italicized, except for essays), edition (if more than one) and year of publication in parentheses, and page number where relevant. Noting the publisher is optional, but it may be included where there are multiple editions of a work. If there are two authors, name both, using last names, connected by "and" (or an ampersand (&) if cite is in parentheses); if there are more than two, list only the first named author followed by "et al." Use the abbreviation "p." for "page" when the citation is in parentheses.

[B] Books

(Rifkin, The Biotechnical Century (1998) pp. 137–139.)
(See Normand et al., Under the Influence: Drugs and the American Work
    Force (1994) pp. 220–223 (hereafter Drugs and the American Work
    Force).)
(Carter, The Culture of Disbelief (1993) p. 100.)
(Williams, Alchemy of Race and Rights (1991) p. 223.)
(Darwin, The Origin of Species (J.M. Dent 1971).)
(Bartlett, Familiar Quotations (11th ed. 1941) p. 98.)
(Madeleine, Monetary and Banking Theories of Jacksonian Democracy
    (1943) pp. 22–24.)
Alderman and Kennedy, The Right to Privacy (1995) pages 131–132.
Evans and Nelson, Wage Justice (1989) page 20.

For the Bible and Shakespeare, see [G], below.

[C] Essays

When citing an individual essay from a book of collected essays, note the author and title of the essay, followed by the word "in," the title and editor of the collection, the date of the book's publication, and the page number. Essay titles are italicized. When citing collections with two editors, name both, using "and" or "&." If there are more than two editors, name only the first and use "et al." for the others. (If the editor is also the essay author, omit the editor notation.)

(Hassoun, *Water Between Arabs and Israelis: Researching Twice-Promised
    Resources* in Water, Culture & Power (Donahue & Johnston edits.,
    1998) p. 313.)
(Lubiano, *Black Ladies, Welfare Queens, and State Minstrels: Ideological
    War by Narrative Means* in Race-ing Justice, En-gendering Power:
    Essays on Anita Hill, Clarence Thomas, and the Construction of Social
    Reality (Morrison edit., 1992) pp. 323, 332.)
Finkelman, *Chief Justice Hornblower of New Jersey and the Fugitive Slave
    Law of 1793* in Slavery and the Law (1997) pages 113–114, . . . *[Note:
    This essay author also edited the book, so no separate notation as editor
    is necessary.]*

[D] Pamphlets

When citing a pamphlet, note the source, title, date of publication, section heading if desired, and page number. Use the abbreviation "p." for page when the citation is in parentheses.

(Cal. Dept. Personnel Admin., Computer User's Handbook (Mar. 1997)
    appen. B.)

(Cal. Public Employees' Retirement System, Understanding CalPERS: A
  Guidebook for Public Officials (1995) Glossary of Terms, p. 35.)
(Nat. Council of Juvenile and Family Ct. Judges, Making Reasonable Efforts:
  Steps for Keeping Families Together (undated) p. 19.)

For ballot pamphlets and other governmental material or legislative history in pamphlet form, see Chapter 2.

[E] Reference works

Cite reference works by giving the title, the edition (if any) and date of publication (in parentheses, unless the date is part of the title), the name of the chapter or table (if desired), and the page number.

(See Cal. Statistical Abstract (1995) table D-12, p. 60.)
(Statistical Abstract of U.S. (94th ed. 1973) table 47, p. 38.)
(Wash. Information Directory 1997–1998, ch. 11, p. 351.)
World Almanac (1996) Employment, Labor Unions, page 157.

For government reports in general, see section 2:32; for Law Revision Commission reports, recommendations, and comments, see section 2:33; for dictionaries, see section 3:4; and for miscellaneous studies, reports, hearings, and manuals, see section 3:14.

[F] Interviews

Cite an interview by giving the name of the article in italics, the person interviewed (in parentheses), the source of the interview (magazine, newspaper, and so forth), the date of the interview, and the page number.

Military Spendings: Impact on Business (interview with David Packard,
  Deputy Sect. of Defense) U.S. News & World Report (Aug. 3, 1970)
  page 44. . . .

[G] The Bible and Shakespeare

Cite the Bible by setting forth the book, chapter, and verse. Adding translation or edition information is optional. The title, the Bible, is not italicized. The names of books of the Bible are not abbreviated.

"thou shalt love him as thyself." (Leviticus 19:33–19:34.)
In the Old Testament (Holy Bible (New Am. Catholic ed. 1950)), the Lord
  spoke to Moses and said . . . ."

When citing Shakespeare, or any play, include the name of the play, the act (in roman numerals), and the scene; the line of the quoted text is optional.

As Shakespeare wrote, "with all my imperfections on my head . . . ."
(Hamlet, act I, scene 5, line 66.)
Moreover, it seems to us that the Board "doth protest too much."
(Shakespeare, Hamlet, act III, scene 2, line 242.)

[H] Films, television shows, songs, and poems

Titles of films are set forth like book titles, in roman type, with initial letters capitalized. The date parenthetical contains the name of the studio that released the film and the date of release. This information is widely available on the Internet.

(Platoon (Hemdale Film Corp. 1986).)
(The Godfather (Paramount Pictures 1972).)
A film called The Sandlot (Twentieth Century Fox 1993) . . .

Titles of television shows and television series are set forth in italics. If relevant, include a parenthetical for the television station or network, and the date of broadcast.

on the daytime television show *The Bold and the Beautiful* .
for a television news show, *Mornings on 2*. After the interviewer . . . .
Roddenberry developed a television series entitled *Star Trek*.
a segment of *On Scene: Emergency Response* (KNBC television broadcast, Sept. 29, 1990) . . . .

Titles of songs and poems are enclosed in quotation marks.

a clip of his performance of the James Brown song "Please, Please, Please."
Emily Dickinson's beautiful poem "Not in Vain."
(Wordsworth (1807) "The World Is Too Much With Us.")
"Long may our land be bright / With freedom's holy light . . . ."
("America," 4th verse.)

§ 3:14 Miscellaneous studies, reports, hearings, manuals, and speeches

Cite the author (if the author is institutional, cite the subunit, if any, listed as the preparer and the general body of which the subunit is a part); the title of the study, report, hearing, manual, or speech; the date (in parentheses); the section heading if desired; and the page number. Use the abbreviation "p." for "page" when the citation is in parentheses.

(ABA Section on Legal Education and Admissions to Bar, ABA Comprehensive Guide to Bar Admission Requirements 1997–98 (1997) chart VII: Foreign Law School Graduates, p. 47.)
(Admin. Off. of U.S. Cts., Electronic Case Files in the Federal Courts (Discussion Draft, Mar. 1997) Authentication, Security, and Preservation of the Litigation Record, p. 23.)

(Nat. Inst. on Drug Abuse, U.S. Dept. Health & Human Services,
    Pharmacokinetics, Metabolism and Pharmaceuticals of Drugs of Abuse,
    NIDA Research Monograph No. 173 (1997) p. 112.)
(Nat. Center for State Cts., 1995 Ann. Rep., p. 6.)
(White House Domestic Policy Council, Health Security: The President's
    Report to the American People (1993) pp. 14–15.)
(Supreme Jud. Ct., Commonwealth of Mass., Reinventing Justice 2022
    (1992) appen., Technology and Justice Task Force Rep., p. 98.)
(Little Hoover Com., Unsafe in Their Own Homes: State Programs Fail to
    Protect Elderly (Nov. 1991) p. 16.)
(See generally U.N. Gen. Assem., Universal Declaration of Human Rights
    (Dec. 1948) Res. No. 217A (111).)
(President's Com. on Law Enforcement and Admin. of Justice, Rep. (1967)
    The Challenge of Crime in a Free Society, p. 143.)
(John N. Turner, Minister of Justice and Atty. Gen. of Canada, address to
    North American Judges Assn. Conf. (Dec. 1, 1969) Justice for the Poor.)
quoting the remarks of Honorable M. McAllister, Associate Justice of the
    Supreme Court of Oregon, which appeared in the Report of Proceedings
    of the National Defender Conference, National Defender Project of the
    National Legal Aid and Defender Association, May 14–16, 1969, pages
    157, 161.
quoting the American Bar Association's Project on Minimum Standards for
    Criminal Justice, Eliminating Frivolous Appeals, Standards Relating to
    Criminal Appeals (Approved Draft 1970) page 63.

§ 3:15 Computer-based sources

Most material treated in this chapter is available in both print-based
and computer-based versions. The computer-based versions are generally
available through the Internet, online legal research services (e.g., Westlaw
and Lexis), or on CD-ROM (i.e., compact disc–read only memory). For citing computer-based versions of opinions, see chapter 1; for online statutory
and legislative materials, see chapter 2.

Computer-based versions are generally cited in the same manner as
print-based versions. If page numbers from print-based versions are not
included in the computer-based version, citing the section, paragraph, or
similar designation will suffice. When citing supplemental update material
from a computer-based source, use the term "supplement" (see also
§ 3:1[B]).

When a CD-ROM is used as the source for a citation, provide the
name of the publisher and date of issuance for the CD-ROM being used, in
parentheses.

(1 Cal. Trial Practice: Civil Procedure During Trial (Cont.Ed.Bar CD-ROM
    Apr. 1998) Handling Trials Efficiently, § 1.9.)

> (94 Cal. Forms of Pleading and Practice (Matthew Bender CD-ROM May
> 1998) Bankruptcy, § 94.10, p. 94-12.)

Some material may only be available from a computer-based source, or the author may wish to signal that a computer-based source was relied upon. In that case, to the extent possible, provide the author, title of the article or other material, publisher or similar entity, and the date. Provide the Westlaw or Lexis cite for material found thereon, or at least identify the database, library, or file on Westlaw or Lexis in which the material is located. For material found on the Internet, provide as much of the Uniform Resource Locator (URL), in angled brackets (< >), as is necessary to facilitate locating the material on the Web site, and the date the material was read or downloaded from the Internet site, which is signalled in parentheses (or brackets if the citation as a whole is parenthetical) by the phrase "as of" in conjunction with the date. If necessary a URL may be divided between lines at any "/" in the address.

> (Levenson, *It's a Criminal Trial, Not a Political Referendum* (Aug. 31,
> 1995) Westlaw, OJ-COMM, 1995 WL 511232.)
> (Alden, Editorial Opinion (May 3, 1998) <http://www.legal.com/
> News/1371editorial.htm> [as of Sept. 21, 1998].)
> (Wilks, *The Community Standards Conundrum in a Borderless World:*
> *Making Sense of Obscenity Law in Cyberspace* (Spring 1998) Institute
> for Cyberspace Law and Policy <http://www.gse.ucla.edu/iclp/
> flwilks.htm> [as of Nov. 3, 1998].)
> in Fenigstein & Kaufman, *Trade Wind: The Arrival of Online Securities*
> *Offerings* (June 1996) Institute for Cyberspace Law and Policy <http://
> www.gse.ucla.edu/iclp/te.html> (as of June 18, 1996).

In addition, capitalize "Internet," "Web," and "World Wide Web." Also, "Web site" is two words. Capitalize "Web," but not "site."

CHAPTER 3
—Notes—

CHAPTER 4

STYLE MECHANICS: CAPITALIZATION, QUOTES, NUMBERS, ITALICS, AND PUNCTUATION

A. CAPITALIZATION

D. ITALICS

E. HYPHENS

F. COMMAS, SEMICOLONS, AND COLONS

A. CAPITALIZATION

§ 4:1　State courts

[A] General guidelines

Capitalize references to state courts when full or accepted formal names are used. Use lowercase when a partial name is given or the reference is to a court or courts generally. Always capitalize partial names when describing the Supreme Court of California (e.g., the Supreme Court) or one of the California Courts of Appeal (e.g., the Court of Appeal, Fourth District, Division Two).

In referring to a trial court, capitalize "department," "law and motion department," etc., only when used as a part of a formal title, as in the caption of a pleading. Otherwise use lowercase, e.g., "The matter was transferred to the law and motion department."

[B] Appellate courts

Supreme Court of California
California Supreme Court
Supreme Court (*capitalize even when standing alone*)
the Florida Supreme Court
the Washington and Oregon courts
the New Mexico Court of Appeals
the state's high court
Court of Appeal, Fourth Appellate District, Division One
Division One of the Court of Appeal, Fourth Appellate District
Court of Appeal (*capitalize even when standing alone*)
Fourth Appellate District (*capitalize even when standing alone*)
Fourth District Court of Appeal
Division Two (*capitalize even when standing alone*)
the court
the appellate court

[C] Trial courts

Superior Court of San Bernardino County
the superior court
the court
Superior Court of the State of California for the County of Tuolumne
San Francisco Superior Court
Lassen Superior Court
El Dorado County Superior Court
unified (or consolidated) superior and municipal courts
the appellate division (or former appellate department)
the superior court appellate division (or former superior court appellate
　　department)

Appellate Division of the Superior Court of Los Angeles County
the Small Claims Division of the Alameda County Superior Court
Juvenile Court of Los Angeles County
the Tehama County Juvenile Court
the probate department of the superior court
the juvenile court
Municipal Court for the Los Angeles Judicial District of Los Angeles County
Municipal Court for the Los Angeles Judicial District
the municipal court
Small Claims Court for the Alameda Judicial District of Alameda County
the small claims court
Small Claims Division of the Municipal Court for the Glendale Judicial
    District of Los Angeles County
the Amador County Small Claims Court

§ 4:2   Federal courts

[A] General guidelines

Capitalize names of federal courts when full or accepted formal titles are used, not when a partial name is given or the reference is to a court or courts generally. Note the exception for the abbreviated reference to the Supreme Court of the United States: Supreme Court is capitalized even when standing alone.

[B] Appellate courts

United States Supreme Court
Supreme Court of the United States
Supreme Court (*capitalize even when standing alone*)
the court
the high court
United States Court of Appeals, Ninth Circuit
Ninth Circuit Court of Appeals
the Ninth Circuit
the circuit court
the circuit court of appeals
the court of appeals

[C] Trial courts

United States District Court
United States District Court for the Eastern District of Arkansas
the district court
the federal district court
United States Court of Federal Claims
the claims court
Tax Court of the United States
the tax court

§ 4:3 Judicial officers

[A] General guidelines

In general, capitalize titles that immediately precede a person's name. Generally, when a personal title is lengthy, it is preferable to place it after the person's name, set off with commas, in lowercase. But capitalize titles of judicial officers, even when used following the person's name, if the complete and formal title of the office is being provided. Capitalize certain formal, complete titles, even when standing alone (e.g., Chief Justice; Attorney General, State Public Defender).

[B] Justices and judges; jurors

Chief Justice William H. Rehnquist
Chief Justice Ronald M. George
Chief Justice *or* Acting Chief
    Justice (*capitalize even when
    standing alone*)
Kathryn M. Werdegar, Associate
    Justice of the California
    Supreme Court
Justice Baxter
the associate justice
the justice
Ming W. Chin, a Supreme Court
    justice
a justice of the Supreme Court
Assigned Justice Arthur G.
    Scotland
the assigned justice
Presiding Justice Roger W. Boren
Presiding Justice of the Court of
    Appeal, Second Appellate
    District, Division Two
the presiding justice
Acting Presiding Justice J. Gary
    Hastings
Acting Presiding Justice of the
    Court of Appeal, First
    Appellate District, Division
    One

the Acting Presiding Justice, the
    Honorable J. Gary Hastings
Associate Justice Richard D. Huffman
Presiding Judge Gary Klausner
the presiding judge
Acting Presiding Judge William
    Hopkins
the acting presiding judge
Judge Mary Jo Levinger
the judge
a judge of the Superior Court of Santa
    Clara County
Temporary Judge John Smith
the temporary judge
Commissioner Beverly
    Daniels-Greenberg
the commissioner
Referee Marilyn Mackel
the referee
a referee of the superior court's
    juvenile dependency division
Juror No. 3
Juror Smith
Prospective Juror Smith
the jurors
the jury
Jury Foreperson Jones

For designating trial judges on filed opinions, see sections 5:28–5:32; for listing appellate justices on filed opinions, see sections 5:33–5:39.

[C] Prosecutors and other attorneys

the Attorney General of California
Attorney General Lockyer
the California Attorney General
the Attorney General (*capitalize even when standing alone*)
Assistant Attorney General Green
Joan Green, an assistant attorney general
Deputy Attorney General Jones
the deputy attorney general, John James
Deputy Attorneys General Janet Smith and Timothy Jones
District Attorney Roth
the district attorney
Assistant District Attorney Brown
the assistant district attorney, Susan Brown
Deputy District Attorney White
a deputy district attorney
John White, the deputy district attorney
the Office of the District Attorney of Monterey County
the Solano County District Attorney's Office
the district attorney's office
the District Attorney of Butte County
the Sutter County District Attorney

the State Public Defender (*capitalize even when standing alone; specific individual's title*)
the Madera County Public Defender
the public defender
San Diego Public Defender John Jimenez
the public defender's office
Contra Costa County Public Defender's Office
James Eli and Mary Moore, deputy state public defenders
Jane Drew, a deputy state public defender
the alternate public defender
County Counsel Anderson
Assistant County Counsel Clark
John Brown, the principal deputy county counsel
Defense Attorney Joyce Davenport
Defense Counsel Jones
Janet Jones, defense counsel
Prosecutor Wong
Dennis Wong, the prosecutor
Attorney Jesse Smith
plaintiff's attorney, Jesse Smith
the chief deputy county counsel, Mary Smith
Reporter of Decisions Office
Reporter of Decisions

§ 4:4   Administrative agencies, bodies, and districts

[A] General guidelines

Capitalize designations of governmental administrative units when using full or accepted formal titles. In general, do not capitalize words such as "commission," "department," "district," or "board" when standing alone, even when referring to a specific governmental unit. When adopted as abbreviated references or short cites, however, such words may be capitalized, at the author's discretion. Many of the following examples include, in parentheses, typical abbreviated references frequently used by opinion authors. For abbreviated or short form references to a state, city, or a geographic unit, see section 4:7; for acronyms, see section 4:64.

[B] State bodies

Board of Prison Terms
Contractors State License Board
    (Board)
State Board of Equalization (SBE)
the board
California Law Revision
    Commission
Law Revision Commission
California State Lands
    Commission (Commission)
Public Utilities Commission (PUC)
the commission
Department of Health Services
    (DHS)
Department of Industrial
    Relations

Department of Transportation
    (Caltrans)
Department of Youth Authority (CYA)
Employment Development
    Department (EDD)
the department
Environmental Protection Agency
    (EPA)
the agency
the Judicial Council of California
Judicial Council
the council
the Administrative Office of the
    Courts (AOC)
Regents of the University of California
the Regents

[C] Local bodies and districts

San Diego Fire Department
the fire department
Stockton Civil Service Commission
the civil service commission
Oakland Police Department
the police department
Grand Jury of San Bernardino
    County
the grand jury
Los Angeles County jail

the Ceres police station
Board of Education of the City of
    Modesto (Board)
Tulare Irrigation District
East Bay Municipal Utility District
    (EBMUD)
the respondent district
Palo Verde Unified School District of
    Riverside County (District)
a school district in Riverside County

[D] The State Bar

State Bar of California
the bar
the bench and bar
California State Bar
the State Bar
the State Bar Court

the court
the Committee of Bar Examiners of
    the State Bar
the committee
the Committee of Bar Examiners

§ 4:5   Executive and administrative officers

[A] General guidelines

Capitalize titles immediately preceding the names of government officers, both executive and administrative. Capitalize full or accepted formal titles, even when standing alone. Capitalize titles denoting unusual preeminence or distinction (e.g., the President, Vice-President, or the Governor) when used as a substitute for the name. Capitalize titles of local officials only when used in an adjective form preceding the officeholder's name or with the name of the political subdivision.

But do not capitalize titles of subordinate executive or administrative officers. Do not capitalize nouns denoting corporate or organizational officers in the private sector. When a title is lengthy, place it after the name, set off with commas, in lowercase.

[B] Federal and state officers

President Grant
the President (*when referring to the President of the United States*)
the president of John Doe Company
former President Carter
President-elect Allyson Jones (*when referring to the president-elect of the United States*)
Vice-President Gore (*when referring to the Vice-President of the United States*)
the vice-president of the firm
Governor Smith
the governor of each state
Goodwin J. Knight, Governor of California
the Governor (*when referring to the Governor of California*)
Cruz Bustamante, the Lieutenant Governor of California

the Lieutenant Governor (*when referring to the Lieutenant Governor of California*)
Chairperson of the State Water Resources Control Board
the chair
the chairperson
Chairman Lucas and Chairwoman Miranda
Commissioner of the Department of Corporations
defendant commissioner
Director of the Department of Alcoholic Beverage Control
Director of the Employment Development Department
C. Green, a deputy director of the Department of Employment Development
Insurance Commissioner
Commissioner Quackenbush

[C] Local and district officers

Mayor Green
the mayor, Charles Green
Mayor of the City and County of San Francisco
City Manager Goldstein
the city manager
assistant city manager James
Chief of Police Chang
the chief of police
Santa Barbara Fire Chief
Chief Ramirez
the fire chief
Los Angeles Police Officer Jones
Jones, a Los Angeles police officer
Sheriff Green

the sheriff
the Sheriff of Los Angeles County
the Sacramento County Sheriff's Department
the Sierra Sheriff
the Sierra County Sheriff
a deputy sheriff of Los Angeles County
the police investigator
district attorney investigator Brian Moore
a Los Angeles County Sheriff's investigator
Water Commissioner Brown
the water commissioner

§ 4:6   Legislative bodies and officers

[A] General guidelines

In general, capitalize titles denoting state or national legislative office both preceding *and* following the name, and when titles are used as a substitute for the name. Titles denoting local office are capitalized only when preceding the name or when the full or accepted formal title is used. Local office titles are generally not otherwise capitalized.

[B] National and state bodies and officers

the United States Congress
Congress
congressional
the Senate
Senator Smith
the Senator (*referring to a specific person*)
the upper house
the House of Representatives
the lower house
the House
the Sixty-third Congress
the 89th Congress
Congressman Twille and Congresswoman Barnes or Congressmember Mendez
the California Legislature
the Legislature (*capitalize even standing alone if referring to the California Legislature*)
Nevada Legislature
Legislature of Nevada
the legislature (*when not referring to California*)

the legislative branch (*whether or not referring to California*)
a legislative department
the Assembly (*when referring to California*)
Assemblyman Brown and Assemblywoman Green or Assemblymember Black
an Assembly member
members of the Assembly
state legislators
the Senate
senatorial districts
Senate district
Senate Committee on the Judiciary
the committee
Assembly Constitutional Amendment Committee
the amendment committee
Joint Budget Committee
a joint committee
the Rules Committee
a rules committee
Committee on Revenue and Taxation
the Jones committee (*not formal title*)

[C] Local bodies and officers

the Board of Supervisors of Marin County
the Mendocino County Board of Supervisors
the board
Boardmember Green (*but* a board member)
Supervisor Blue
the supervisor
Chairman Adams and Chairwoman Lee

the City Council of Berkeley
the Berkeley City Council
the council
the city council
Councilmember Elizabeth Gee (*but* a council member)
John Smith, chair of the city's civil service board
chair of the civil service board

§ 4:7 States, counties, cities, towns, and geographic terms

In general, capitalize words such as "state," "city," "town," etc., only when part of a proper name. When adopted as abbreviated references or short cites, however, such words may be capitalized at the author's discretion. A few of the following examples include, in parentheses, typical abbreviated references. For abbreviated or short cite references to administrative agencies, districts, etc., see section 4:4.

[A] States and counties

State of California	the county
the state	County of Solano (County)
the Commonwealth of Virginia	appellant county
New York State	Los Angeles and Riverside Counties
a state	defendant counties
States of Nevada and California	City and County of San Francisco
respondent states	(S.F.)
several western states	respondent city and county
Solano County	

[B] Cities and towns

Redwood City	the town
defendant city	City of Los Angeles
Town of Arnold (Town)	City of Rancho Mirage (City)

[C] Geographic terms

Capitalize geographic terms that are commonly used as proper names (e.g., the Bay Area). Use lowercase for other geographic descriptions that do not apply to one geographic entity or have not been commonly accepted as proper names (e.g., the northwest).

Pacific Ocean	Southern California
the West	Port of Los Angeles
west, western	the harbor
the Pacific Northwest	San Fernando Valley
the northwest	San Joaquin Delta
the North Coast	American River
northern coast	Sacramento and San Joaquin Rivers
Sierra Nevada	Monterey Bay
Big Sur	the bay
the Bay Area	Clear Lake
the La Jolla area of San Diego	Lakes Tahoe and Arrowhead
the bay region	the lake
the East Bay	Oakland Estuary
San Joaquin Valley	Santa Monica Beach
the valley	Griffith Park
the Central Valley	the park

§ 4:8   Proper names, derivative words, numbered items, and labeled items

Capitalize otherwise common nouns and adjectives (and their plural forms) when part of a proper name. In some instances a company, newspaper, periodical, etc., will employ, and become commonly recognized by, "The" as a part of its proper name. To facilitate indexing, "the" is disregarded in tables, indexes, and running heads, but "the" may be capitalized in text if it facilitates recognition.

State of California	San Bernardino Freeway
Folsom State Prison	the freeway
the state prison at Folsom	State Route 99 *or* Route 99
Folsom Prison	Interstate Highway 5 *or* Interstate 5
San Francisco County Jail (*but* Los Angeles County jail	U.S. Highway 101
the county jail	The Hartford
Alameda County	the highway
the County of Alameda	the Democratic Party
the Bay Bridge	the party
Roosevelt Dam	The New York Times
Market Street	the Page Investment Co. (*"the"* not
Sunset Boulevard	*part of proper name, nor does it*
Santa Monica Boulevard	*facilitate recognition*)

Common words derived from proper nouns are generally not capitalized.

anglicized	pasteurize
arabic numbers	quixotic
biblical	roman numerals
herculean	venetian blinds
french fries	

Adding a number, letter, or date to a common noun to indicate sequence, or for convenience in referring to material, does not form a proper noun; therefore do not capitalize that noun. (But follow the numbering style used in the complaint when referring to its paragraphs or counts; i.e., spelling out, or using arabic numbers or roman numerals.)

appendix A	exhibit A
article I	July 9th order
chapter 6	paragraph 17
clause 4	part 2
count one	room 28
count II	rule 12
division 3 (*but* Division Three	schedule A
when referring to a California	section 12
appellate court)	title VI
	volume 9

§ 4:9 Headings and subheadings

Use the same styling for all headings at the same heading level; and use different styles for different heading levels. For example, if major headings are all uppercase (all capital letters), then headings at the next level down (subheadings) should be a style other than all uppercase. Capitalization, italicization, and other style elements for headings and subheadings are otherwise at the author's discretion.

When using initial capitals as part of a heading or subheading, capitalize all words *except* (1) articles ("a," "an," "the"), (2) coordinating conjunctions ("or," "and," etc.), (3) prepositions of four letters or fewer ("into," "from," "of," "for," "to," etc.), and (4) any word preceded by a connective hyphen, such as the word "murder" in "Felony-murder Rule." Capitalize the first and last words regardless of what part of speech they are; for example, Was the Evidence All In? *or* An Option Was Not Exercised. Capitalize the first word following a colon, dash, or similar break; for example, Comparative Negligence: A New Theory.

Extended headings or subheadings normally are more in the nature of complete sentences rather than abbreviated topic titles. The preferred style is to use italics and to capitalize only the first word of the heading. (See, e.g., *San Clemente Ranch, Ltd. v. Agricultural Labor Relations Board* (1981) 29 Cal.3d 874, 883.)

§ 4:10 Constitutions, amendments, statutes, and rules

[A] Constitutions and amendments

Capitalize the word "Constitution" when referring to a specific constitution, including both the California and federal Constitutions, but not when referring to constitutions in general. Derivative words such as "constitutional" are not capitalized, nor are "federal" and "state" capitalized when preceding "Constitution."

> Prosecution by information, authorized by the state Constitution, is not in contravention of the federal Constitution. Several other state constitutions have similar language. Notwithstanding the constitutional right . . . .

Constitutions, constitutional amendments, and parts thereof are capitalized in the following manner:

> United States Constitution
> the Constitution of the United States
> the California Constitution
> the New York Constitution
> article VI, clause 2 of the United States Constitution

Fourteenth Amendment to [of] the United States Constitution
Fifth, Sixth, and Fourteenth Amendments
14th Amendment
the Bill of Rights (*but* a patients' bill of rights)
equal protection clause
supremacy clause
commerce clause of the United States Constitution
due process clause
section 8 of article I of the California Constitution
article I, section 8 of the California Constitution
former section 2 3/4 of article II of the California Constitution

For citation styles for constitutions, see sections 2:1–2:4.

[B] Statutes, popular names, government programs, and familiar doctrines

Capitalize all official titles of statutes, popular names, uniform laws, and government programs. (See § 2:15 for statutes, § 2:34 for initiative measures.)

Aid to Families With Dependent Children (AFDC)
 (*now* Temporary Assistance for Needy Families [TANF])
Beverly-Killea Limited Liability Company Act
California Environmental Quality Act (CEQA)
California Law Enforcement Telecommunications System (CLETS)
California Public Records Act
California Tort Claims Act
California Uniform Commercial Code
California Work Opportunity and Responsibility to Kids Act (CalWORKS)
Civil Action Mediation Act
Civil Discovery Act of 1986
Consumer Legal Remedies Act
Crime Victims Justice Reform Act (Prop. 115)
Determinate Sentencing Act of 1976
Determinate Sentencing Act (*but* determinate sentencing law)
Domestic Violence Prevention Law
Employee Retirement Income Security Act (ERISA)
Enforcement of Judgments Law
Fair Employment and Housing Act (FEHA)
Lanterman-Petris-Short Act (LPS)
Meyers-Milias-Brown Act
Parental Kidnapping Prevention Act
Restitution Fund
Social Security
Social Security Act (*but* Social Security number)
State Civil Service Act

Temporary Assistance for Needy Families (TANF) (*formerly* Aid to Families With Dependent Children [AFDC])
"Three Strikes" law (*quotation marks omitted after first usage; capitalization retained throughout; see § 2:34*)
three strikes law (*no quotation marks; see § 2:34*)
Tort Claims Act
Trial Court Delay Reduction Act of 1986
Uniform Interstate Family Support Act (UIFSA)
Unfair Practices Act (*but* unfair competition law)
Uniform Limited Partnership Act
Uniform Parentage Act (UPA)
Uniform Reciprocal Enforcement of Support Act (URESA)
Unruh Act (*applying to retail installment sales*)
Unruh Civil Rights Act (Civ. Code, § 51 et seq.) (*Note: Do not short cite as* "Unruh Act," *to avoid confusion with* Unruh Act *relating to retail installment sales*)
Usury Law
Workers' Compensation Act (*but* workers' compensation law)

In referring to a particular statute previously cited by its full name, do not capitalize "act," "statute," or "code" when it stands alone (e.g., "The act provides: . . ."). The author may, however, adopt "Act," "Statute," etc., as a short form of citation following the full cite. Do not capitalize "federal" or "state" preceding the name of the statute unless it is in the official name; for example, "federal Social Security Act."

Do not capitalize names of familiar doctrines or the unofficial or generic names of statutes.

the last clear chance doctrine
the lemon law
the statute of frauds
the statute of limitations
res ipsa loquitur

[C] Rules

Capitalize "Rule" when it is part of a proper name, but not when it precedes a number: for example, "The California Rules of Court," but "Under rule 5-104 of the Rules of Professional Conduct . . . ."

For citation styles for state and local rules, see sections 2:18–2:23.

[D] Title, division, part, chapter, article, section

Capitalize "title," "division," "part," "chapter," "article," "section," "appendix" and so forth only when used as part of an actual title or heading. Do not capitalize the words or their abbreviations when merely referring to them or using them as part of a citation: for example, "(Cal. Const., art. VI, § 4)." However, when a word starts a citation within parentheses after the end of a full sentence, that word begins a sentence, and it should be capitalized; for example, "The Constitution limits the power to grant pardons. (Art. V, § 8.)"

For abbreviations for constitutional citations, see section 2:3; for statutory code abbreviations, see section 2:8; for capitalization of proper names and numbered or labeled items, see section 4:8.

§ 4:11 Party designations

[A] People as party

When the People of the State of California is a party litigant, the word "People" is capitalized when standing alone. Do not capitalize "people" if the reference is to the people as a group and not as a party to litigation. For example:

> Evidence was introduced by the People.
> The people have not voted on that issue.

[B] Substitute designations for parties

Ordinarily, a party's trial designation is not capitalized in text (plaintiff, defendant, appellant, respondent, personal representative, etc.), whether the designation is used alone or in conjunction with a party's name.

> He pointed to plaintiff Jones.
> He was substituted for a Doe defendant.
> They attempted to serve the defendant but were unsuccessful.

When a case involves a party or entity with a long, cumbersome name, the author may, for convenience, adopt a short form of the name for subsequent references.

> Bridge and Construction Company (hereafter Plaintiff) entered into a contract with American British Commercial Bank and Trust Company (hereafter Bank) and Waste Management of the Desert (hereafter Waste Management). (*Subsequent references to "Plaintiff," "Bank," and "Waste Management" would be capitalized, consistent with the adopted form.*)

B. QUOTED MATERIAL

§ 4:12 Exact correspondence with original; fragments

Quoted material should correspond exactly with its original source in wording, spelling, capitalization, internal punctuation, and citation style.

Any deviations must be indicated or explained. Explanatory or other material inserted within the quotation must be placed in brackets or otherwise noted.

When a source is not quoted in full, care must be taken to convey this' fact to the reader. Any break in the sequence of quoted words or other quoted matter must be noted (see §§ 4:13–4:18). But if only a fragment or short clause is quoted, it is not necessary to signal that portions are missing before or after, as long as the reader will not be misled. For example:

> Section 820, subdivision (a) expressly declares that "[e]xcept as otherwise provided by statute," a public employee is liable for injurious acts or omissions "to the same extent as a private person."

Similarly, there is no need to note the omission of material preceding or following a quoted complete sentence or sentences. Some situations, however, may call for indicating such omissions; as, for example, where an author quotes a single sentence from a legal document, trial testimony, or a statute with multiple sentences, and desires to signal that the original passage is more extensive than quoted (see § 4:13[D]).

For placement of commas, semicolons, and other punctuation with quotation marks, see section 4:49.

§ 4:13 Noting omissions

[A] Omission at beginning of quoted sentence

If material is omitted from the beginning of a quoted sentence, and the quote starts a sentence in the quoting document, capitalize the quote's first letter and place it within brackets. An ellipsis is not needed, as the capital letter in brackets signals the omission. If the quoted material does not start a sentence, retain the lowercase for the first letter of the quote; again, an ellipsis is not necessary, as using lowercase for the quote's first letter signals the omission. (For adjusting a quotation to fit the author's sentence, see § 4:18.)

> "[T]he motive, as noted, is not an element of arson."
> On the other hand, "the motive, as noted, is not an element of arson."

[B] Omission in middle of quoted sentence

If material is omitted from the middle of a quoted sentence, note the omission with an ellipsis set off by a space before the first ellipsis point and after the last ellipsis point.

> "A valid defense . . . is indicated."
> The contract provides: "Lessor shall pay taxes . . . and other governmental levies."

[C] Omission at end of quoted sentence

If material is omitted from the end of a quoted sentence, the omission should be noted with a space, an ellipsis, another space, a period, and the closing quotation mark. In this case, there is no space between the final period and the closing quotation mark. For other punctuation with quotation marks, see section 4:23.

> "For these reasons, we conclude that section 1385(a) does permit a
>   court acting on its own motion to strike prior felony conviction
>   allegations . . . ."
> The "plaintiff in a small claims action shall have no right to appeal the
>   judgment on the plaintiff's claim . . . ." (Code Civ. Proc., § 116.710,
>   subd. (a).)

If the quoted portion of the sentence ends with punctuation (for example, a comma or semicolon), the preferred approach is to terminate the quotation before the punctuation and add the punctuation that is appropriate to the quoting sentence (see § 4:49). If, however, the author wishes to retain the punctuation, an ellipsis is inserted after the punctuation. (Thus, the quote's punctuation substitutes for the first ellipsis point, and is followed by two ellipsis points and the sentence's period.)

> The court noted, "The complaint was ignored . . . ."
> The court noted, "The complaint was ignored, . . ."
> The court noted, "The complaint was ignored; . . ."

[D] Omission following a quoted complete sentence

If a complete sentence is quoted, there is no need to indicate that the text continues after the portion quoted. If so desired, however, signal the omission of continuing material by using an ellipsis immediately after the quoted sentence's period. There is no space between the final ellipsis point and the closing quotation mark.

> The court noted, "The facts are distinguishable." [or]
> The court noted, "The facts are distinguishable. . . ."

[E] Omission of significant portions of intervening material

[1] Omission from single paragraph

If two or more quoted phrases or sentences from a single paragraph are not quoted in the same order as in the original, they may not be combined in one set of quotation marks, but must instead be enclosed in separate quotation marks. If the phrases or sentences do appear in the same order as in the original, signal the omission of intervening material by using an ellipsis, or else enclose each phrase or sentence in separate quotation marks. However, combining phrases from several sentences of the original into a single quotation is discouraged, even when omissions are appropriately signaled. The author should instead paraphrase with appropriate attribution, or use separate quoted phrases.

[2] Omissions from consecutive paragraphs

When quoting a portion of one paragraph and a portion from the following paragraph, without following the source's original paragraph formatting, use the paragraph symbol in brackets [¶] to signal where text from the new paragraph begins.

> The relevant portion of the letter provides: "Acme was prepared to go forward with performance on the 23d. [¶] However, the goods were not ready for shipment until the 29th. . . . [¶] We deny that we are responsible for the delay."
> "As a general guide, those convictions that are for the same crime should be admitted sparingly . . . . [¶] . . . One important consideration . . . is the magnified effect of such convictions."

For consolidating original paragraphs, see section 4:19; for multiparagraph quotations, see section 4:21.

[3] Omission of entire paragraphs

When omitting one or more paragraphs from a quoted passage, use two bracketed paragraph symbols separated by an ellipsis.

> "Duress consists in: [¶] . . . [¶] 2. Unlawful detention of the property of any such person."

[F] Omission of citations

To note the omission of citations, use the word "citation" or "citations" in brackets at the point of each omitted citation or string of citations.

> "This is the general rule. [Citations.] However, . . ."
> "All the elements are present, including evidence of a threat [citations] and prior presence in the building [citation]."

It is also permissible, although not preferred, to note "citation omitted" after the quotation's citation, provided that ellipses are inserted at each point where citations were omitted. This method is discouraged because it does not signal to the reader whether the ellipses mean omitted text or omitted citations, or both.

> "This is the general rule. . . . However, exceptions abound." (*People v. Ross* (1978) 44 Cal.3d 25, 28, citations omitted.)

[G] Omission of footnotes

Indicate that footnotes have been omitted from within a quotation by placing "Fn. omitted" or "Fns. omitted" in brackets before the closing quotation marks, or by placing "fn. omitted" or "fns. omitted" within parentheses after the citation.

> "We follow the established rule. [Fn. omitted.]" (*A v. B* (1990) 50 Cal.3d 100.)
>
> "We follow the established rule." (*C v. D*. (1980) 100 Cal.App.3d 100, fn. omitted.)

§ 4:14 Bracketed substitutions for omissions

Quoted material can be omitted, and new material substituted for it, by enclosing the substitution in brackets when it is clear that the bracketed material replaces what appeared in the original. Do not use ellipses in conjunction with brackets when there is a deletion and substitution of material within a quote. For explanatory bracketed insertions, see section 4:16; for adjusting the quote to fit the author's sentence, see section 4:18.

> *Original:* "It is provided that the Bureau of Labor Statistics of the United States Department of Labor shall determine the proper ratio."
>
> *With substitution:* "It is provided that the [bureau] shall determine the proper ratio."

§ 4:15 Error in quoted source

[A] Quote exactly

Even when the original contains an obvious error, quote it exactly but note that the error is intentionally quoted, or insert a correction, using one of the following methods.

[B] Misspelled words

Indicate by inserting "[*sic*]" after the error. Alternatively, the author may substitute the correctly spelled word in brackets, if the author is certain of what was meant.

> "The judgment was a bar to those preceedings [*sic*]."
>
> "The court exercised it's [*sic*] discretion."
>
> "The court exercised [its] discretion."

Do not indicate a spelling error by spelling the word correctly and italicizing the corrected letter or letters; the reader does not know if the italicized letter is a printer's error, was italicized in the original, or is in lieu of an undisclosed letter.

[C] Error obvious

When a passage does not read properly or the tense of a verb is incorrect or some other *obvious* flaw appears, indicate the error by inserting "[*sic*]" within the quote following the error or by inserting "(*Sic.*)" after the quotation. Be careful that there is in fact an error and not merely a change in usage or an alternative usage.

> "The judgment were [*sic*] annulled."
> "By count three charged the defendant was with arson." (*Sic.*)
> "The majority have misconstrued the statute." (Note: No [*sic*]; alternate usage.)

[D] Error not obvious

When the error is not obvious, insert correcting information in brackets within the quotation or, in parentheses or a footnote, provide the changes or explanations necessary to clarify the passage.

> "Section 1234 of the Penal Code is not applicable." (The intended citation is to section 1324, not section 1234.)
> "Section 1234[1] of the Penal Code is not applicable."

> ---
> [1]The intended citation is to section 1324, not section 1234.

[E] Multiple errors

When a quoted document contains many errors, such as might be found in the will or a letter of an illiterate person, it may be preferable to indicate the errors by italicizing or underlining the erroneous portions. Notify the reader of the technique adopted in an explanatory parenthetical note or a footnote.

> The testamentary document involved is set out below.[1] [*Or, instead of a footnote:*]
> The testamentary document involved is set out below. (Italicized portions denote spelling and grammatical errors in the original.)
>
> "May 19, 1873,
> Fresno, California
> "I John Brown *herebye* give my *hole* estate to my wife. *Aul* other *ayers* get nothing. . . ."

> ---
> [1] Italicized portions denote spelling and grammatical errors in the original.

[F] Error of omission

Note an error of omission by inserting the missing letter or word in brackets.

"The court[s] have followed the rule."
"The patient then [began] hemorrhaging."

§ 4:16 Explanatory insertions in quoted material

If it is necessary to insert a word or short clause to explain or clarify the meaning of the quotation, place the inserted matter in brackets. This technique for explaining or clarifying within quoted matter should not, however, be employed to rewrite or to accomplish a de facto paraphrasing of the original language.

"Such an order [denying a new trial] is not appealable."
"The reason offered in this case [for the late filing] was unconvincing."

When the source quoted already has material in brackets and the author wishes to add more material, note the distinction between the old and the new.

The court determined, therefore, that she should not "be placed in the dilemma of awaiting 'jurisdictional' decisions [of one tribunal] while the clock of limitations tick[ed] in her ears." (A v. B (1990) 225 Cal.App.3d 100, 110, first bracketed insertion added.)

Another way to indicate which brackets are from the original and which are added is to use an explanatory footnote.

[1] Insertions added by this court are placed in brackets and italicized to distinguish them from the bracketed insertions appearing in the original material.

§ 4:17 Completing citations within quoted material

When quoting a sentence that cites a case by name or by short cite only, or with an incomplete citation (e.g., "In *People v. Hart, supra,* 65 Cal.App.4th at p. 905, defendant contended . . . ."), and the case has not already been cited in the quoting document, complete the citation in brackets, with appropriate punctuation. For example, a citation in a quoted sentence that reads, "This is the holding of *People v. Hines, supra,* 15 Cal.4th at pp. 1044–1045" should be completed by adding the date and any parallel citations, in brackets.

As that court noted, "This is the holding of *People v. Hines* [(1997)] 15 Cal.4th [997,] 1044–1045 [64 Cal.Rptr.2d 594, 938 P.2d 388]."

Similarly, an original quote that reads, "for the reasons stated in *Agnello* and the explanation of that decision in *Wolder* . . . ." would be adjusted by completing the citations, in brackets.

> This court reversed Smith's conviction, holding that "for the reasons stated in *Agnello [v. United States* (1925) 269 U.S. 20 [46 S.Ct. 4, 70 L.Ed. 145]] and the explanation of that decision in *Wolder [v. United States* (1954) 347 U.S. 62 [74 S.Ct. 354, 98 L.Ed. 503]] . . . ." *(Note: If the author later cites the same case outside the quoted passage, it will not be necessary to repeat the complete citation. The completed full citation within the quote will serve as the opinion author's initial cite, and the author may use "supra" for subsequent cites to the same opinion.)*

§ 4:18 Adjusting quoted sentence for author's sentence

When a quoted sentence, or the beginning of a quoted sentence, falls in the middle of the author's sentence, the quoted sentence or beginning of sentence should follow copy and start with a capital letter. If only a fragment of the original sentence is quoted, however, it need not retain the original capital letter; instead, readability is enhanced by putting the first letter in lowercase, in brackets.

> The court rejected the argument, stating, "Nor does section 1281.6 excuse respondent's alleged misfeasance."
> The concurring opinion discussed other aspects of "[u]nfairness in arbitration sufficiently extreme to justify court intervention."

Similar minor adjustments may be made to adjust verb tense, plurals, etc., of the quoted sentence to fit the author's text:

> These rules are little more than the "outmoded carryover[s] of the past."

§ 4:19 Original paragraph formatting not followed

While it is best to follow the paragraph formatting of the original material, it is sometimes necessary to consolidate into one paragraph a quote consisting of multiple short paragraphs, such as a numbered list or a statute with several short subdivisions. When consolidating several quoted paragraphs into one paragraph, insert the symbol [¶] in brackets at the appropriate location.

> "The remoteness of the prior conviction is a factor. [¶] A special and even more difficult problem arises . . . ."
> "The department concluded that: [¶] 1. The premises sought to be licensed are in a residential area; [¶] 2. Issuance of the license would aggravate an existing police problem."

§ 4:20 Line spacing and margins; multiparagraph quotes and block quotes

Quoted matter may either use the same line spacing and margins as the rest of the text, or may be block-indented. (For judicial opinion authors, see § 4:21.)

When the quotation uses the same margins and line spacing as the text and is more than one paragraph long, the entire quotation, including the initial paragraph, should be set forth in separate paragraphs, using the original paragraphing. An opening quotation mark precedes each quoted paragraph, and a closing quotation mark follows the last quoted paragraph only. As with shorter quotes, the citation may precede or follow the quote; if the citation follows the quote, include it in the quote's last paragraph, immediately after the closing quotation mark.

To block-indent a quote, indent from both left and right margins. Further indent the first line of the blocked quote if the quoted material starts a new paragraph in the original. Single-space each paragraph, but double-space between paragraphs. Do not enclose block quotes in quotation marks (except, of course, for quotation marks in the original). If the citation follows the quote, it is not indented, but is placed at the left-hand margin of the next line after the quote.

See also California Rules of Court, rules 15 (quotations longer than two lines in appellate briefs), and 201(c) (line spacing in papers filed in superior court), and any local court rules.

§ 4:21 Multiparagraph quotes and adopted opinions, for opinion authors

[A] Multiparagraph quotes

To quote several paragraphs from another source, judicial opinion authors should observe the rules set forth in section 4:20 for multiparagraph quotes that are not indented. (See, e.g., *Manufacturers Life Ins. Co. v. Superior Court* (1995) 10 Cal.4th 257, 286–289 (conc. opn. of Mosk, J.).)

The block quote is not recommended for opinion authors, as opinions published in the Official Reports do not use the block quote format, regardless of the quote's length. If an opinion author nevertheless wishes to use a block quote for a filed opinion, follow the rules for block quotes set forth in the preceding section, with one exception: Because the Official Reports publisher automatically converts block-indented quotes to unindented quotes, opinion authors must use quotation marks with block quotes, observing the same punctuation rules as for quotes that are not indented (i.e., opening quotes before each separate paragraph; closing quotation marks after the last paragraph only; reversing quotation marks for internal quotes, etc.). (See § 4:22.) If the quote's citation follows the quote, place it following the closing quotation mark, in the last indented paragraph, not in a new paragraph.

[B] Adopted opinions

When a court adopts a prior opinion or quotes extensively from a cited decision, opinion authors may omit quotation marks entirely, using instead a footnote or an explanatory note in the text to inform the reader that the matter presented is quoted. (See, e.g., *Municipal Court v. Superior Court (Gonzalez)* (1993) 5 Cal.4th 1126, 1129.) After notifying the reader that customary quotation marks will not be used, follow the original exactly except for material that, if quoted directly from the original, would be out of context. For example, if a Supreme Court opinion adopts a lengthy quotation from a Court of Appeal opinion that refers to "this court," the author of the Supreme Court opinion should adjust it to "[the Court of Appeal]."

If the context of the opinion does not clearly signal the point at which the lengthy quotation concludes, note the end before continuing with the opinion text, as in the following examples:

> [End of quotation from the opinion of Justice Mosk.]
> [We end our quotation from the Court of Appeal opinion.]

If an author wants to delete portions of a lengthy quotation or adopted opinion, or make additions, or both, an explanatory footnote can be used.

> [1] Empty brackets [ ] denote deletions from the Court of Appeal opinion.
> [1] Brackets enclosing material (other than parallel citations) denote insertions or additions by this court, unless otherwise specified.
> [1] Empty brackets [ ] indicate deletions from the Court of Appeal opinion; brackets with material enclosed (aside from parallel citations) indicate matter added by this court, unless otherwise specified.

If, after adopting one of the foregoing footnotes, the opinion author adds a new disposition sentence or paragraph to an adopted opinion, the author should enclose the new material in brackets, following empty brackets, to signal that the original disposition or paragraph was deleted and that the bracketed disposition or paragraph was not part of the original opinion.

> we have determined that no action lies. [ ] [The judgment is accordingly reversed.]

See generally, as illustrations of adopted opinions, *Arriaga v. County of Alameda* (1995) 9 Cal.4th 1055, 1059; *Municipal Court v. Superior Court (Gonzalez)* (1993) 5 Cal.4th 1126, 1129; *O'Hare v. Superior Court* (1987) 43 Cal.3d 86, 90; *Estate of McDill* (1975) 14 Cal.3d 831, 833–834; *People v. Cantrell* (1973) 8 Cal.3d 672, 677; see also section 4:25 (footnotes in quoted material).

§ 4:22 Quotations within quoted material

After the opening quotation mark, alternate single and double quotation marks to indicate internal quotations within quotations. Under this practice, the quoting author reverses the quotation marks that appear in the quoted source: A double mark becomes a single mark and a single becomes a double. Use alternating quotation marks in this manner for each level of internal quote, even if several reversals are required. Internal quotation marks may not be omitted.

> *Original:* A state law implicates the right to travel when it actually deters such travel [citations], when impeding travel is its primary objective [citations], or when it "uses any classification" that serves to "penalize the exercise of that right."
>
> *Quotation:* The court held: "A state law implicates the right to travel when it actually deters such travel [citations], when impeding travel is its primary objective [citations], or when it 'uses any classification' that serves to 'penalize the exercise of that right.'"

§ 4:23 Quotation marks with other punctuation

Place the final period and the comma, whether present in the original or added by the author, within the closing quotation marks. Place other punctuation marks within quotation marks only if they are present in the original.

> The officer's testimony was "really very weak," since the prosecutor was unable to "trace it back to its source."
>
> One note read, "We are . . . entitled to a refund"; another, "Unfair tax!"; still another, "Why not waive nonpayment?"
>
> "Who was present?" the witness was asked.
>
> Was the witness asked, "Who was present?" (*Note that no additional question mark is needed.*)
>
> Was the defendant heard to say, "I confess"?
>
> The officer shouted, "Halt!"

For omissions at end of quoted sentence, see section 4:13[C]; for use of commas, semicolons, and colons with quotation marks, see section 4:49.

§ 4:24 Quotation marks for emphasis

Quotation marks are sometimes used to emphasize words or phrases, although most authorities now discourage the practice. Italic typeface is generally better used for this purpose. Quotation marks may also be used when referring to a word as a word (e.g., the word "insured" means . . .), for unfamiliar or slang words, or for words used ironically.

The "better" theory is . . . .
He "bookmarked" the Web site.
The city passed an "anticonversion" ordinance covering residential hotels.

Whether quotation marks should be used for emphasis, and when, are within the author's discretion, but extensive use for emphasis dilutes the effect and can be distracting for the reader. Further, the reader may be confused if quotation marks for emphasis are used in conjunction with actual quotations.

§ 4:25 Footnotes in quoted material

[A] Footnotes in original included

To include an original footnote from a quote, replace the original footnote number in the quote with a new footnote number, in brackets, in sequence with the author's footnotes. Then, at the bottom of the page, after the footnote number, either (1) insert the original footnote's text, in quotes (see, e.g., *Manufacturers Life Ins. Co. v. Superior Court* (1995) 10 Cal.4th 257, 286–289 (conc. opn. of Mosk, J.)), or (2) paraphrase the original footnote as an indirect quote, without quotation marks. Do not enclose the footnote number at the bottom of the page in brackets.

The following example shows the footnote number in brackets within the quote, and the two possible methods for setting forth the quoted footnote, at the bottom of the page:

The court was unpersuaded. "Dismissal of the felony-murder . . . special circumstance constituted no bar under any of the principles defendant suggests—whether double jeopardy, res judicata, or collateral estoppel.[3]" (*People v. Davis* (1995) 10 Cal.4th 463, 514.)

---

[3] "Dismissal of the charges put defendant in the same position he would have been in if they had not been filed." [*or*]

[3] In a footnote at this point, the court noted that dismissal of those charges put defendant in the same position he would otherwise have been in if they had not been filed.

[B] Footnotes added to original

To add a footnote to a quotation, number the footnote consecutively with others in the text. Then place the footnote number in the quote, enclosing the number in brackets to signal that it is an addition. At the bottom of the page, the brackets are omitted and the footnote is treated as any other. (See, e.g., *City of Los Angeles v. Public Utilities Com.* (1975) 15 Cal.3d 680, 688, fn. 10.) The following example illustrates a quote to which a footnote has been added, in sequence with another footnote:

"The net receipts directly[3] attributable to Smith, Inc. are to be paid to it."
(Smith-Jones contract, p. 3.) The contract as initially signed was filed in
the Shasta County Recorder's office.[4]

---

[3]The word "directly" was added on July 10.
[4]The record establishes that the filing took place on July 12.

For omitting footnotes from original quoted language, see section
4:13[G]; for placement of footnote number, see section 4:66.

[C] Footnotes added when adopting major portion of another text

See, e.g., *O'Hare v. Superior Court* (1987) 43 Cal.3d 86, 99, footnotes
12–13; *Mehl v. People* ex rel. *Dept. Pub. Wks.* (1975) 13 Cal.3d 710, 714,
717–718, footnotes 1–4; *People v. Rojas* (1975) 15 Cal.3d 540, 544–545,
footnote 2, 551, footnote 7. For lengthy quotations and adopted opinions,
see section 4:21; for footnote placement, see section 4:66.

§ 4:26 Strike-out type in quoted material

When a quotation contains strike-out type, use the word processor's
strike-out feature or draw a line through the middle of the words to appear
as strike-out type. For example:

". . . the trustee to distribute the ~~corpus of the trust~~ principal on the death
of the beneficiary."

§ 4:27 Italics and underscoring in quoted material

[A] Emphasis in original

If the matter quoted contains words or phrases that are italicized or
underscored (or both) in the original, follow the original italics or underscoring exactly. The quotation marks themselves signal that the quotation is identical to the original source in all respects, including the emphasis; thus, it is
unnecessary to add "original italics," or similar language, after the quote. In
rare instances, where the context requires, the author may wish to add a parenthetical note after the quote to clarify the source of italics or to stress that
even the original author stressed the emphasized language. For example:

The court observed that what was involved was not a contractual deadline,
but a "time schedule with respect to the filing and processing of
grievances." (98 Cal.App.3d at p. 270, original italics.)

By the same token, if original italics or underscoring is not needed,
they may be omitted, with a parenthetical note to that effect, such as "italics
omitted" or "italics and underscoring omitted," at the end of the quote.

> The court observed that what was involved was not a contractual deadline, but a "time schedule with respect to the filing and processing of grievances." (98 Cal.App.3d at p. 270, italics omitted.)

When quoted matter itself contains a quotation with italics, signal the source of the italicized phrase, using a parenthetical note, such as "italics added by [*name of case*]." The phrase "original italics" is confusing in this context and should not be used.

[B] Emphasis added to quoted material

If italics are added to quoted matter, insert a parenthetical note after the quoted passage. The notation is placed at the end of the entire quotation, not directly following the italicized word or expression.

> Section 6012, subdivision (a)(3) specifically provides that the "*gross receipts*" should not be reduced by the cost of "materials, labor . . . or any other expense." (Italics added.)
> Under this set of circumstances we decline to extend liability to "an independent contractor of the *public entity*." (§ 814:4, italics added.)

When adding italics to quoted material that already contains italics, insert a parenthetical note at the end of the quotation to indicate which italicized portions are new. For example:

> The case is distinguished on the ground that "there the action was *solely* to prevent the doing of certain acts by such officials and by the other defendants *in the future*." (59 Cal.App.2d at p. 797, second italics added.)
> Damages for fear of cancer are recoverable upon proof that (1) due to defendant's negligence, "plaintiff is exposed to a toxic substance which threatens cancer; *and* (2) the plaintiff's fear stems from a knowledge, *corroborated by reliable medical or scientific opinion*," that, more likely than not, the plaintiff will develop cancer due to the exposure. (13 Cal.4th at p. 913, first italics in original, second italics added.)

For other insertions into quoted matter, see section 4:16.

C. NUMBERS

§ 4:28 General rules governing numbers

The following styles are used in the Official Reports, to achieve consistency and uniformity. These rules indicate when numbers are to be spelled out and when they are to be written as figures. The rules may be varied for emphasis, to maintain uniformity in a series of numbers (14 apples, 21 oranges, and 7 bananas), or for consistency when quoted matter has followed a different rule. General rules are indicated first, followed by narrower rules applicable to specific circumstances. When a conflict exists, follow the more specific rule.

1. Follow copy exactly when quoting.
2. Use words for numbers that start sentences.
3. Use words for numerals zero to nine (except for dates, percentages, numbers with decimals, clock time, money, or technical, scientific, or statistical matter).
4. Use figures for the numbers 10 and greater, except when beginning a sentence.
5. Use figures in all tabular work.
6. When one number follows another, use a comma to separate them (e.g., of the 500, 300 did not vote).
7. Where two numbers describing the same item occur together, express one of them with a figure to avoid confusion (e.g., there were six 5-foot logs; twenty $5 bills).

For hyphens with compound numbers (e.g., forty-five, twenty-one), see section 4:42; for commas with numbers and figures, see section 4:51; for apostrophes with numbers and figures, see section 4:62.

§ 4:29 Dates

Use figures for dates and spell out holidays (the 1930's, the '30's, the Fourth of July, Cinco de Mayo); but note: the 4th of July (when not referred to as a holiday).

When only the month and day are given, the date may be July 25 (preferred), or July 25th, or the 25th of July. If the year is added, use July 25, 1994; avoid the use in text of July 25th, 1994, 25 July 1994, or 7/25/94. When only the month and year are given, no comma separates them: July 2001, *not* July, 2001.

When an author adds an ordinal suffix such as "th" to the day of the month, the abbreviations are 1st, 2d (*not* 2nd), 3d (*not* 3rd), 4th, 5th, and so forth.

To denote a span of time, the author should use either the "en" dash (the shorter dash on a word processor, or one hyphen), or the word "to." Note that the closing year in a span of years is given in its entirety, not abbreviated to the last two digits.

    1996 to 1997; 1996–1997 (*not* 1996–97)
    April to August
    June to August 1997
    June–August 1997
    June 1, 2002, to August 1, 2003
    June 1, 2002–August 1, 2003

When a sequence of month, day, and year is not immediately followed by a period, semicolon, colon, dash, bracket, or parenthesis, insert a comma after the year. When a date is used as a modifier, the comma after the year is strongly preferred, but it may be omitted. For more examples of commas with dates, see section 4:49.

> The meeting on July 10, 1999, was the committee's last. [*but*]
> The March 23, 1999, report so stated. [*or*]
> The March 23, 1999 report so stated.

§ 4:30 Time

Use figures for clock time. Use "p.m." and "a.m.," not "P.M." and "A.M." (Writing the time with a colon and two additional characters is preferred: e.g., 12:00 noon is preferred to 12 noon; 1:00 p.m. is preferred to 1 p.m.)

> 4:05 p.m.
> 10:00 o'clock in the evening (*not* 10:00 o'clock p.m.)
> 10:00 p.m. and 2:00 a.m.
> about 6:00 p.m. (*not* at about 6:00 p.m. *or* at about 6 p.m.)

When referring to a period of time composed of several parts (years, months, days, etc.), do not separate the parts with commas.

> He was sentenced to 10 years 11 months and 2 days.
> He served 10 years 11 months.

§ 4:31 Numbers indicating sequence

Use figures with numbers indicating sequence (as distinct from numbers indicating amount, length, or other measure). Note that commas are generally not used in numbers indicating sequence (i.e., section 25003, *not* section 25,003).

> order 9
> count 2
> paragraph No. 21
> interrogatory No. 6
> docket No. 2160
> item 4
> part III
> S.F. No. 18761; Civ. No. 10280; case No. A012345
> page 4, pages 278–288 (*not* pages 278–88)

§ 4:32 Percentages, fractions, and ordinals

Use figures for percentages. The word "percent" is spelled out except in tables, which use the percent symbol (%).

6 percent
6.5 percent (*not* 6.5% except in tables)
21 percent
the bonus was between 2 and 10 percent [*the word "percent" follows the last number*]
0.10 percent, or more, of alcohol (or 0.1 percent)

Spell out fractions standing alone (e.g., one-half, one-third, etc.) or when followed by "of a" or "of an" (or where these expressions are implied). Insert a hyphen between the numerator and denominator of a fraction, unless either element already contains a hyphen (for compound numbers, see § 4:42). Do not spell out a portion of a fraction and express the other part as a figure. Use figures for fractions with numbers 10 and higher.

two-thirds of a foot (*not* 2-thirds foot or ⅔ of a foot)
one-half inch
two-thirds majority
five-hundredths (*but* 5 one-hundredths)
45/50
21/35
a half-inch
a half-hour
a half-mile
half an inch
half a dozen
three and one-half (*but* 10½)

For ordinals, apply the rules in section 4:28 (general rules governing numbers), and spell out numbers first through ninth.

first	22d
second	23d
third	24th
fourth	third century
10th	20th century
21st	

§ 4:33 Money

Use figures for units of currency. Use the dollar sign ($) rather than the word "dollars," but spell out "cents."

4 cents (*not* 4¢)	$1 bill
$0.04	$5 bills (*but* twenty $5 bills)
85 cents	$17.95
$0.85	$179.95
$2 (*not* $2.00)	$1,000 (*not* a thousand dollars)

Exceptions: Spell out indefinite sums of money (e.g., thousands of dollars); and for round amounts of $1 million and greater, use figures together with the words "million" or "billion," to enhance readability.

> $4 million (*not* $4,000,000)
> $4.6 million (*not* $4,600,000 *or* 4.6 million dollars)
> $4.5 million (*not* four and one-half million)
> but $4,567,785
> $950,000 to $1 million
> $500,000 (*not* $500 thousand)
> a $200-a-week job
> a $5,000 grant
> $2,000-$3,000 (*the dollar sign is used with both figures*)
> $8 billion (*not* $8,000,000,000)
> $8.2 billion (*not* $8,200,000,000 or 8.2 billion dollars)
> $4.25 billion (*not* four and one-quarter billion dollars)
> The claim involved many thousands of dollars; but he earned millions.

Numbers written with "million" or "billion" are usually limited to one place beyond the decimal point, but exceptions may be made for readability.

> The buyer offered $1.8 million, and the seller made a counteroffer of $1.85 million.

D. ITALICS

§ 4:34 Consistent use of italics

Because italics are used extensively in legal writing, consistent use is essential. The following sections indicate approved styles. Keep in mind, however, that the modern tendency is to minimize the use of italics.

§ 4:35 Indicating italics in manuscript

Italics is the normal convention for providing emphasis. Generally, do not use underscoring to signal italics if word processing software provides an italics font. There are, however, some special circumstances where underscoring might be used, even though an italics font is available (e.g., to provide special emphasis, or where it is added to quoted matter that is already italicized).

> Under the circumstances the trial court "*correctly concluded that section 832 of the Civil Code does not absolve a negligent excavator.*" (Underscoring added.)

For adding emphasis to quoted material, see section 4:27.

§ 4:36 Italicizing Latin and foreign language words and phrases

[A] Modern usage

In legal writing many Latin and foreign words and phrases are in such common use that they have now become a part of the legal idiom and do not need to be distinguished by italics. If the word or phrase is not in common usage, italics are used. If emphasis is desired, italics are used whether or not the word is otherwise italicized.

The following lists contain many of the Latin and foreign words and phrases that are used with some frequency in legal writing. They are divided into those words that should not be italicized and those that should be.

[B] Latin and other foreign terms that are not italicized

actus reus	de minimis	in propria persona
addendum	de novo	(in pro. per.)
ad hoc	dicta	in rem
ad hominem	dictum	in situ
ad infinitum	duces tecum	inter alia
ad litem	e.g.	interim
ad valorem	en banc	in terrorem
a fortiori	ergo	inter vivos
alias	errata	in toto
alter ego	erratum	ipse dixit
amici curiae	et al.	ipso facto
amicus curiae	et cetera, etc.	laissez faire (n.)
anno Domini	et seq.	laissez-faire (adj.)
antebellum	ex contractu	lis pendens
a priori	ex delicto	mala in se
apropos	ex officio	mala prohibita
arguendo	ex parte	malum in se
assumpsit	ex post facto	malum prohibitum
attaché	fait accompli	mandamus
bona fide	forum non conveniens	mens rea
caveat emptor	habeas corpus	mesne profits
certiorari	i.e.	modus operandi
cf.	in camera	née (or né)
chose	in extenso	nisi
chose in action	in extremis	nisi prius
circa	in forma pauperis	nolle prosequi
compos mentis	in futuro	nolo contendere
consortium	in haec verba	nom de plume
contra	in limine	non compos mentis
corpus	in loco parentis	non sequitur
corpus delicti	in pari delicto	nunc pro tunc
coup de grâce	in pari materia	obiter
de facto	in personam	obiter dictum
de jure		

onus
pendente lite
per annum
per capita
per diem
per se
per stirpes
petit larceny
post hoc
postmortem
prima facie
pro bono
pro bono publico
pro forma
propria persona (pro. per.)
pro rata
pro se
pro tanto

pro tempore
quantum meruit
quasi
quid pro quo
quo warranto
ratio decidendi
res
res gestae
res ipsa loquitur
res judicata
respondeat superior
résumé
scienter
seriatim
sine qua non
situs
stare decisis
status quo

status quo
ante
sua sponte
sub silentio
sui generis
sui juris
supersedeas
ultimatum
ultra vires
verbatim
versus
via
vice
vice versa
vis-à-vis
viva voce
viz.
voir dire

[C] Latin and other foreign terms that are italicized

ab ante
ab initio
ad damnum
ad diem
ad finem
ad idem
alterius
animo revocandi
animus
ante
a posteriori
autrefois acquit
autrefois convict
causa mortis
conditio sine qua non
consideratum est per curiam
coram nobis
coram vobis
cum testamento annexo
cy près
damnum absque injuria
de bene esse
del credere
de son tort
donatio causa mortis
ejusdem generis
en masse
ex curia
expressio unius

ex proprio vigore
ferae naturae
ff.
functus officio
haec verba
ibid.
id.
idem
idem sonans
in capite
in curia
inclusio unius est exclusio alterius
in esse
infra
in perpetuum
in posse
in praesenti
in re
in statu quo
interesse
inter se
inter sese
judgment *non obstante veredicto*
lex domicilii
lex locus contractus
lex non scripta
loc. cit.
locus delicti
locus in quo

locus poenitentiae	*quare clausum fregit*
mala fide	*quo animo*
mobilia sequuntur personam	*quoad hoc*
ne plus ultra	*raison d'être*
op. cit.	*scire facias*
parens patriae	*semble*
pari ratione	*sic*
passim	*simpliciter*
per autre vie	*stet processus*
per curiam	*sub judice*
post	*sub nom.*
post facto	*supra*
post-factum	*ubi supra*
profit à prendre	*ut infra*
pro hac vice	*ut supra*
qua	*vide ut supra*
quaere	

§ 4:37   Use with anglicized words

A foreign language phrase is generally treated as a single unit. Either italicize the whole phrase or none of it, depending on whether or not the phrase as a whole has become anglicized. Take care to determine how much of a phrase is foreign; only the foreign portion is italicized.

administrator *de son tort*

§ 4:38   Italics for emphasis

Italics are frequently employed to give emphasis or prominence to words or expressions. Whether italics should be used for emphasis, and when, are within the author's discretion, but extensive use of italics for emphasis is generally disfavored.

§ 4:39   Italics with citations

[A] Case names

Case names are italicized whether or not they are within a citation. This rule applies to trial court case names (see § 1:16) as well as appellate cases (see § 1:14).

a pre-*Boykin* decision
Notwithstanding *Smith*
a *Jones* instruction
Defendant was given *Miranda* warnings
the trial court action, *Garcia v. Superior Court* (Super. Ct. S.F., 1999, No. 994499)

[B] Citation cross-references

The cross-reference words *ante, ibid., id., infra, post,* and *supra* are always italicized. For use of these words with case authority, see chapter 1; for use with secondary authority, see chapter 3.

[C] Subsequent history references

Words denoting the subsequent history of cited opinions (see § 1:11) and the abbreviated forms of these words are generally not italicized. A few such words are italicized by tradition (e.g., *sub nom., per curiam*).

[D] Statutes and session laws

Do not italicize the following words or their abbreviations: article, chapter, clause, division, section, subdivision, subsection, title. If these words appear italicized in quoted matter, however, follow the original (see § 4:27). Also follow copy where the letters *l* and *o* are italicized to avoid confusion with their look-alike digits. (See, e.g., Pen. Code, § 602.2, subd. (*l*); 15 U.S.C. § 1681*o*.)

E. HYPHENS

§ 4:40 General guidelines

Avoid using hyphens except when they improve the flow of the sentence, resolve ambiguity, or assist the reader in comprehending the author's meaning. When in doubt about hyphenating a word or phrase, first check the dictionary for use or nonuse of hyphens. Otherwise, the following sections provide guidelines on hyphenation for California legal writing, and the United States Government Printing Office Style Manual (1984 ed.) provides comprehensive information and lists on hyphenation.

§ 4:41 Compound adjectives

When two or more words combine to serve as a compound adjective (or adjective phrase), they are often connected by a hyphen. If one of the words contains a prefix, the entire adjective phrase, including the prefix, may require hyphens to avoid ambiguity. If the result is too cumbersome, consider using a different construction.

agreed-upon price
ready-to-wear garment
13-day period
two-year-old boy
non-revenue-producing plant (*but* nonrevenue reasons)

non-civil-service position
non-death-qualified jurors
anti-death-penalty views (*but* antisympathy instruction)
anti-speed-trap law
non-interest-bearing account

If a sentence containing a compound adjective is readable and clear without a hyphen, however, then omit the hyphen. A hyphen is not used with common legal terms (see § 4:44).

A civil rights bill was introduced.
This public utility rule is fundamental.
The civil service examination was held as scheduled.
The topic of the lecture was land use planning.
Many public school districts were affected.

Do not hyphenate compound adjectives containing an adverb ending in "ly."

highly refined material
fully discounted note
constitutionally required admonition
federally mandated payment

If a compound adjective is not *customarily* spelled with a hyphen, and the phrase follows the noun modified, the hyphen is deleted, as in the following examples:

Before noun: The court by a four-to-three vote affirmed the judgment.
After noun: The court's vote of four to three affirmed the judgment.
Before noun: He drank the crystal-clear spring water.
After noun: The spring water was crystal clear.
Before noun: They ordered fire-tested synthetic material.
After noun: The material had been fire tested.
BUT:
Before noun: Just an old-fashioned love song.
After noun: We're old-fashioned.

§ 4:42 Compound numbers and units of measurement

Hyphenate compound numbers from twenty-one to ninety-nine if spelling out those numbers. Also hyphenate modifying phrases that contain numerical first elements. Fractions are hyphenated when spelled out, but no additional hyphen is used between the numerator and the denominator when either is already hyphenated. Technical units of measurement are generally hyphenated. For spelling out numbers, see section 4:28; for spelling out fractions and percentages, see section 4:32.

Compound numbers
forty-five
one hundred forty-five (*but* one hundred forty)

Adjectives with numerical first elements
an eight-hour day
four-to-three vote
three-to-one ratio
12-inch ruler
.45-caliber gun
12-gauge shotgun
nine-millimeter handgun
two-sided issue (*but* twofold)
60-day note
four-week vacation (*but* four weeks' vacation *or* one year's probation; see
   § 4:60[B])
19th-century weapon
$5-per-bushel wheat
110-volt line
five-gallon jug
four-month continuance
six-foot man (*but* six feet tall, *and* 5 feet 10 or 11 inches tall)
five-year-old boy (*but* a two year old)
7-Eleven store (*correct name*)

Fractions
three five-hundredths (if spelling out; *normally* 3/500ths)
three-fourths
a half-inch; half an inch
a half-mile; half a mile
a half-hour; one-half hour
half an hour
two and one-half to three hours (*or* two and a half to three hours)
half a mile
half a dozen
Three and one-half shares of stock were delivered.
The officer found one-half ounce of heroin.
The window was open one-third of an inch.

Avoid the construction "half of 1 percent"; use 0.5 percent instead.
(Adding the zero makes the decimal more visible.)

Technical units of measurement
passenger-mile
board-foot
kilowatt-hour
foot-pounds

Number compounds

Hyphens are used in both parts of number compounds having a common element that is only expressed once.

> three- and four-foot lengths
> 10- to 20-unit apartment house
> three- to six-pound bags
> three-, four-, and five-inch openings
> *but* three to four feet wide

§ 4:43 Other common uses of hyphens

[A] General rules

Hyphens are often used in the following situations:

1. With compounds composed of nouns and prepositions.

> case-in-chief
> face-to-face
> hand-to-hand

2. To avoid ambiguity of meaning.

> re-collect (*as distinct from* recollect)
> re-cover (*as distinct from* recover)

3. To join certain prefixes to words.

> cross- (*as in* cross-defendant, cross-complaint)
> self- (*as in* self-incrimination)
> quasi- (*as in* quasi-community property)

4. To join prefixes to a capitalized word.

> pro-British　　　　mid-June
> anti-French　　　　all-American

5. To join a single capital letter to form a common word (a letter compound).

> A-bomb　　　　S-curve
> D-Day　　　　　T-square
> I-beam　　　　　X-ray

6. "Felony-murder" and like constructions used as compound adjectives.

> felony murder (noun)
> felony-murder rule (adj.)
> felony-murder robbery (adj.)
> felony-murder special circumstances (adj.)
> felony-murder special-circumstance allegation (adj.)
> felony-murder-robbery special-circumstance rule (adj.)
> *but* robbery felony murder (noun)
> felony-murder-robbery special circumstances (adj.)
> multiple-murder conviction (adj.)

multiple-murder special-circumstance instruction (adj.)
robbery murder (noun)
robbery-murder instruction (adj.)

7. To join a prefix to a number.

post-1995 amendment
pre-1960 conviction

[B] Hyphenated terms

The following terms should be hyphenated unless they appear in quoted matter and were not hyphenated in the original:

alcohol-related (adj.)	cross-purpose
all-American	cross-question
all-or-nothing (adj.)	cross-reference
anti-abortion	cross-section
attorney-client relationship	ex-contemner
at-will employee	ex-felon
blood-alcohol level (adj.)	ex-Governor
blood-to-breath partition ratio (adj.)	ex-husband
brother-in-law (etc.)	ex-servicemember
by-product	ex-wife
case-in-chief	ex-vice-president
co-administrator	great-grandparent
co-author	I-beam
co-executor	in-laws
co-obligor	long-standing (adj.)
co-occupant	long-term (adj.) (*but* longtime)
co-op	mid-Atlantic
co-owner	mid-June
court-appointed (adj.)	mother-in-law (etc.)
court-martial	multiple-murder rule (adj.)
cross-appeal	murder-for-hire law (adj.)
cross-bidding	off-duty (adj.)
cross-check	off-hours
cross-claim (noun or verb)	off-ramp and on-ramp (of a
cross-complainant	freeway)
cross-complaint	off-season
cross-country	off-street (adj.)
cross-date	off-the-record (adj.)
cross-defendant	out-of-date
cross-examination	out-of-state (adj.)
cross-examine	parent-child relationship
cross-immunity	pre-1900
cross-index	quasi-community property
cross-interrogate	quasi-contract
cross-interrogatory	quasi-corporation

quasi-specific performance
re-advised
rear-end collision
recross-examination
right-angle intersection
right-hand (adj.)
right-of-way (noun)
safe-deposit box
second-guess
self-control
self-defense
self-imposed
self-incrimination
7-Eleven store (*but* Kmart store)
single-family dwelling
sister-in-law
so-called

to tape-record (verb)
tape-recorded (adj.)
but a tape recording
time-barred
un-American
vice-president
V-shaped
Wal-Mart stores
well-being
well-informed (adj. preceding noun)
well-known (adj. preceding noun,
    but "it was well known.")
well-off (adj. preceding noun)
well-settled (adj. preceding noun)
well-spoken (adj. preceding noun)
X-ray

§ 4:44 Hyphens not used

[A] General rules

Hyphens are not used in the following situations:

1. With compound verbs, if the meaning is unambiguous. However, compound verbs that are used to modify an immediately following noun *are* hyphenated.

   The defendant was forum shopping. (*but* a forum-shopping litigant)
   The process server hand delivered the summons. (*but* a hand-delivered invitation)
   The attorney and the judge doubled up on the witness. (*but* doubled-up accommodations)

2. With compound adjectives that have a number or letter as a second element.

   section 21 situation   Class B regulation

3. With compound adjectives in quotation marks, unless the compound is customarily hyphenated.

   "blue sky" law   *but* "ill-humored" judges

4. With compound adjectives whose first word is a comparative or superlative, unless a hyphen is necessary to avoid ambiguity.

   the greatest income period
   the lowest production group
   a lesser known exception
   the most wanted fugitive
   the more qualified candidate (*but* the more-polished apples)

5. With a series of adjectives before a noun when the adjectives do not convey a single concept. For commas with adjectives, see section 4:54.

a brown thatched cottage
but a black-and-white TV; a brown-eyed child

6. With certain common prefixes used before nouns, unless a hyphen is necessary to separate two adjacent vowels.

antitrust	coworker
midterm	*but* co-owner
nonrefundable	pretrial, posttrial

7. With common phrases and legal terms of art when used as adjectives.

case law	land use
child support	law of the case
civil rights	penalty phase
civil service	public utilities
common law	state law
due process	successor in interest
equal protection	tenant in common
guilt phase	third party
just compensation	work product

[B] Nonhyphenated terms

The following terms should not be hyphenated, unless they appear in quoted matter and were hyphenated in the original:

above described	coconspirator
above quoted	cocounsel
above referred to	codefendant
airmail	coemployee
antenuptial	colessee
antisympathy instruction	colessor
antitrust	commingle
attorney at law	common law (adj. or noun)
audiotape	common sense (noun)
backlog	commonsense (adj.)
backpay	cooperative
bank book	coparty
bloodstain	coplaintiff
board member	cosign
boilerplate	cotenants
bondsman	cotrustor
bylaw	counteraffidavit
case law	courthouse

155

courtroom
coworkers
decision maker
decisionmaking
double counting
extrahazardous
eyewitness
fact finder
but factfinding (adj.)
felony murder (noun)
but felony-murder rule (adj.)
fingerprint
firefighter
firefighting
first degree (adj.)
first degree felony murder
but first degree felony-murder
    instruction
first degree murder
first degree murder instruction
footprint
getaway
grand theft auto
guilt phase error
half brother (etc.)
jailhouse
judgment roll
Kmart store
but 7-Eleven store
land use (adj.)
layperson
lineup
midterm
minibike
misdemeanor manslaughter (noun)
but misdemeanor-manslaughter
    rule (adj.)
mobilehome
motor home
no contest
nonpayment
nosebleed
note taker
but notetaking
palm print
passerby
patdown
patsearch

penalty phase error
postmortem (adj.)
postoffense
posttraumatic
posttrial
postverdict
preempt
pretrial
pro rata
purchase money
redirect examination
reenter
reexamine
second degree (adj.)
shoe print
soleprint
special circumstances
special circumstance
    instruction
and felony-murder special
    circumstance
but felony-murder special-
    circumstance instruction
statewide
stepchild (etc.)
stickup
streetcar
subject matter
successor in interest
tenant in common
third party claim
tortfeasor
torture murder (noun)
but torture-murder allegation
    (adj.)
to wit
twofold
venire member
but venirepersons
videotape
voiceprint
whistleblower
word processing
word processor
work product
work product doctrine (adj.)

§ 4:45 Word division

Never manually divide words for cosmetic effect at the end of lines in a computer word processing environment. If word processing software has a utility for dividing words in that context, it may be used in lieu of manually dividing words, although clarity is enhanced by avoiding the division of words at the ends of lines under any circumstances.

F. COMMAS, SEMICOLONS, AND COLONS

§ 4:46 General use of commas, semicolons, and colons

The comma is an indispensable tool in conveying meaning and in emphasizing or de-emphasizing thought. The present trend is to avoid using a comma when it does not improve clarity or enhance the flow of the ideas presented, particularly in shorter sentences. In more complex sentences, however, commas are often necessary to create clear associations between modifying phrases or clauses and the parts of the sentence modified. When the use of a comma becomes critical to the meaning of a document or other text, or creates an ambiguity, it is better to recast the sentence to avoid any interpretation problems. (See *Russell v. Bankers Life Co.* (1975) 46 Cal.App.3d 405, 411, 415.)

The semicolon is often used to join together ideas too closely related in meaning for each to stand as a separate sentence, but not closely related enough for a comma, such as statements of contrast. It may also be used as a "full stop" pause to divide distinct thoughts joined in a single sentence; to separate long sentences with multiple clauses following a colon; and to prevent ideas, words, phrases, or clauses from running together. It demonstrates greater emphasis than is available with the comma. In its most common use, a semicolon divides a series when there is a comma in one or more sections of the series.

A colon is often used to introduce a formal statement, a quotation, or a series or list. Traditionally it also was used between two related clauses that formed a single sentence, or before a clause that illustrated the preceding clause. Current usage often separates such clauses with a semicolon or breaks the clauses into separate sentences. If the clause following a colon would, if standing alone, constitute a complete sentence, the clause should generally commence with a capital letter.

§ 4:47 Commas with names

Use commas before and after "Jr." and "Sr." when they follow a person's name. Commas are also used to set off academic degrees, such as

"M.D." and "Ph.D." from the name. Commas are not used when roman numerals follow the name.

> Frank Jones, Jr., appeared for the defendants.
> Walter Hunter, M.D., signed the death certificate.
> Peter Smith III appeared for appellants.

§ 4:48 Commas, semicolons, and colons in series

The use of a comma before "and," "or," or "nor" when these conjunctions precede the last of a series of three or more words, phrases, letters, or figures is optional unless required for clarity.

> one, two, three, and four
> one, two, three or four, and five

When a series contains lengthy or complex items, or when one or more items contains a comma, the items should be separated by semicolons, not commas. In a series separated by semicolons, use a semicolon before the last "and." A colon is often used to introduce such a series or list.

> *Rocco* speaks of "three elements: (1) neglectful conduct by the parent in
> one of the specified forms; (2) causation; and (3) 'serious physical harm
> or illness' to the minor, or a 'substantial risk' of such harm or illness."

A colon is not used, however, when a series or list is preceded by an introductory phrase, e.g., "namely," "for instance," or "that is," and the phrases in the series are not grammatically complete, or when the list is a complement or object of an element in the introductory phrase.

> Defendants had alternative courses of conduct to avoid tort liability,
> namely, (1) writing a "full disclosure" letter revealing all relevant facts
> regarding the employee's background, or (2) writing a "no comment"
> letter omitting any affirmative representations.
> Dr. Chong would testify (1) that radiation therapy combined with a radical
> hysterectomy is just as successful a method of treatment, and (2) that
> the applicable standard of care required defendant to discuss this and
> other options with plaintiff prior to surgery.

For the use of commas in a series of citations, see section 1:7.

§ 4:49 Commas, semicolons, and colons with quotation marks

Use commas to set off direct quotes, unless the sentence flows into the quote. Commas are not used with indirect quotes.

> The witness testified, "I saw nobody."
> The witness testified that she "saw nobody."
> The witness testified that she saw nobody.

If a comma immediately follows a quoted word or phrase, place the comma inside the closing quotation mark. Place a semicolon or colon outside quotation marks.

> "Counsel," said the judge, "please limit your argument."
> One note read, "We protest this unfair tax"; another, "Boycott!"

If a quoted phrase ends with a semicolon, end the quote before the semicolon, and add the punctuation mark appropriate to the quoting sentence, such as a period or comma. The following example illustrates a quoted fragment whose original semicolon is replaced by a comma:

> *Original:* "Destruction was total; nothing was spared."
> *Quoted fragment:* Observing, "Destruction was total," the court upheld the verdict.

For use of ellipses at the end of a quoted sentence, see section 4:13[C]; for use of other punctuation with quotation marks, see section 4:23.

§ 4:50 Commas with dates

When the month, day, and year are given (see § 4:29), commas should be placed before and after the year. When a date is used as a modifier, the comma after the year is strongly preferred, but it may be omitted. If only the month and year are noted, no commas are used.

> The accident occurred on April 10, 1998, in San Diego.
> The accident occurred in April 1998 in San Diego.
> The November 24, 1998, codicil provided that . . . .
> The November 24, 1998 codicil . . . . (*comma optional*)

§ 4:51 Commas with numbers and figures

Use a comma to separate numbers to avoid confusion.

> Of the 100, 42 were present.
> Instead of three, four appealed.

In adjective phrases, do not use a comma between parts of an expression of time.

> a five-year four-month period
> a sentence of 3 years 11 months 15 days

Use a comma in numbers having four or more digits.

> 1,200
> 12,000
> 120,000

Do not use commas with numbers that indicate sequence (see § 4:31):

page 1003
section 25003
docket No. 15167
S.F. No. 22861
Civ. No. 11260

Fractions do not take commas unless one number is five or more digits. For rules on when to spell out fractions, see section 4:32.

60/2500
60/25,000

§ 4:52 Commas or colons following introductory phrases

A comma is generally used after introductory participial, adverbial, or prepositional phrases, and after introductory dependent clauses.

Anticipating later developments, counsel agreed to the stipulation.
Without further ceremony, we shall dispose of the final issue by observing that . . . .
Around the corner, defendant was hiding with the contraband.
While Rome burned, Nero fiddled.

A colon is used to introduce a formal statement or extract.

The earliest public nuisance statute thus bore a feature that marks the entire field even today: Public nuisances are offenses against, or interferences with, the exercise of rights common to the public.

§ 4:53 Capital letter following colon

If material following a colon is a quotation or a formal statement, capitalize the first word following the colon.

After quoting the text of section 370, we observed: "[T]he prescribed act may be anything which alternatively is injurious to health *or* is indecent, *or* offensive to the senses . . . ."
The task force has concluded as follows: The application to the committee on tenure and retention should be approved.

§ 4:54 Commas with adjectives

Use commas when the adjectives are both of the same degree; that is, the word "and" could replace the comma without changing the phrase's meaning. For use of hyphens with compound adjectives, see section 4:41; for omitting hyphens with adjectives, see section 4:44[A].

a short, decisive opinion
a long, meritless complaint

Do not use commas when the last adjective and the noun are so closely related that together they form a noun phrase or a single idea.

light denim jacket (*denim jacket is a noun phrase*)
cheap fur coat (*fur coat is a noun phrase*)

§ 4:55 Semicolons separating independent clauses

When a word such as "then," "however," "hence," "indeed," or "accordingly" is used as a transitional adverb between independent clauses of a compound sentence, place a semicolon before it. Some authors may prefer to convert the clauses into separate sentences.

Those prerequisites are lacking in this case; accordingly, we reverse.

G. PARENTHESES AND BRACKETS

§ 4:56 General use of parentheses and brackets

Parentheses and brackets are used to indicate extraneous, explanatory, incidental, and interpolated matter. Use brackets, not parentheses, to insert matter into a quote. Brackets may also be used to indicate a second parenthetical statement within parentheses, although the preference, for stylistic reasons, is that sentences so structured be recast.

Insertions by author in own text:

The first defendant (Smith) was found not guilty.
The first defendant (Smith [charged with manslaughter]) was found not guilty.

Insertion by author into quoted matter:

"The first defendant [Smith] was found not guilty."

Parenthetical descriptive statements following case citations in parentheses are enclosed in brackets. For example:

(*Commonwealth Coatings Corp. v. Continental Casualty Co.* (1968) 393 U.S. 145, 148–149 [89 S.Ct. 337, 21 L.Ed.2d 301] [observing that arbitration may require greater oversight than judicial proceedings].)

Alternate parentheses with brackets for multiple parentheses within parentheses.

The penalties imposed for those offenses (Pen. Code, § 207 [one to 25 years in prison (see Pen. Code, § 208)]; Pen. Code, § 261, subds. 2 and 3 [three years to life (Pen. Code, §§ 264, 671)]) are indeed severe.

Exceptions that always use parentheses within parentheses: Always use parentheses for references to opinion authors (see § 4:58), adopting a short form or abbreviated reference (see § 5:8), and certain citational elements (e.g., dates), even when occurring within parentheses. For example:

> (*Toland v. Sunland Housing Group* (1998) 18 Cal.4th 253 (hereafter *Toland*).)
>
> (*Toland, supra,* 18 Cal. 4th at p. 281 (conc. & dis. opn. of Werdegar, J.).)

§ 4:57 Citations

In general, use parentheses around a citation, whether it appears within a sentence or following the end, and use brackets to enclose any unofficial parallel citations. If the citation forms an integral part of the sentence, do not use parentheses around it, but brackets are still used around any parallel citations. In addition, abbreviated case references expressly adopted by the author are always placed in parentheses, whether they appear within text or within a citation.

> "When statutory language is clear and unambiguous, there is no need for construction and courts should not indulge in it." (*People v. Overstreet* (1986) 42 Cal.3d 891, 895 [231 Cal.Rptr. 213, 726 P.2d 1288]; see also *People v. Valladoli* (1996) 13 Cal.4th 590, 597 [54 Cal.Rptr.2d 695, 918 P.2d 999].)
>
> One such legal barrier exists "where . . . a parent of the foster child or stepchild" "refuses to consent to the adoption." (Sen. Com. on Judiciary, Rep. on Assem. Bills Nos. 25 & 68 (1983–1984 Reg. Sess.) 3 Sen. J. (1983–1984 Reg. Sess.) p. 4882 (hereafter Senate Committee on Judiciary Report).)
>
> In *American Academy of Pediatrics v. Lungren* (1997) 16 Cal.4th 307 [66 Cal.Rptr.2d 210, 940 P.2d 797], the California Supreme Court considered this very question.

§ 4:58 Designation of opinion authors

Enclose references to opinion authors in parentheses, even if the case citation appears within parentheses. For citation of lead, plurality, concurring, and dissenting opinions, see section 1:10.

> *Stop Youth Addiction, Inc. v. Lucky Stores, Inc.* (1998) 17 Cal.4th 553, 578 (conc. opn. of Baxter, J.).
>
> (*People* ex rel. *Gallo v. Acuna* (1997) 14 Cal.4th 1090, 1132 (dis. opn. of Mosk, J.).)
>
> (See *Harris, supra,* 401 U.S. at p. 232 [91 S.Ct. at p. 649] (dis. opn. of Brennan, J.); *People v. May, supra,* 44 Cal.3d at pp. 333–334 (dis. opn. of Mosk, J.); *People v. Disbrow* (1976) 16 Cal.3d 101, 113 [127 Cal.Rptr. 360, 545 P.2d 272]; *id.* at p. 116 (conc. opn. of Wright, C. J.); see also *State v. Durepo* (Me. 1984) 472 A.2d 919, 927 (conc. & dis. opn. of Glassman, J.).)

§ 4:59 Brackets, summarized

In pairs, brackets indicate that the material enclosed within is one of the following:

1. An author's explanatory insertion into a quotation (for insertions, see § 4:16; for adding footnotes, see § 4:25[B]).
2. A correction or notation of an error in a quotation (see § 4:15).
3. A parenthetical statement within parentheses (see § 4:56).
4. A parallel citation (see § 1:1[F]), whether in parentheses or in the body of a sentence (see § 4:56).
5. A signal showing the original paragraph formatting of a quoted passage, where significant portions are omitted (see § 4:13[E]), or where paragraphs are consolidated (see § 4:19).
6. A capitalization (see § 4:13[A]) or other adjustment of a quote (see § 4:18).
7. A substitution for an omission in quoted material (see § 4:14).
8. The completion of a citation within a quotation (see § 4:17).
9. A signal to introduce and conclude a lengthy quotation (see § 4:21).

H. APOSTROPHES

§ 4:60 Apostrophe with possessives

[A] Possessive of singular nouns

To form the possessive of singular nouns (including proper names), the general rule is to add an apostrophe and an *s*, whether or not the word itself ends in an *s* or *s*-sound.

Burns's poems	press's deadline
day's trip	UPS's responsibility
driver's permit	witness's affidavit
horse's mouth	a year's probation
Mr. Jones's lawsuit	

The term "attorney fees" is preferred, but "attorney's fees" or "attorneys' fees" may be used at the author's discretion. Whichever term is used, consistency within the document is required.

[B] Possessive of plural nouns

To form the possessive of plural nouns (including proper names) that end in an *s*, add an apostrophe only. For plural nouns *not* ending in an *s*, add an apostrophe *and* an *s*.

plaintiffs' arguments	the Joneses' lawsuit
experts' opinions	the Regents' compensation
doctors' reports	two weeks' vacation
jurors' hostility	*but* a two-week vacation
in five years' time	witnesses' affidavits
women's club	children's rights

[C] Joint and individual possession

To note joint possession, the apostrophe is used with the last element of the series. To note individual possession, the apostrophe is used with each element.

Wah and Green's assets (*the assets they possess together*)
Wah's and Green's assets (*the assets they each individually possess*)

[D] Possessive of compound nouns

Place the "apostrophe s" ('s) nearest to the thing possessed.

attorney at law's oath
Attorney General's report
Al Martinez, Jr.'s objections
sister-in-law's property
somebody else's problem
the wife's attorney's delay
the Administrative Office of the Court's (AOC) standard procedures

[E] Possessive pronouns, adjectives, and nouns before gerunds

Possessive pronouns such as "hers," "ours," "theirs," "yours," "its," "itself," and "whose" do not take an apostrophe. Possessive adjectives such as "another's," "each other's," "one's," "someone's," and "somebody's" take an apostrophe, as do nouns before gerunds.

The court relied on its prior holding. (*possessive pronoun*)
Each took the deposition of the other's expert witness. (*possessive adjective*)
The district attorney's removing his coat was part of his trial strategy. (*gerund*)

§ 4:61 Apostrophe with established designations

Whether an apostrophe is to be used with the name of a firm, organization, institution, book, or place depends entirely upon the official designation of the firm or organization. For example, if a firm is incorporated as and uses the name "Blacks Elevator Company" rather than "Black's Elevator Company," do not add an apostrophe. However, where the authentic title is not ascertainable from the record or otherwise, use the normal possessive forms.

The apostrophe should not be used with names of countries and other organized bodies ending in an "s" or after words more descriptive than possessive.

> editors handbook
> homeowners association
> House of Representatives committee
> Massachusetts laws
> merchants exchange
> Reporter of Decisions Office
> technicians guide
> United States possessions
> Department of Veterans Affairs (*formerly* Veterans Administration)

§ 4:62 Apostrophe with numbers, letters, acronyms, and abbreviations

Use an apostrophe and an "s" to form plurals of numbers and letters.

> The 6's were not legible.
> Her name is spelled with two l's.
> He was born in the 1960's.

For acronyms and abbreviations, use an apostrophe and an "s" to form the plural and to form the possessive.

> The covenants, conditions, and restrictions (CC&R's) . . . .
> All environmental impact reports (EIR's) must comply with the provisions of the California Environmental Quality Act (CEQA). CEQA's requirements include . . . .
> California Federal Savings and Loan (Cal. Fed.) generally requires a minimum deposit of $2,000. Cal. Fed.'s requirements . . . .

§ 4:63 Apostrophe with contractions

The apostrophe is used to note the omission of letters or numbers in contracted expressions. Although occasionally used with numbers, contractions are generally not otherwise used in formal legal writing.

> they're   the summer of '99   the '80's (*preferred:* the 1980's)
> o'clock   spirit of '76   it's ("it is," not the possessive)

Do not use an apostrophe to denote omissions to form abbreviations such as "ass'n," "comm'n." and "comm'rs." (*Use:* "assn.," "com.," and "comrs.")

I. MISCELLANEOUS RULES

§ 4:64 Acronyms

The periods and spaces in acronyms of governmental agencies and other organized bodies are usually omitted.

> AFL-CIO (American Federation of Labor and Congress of Industrial
>   Organizations)
> GM (General Motors)
> MIT (Massachusetts Institute of Technology)
> NLRB (National Labor Relations Board)
> UCLA (University of California at Los Angeles)

If an acronym is commonly known and appears in dictionaries, no parenthetical designation is required.

> AIDS.　　　IRS
> CIA　　　　LSD
> FBI　　　　PCP
> HIV

The first reference to lesser known abbreviated designations should either be preceded or followed by a spelled-out reference. Thereafter only the abbreviated form is used.

> The VA (Department of Veterans Affairs) was not represented at the
>   hearing.
> The California Environmental Quality Act's (CEQA) main provisions . . . .
> The compact disc (CD) was distributed.
> The program could be uploaded from a CD-ROM (compact disc-read only
>   memory).

Use restraint in adopting acronyms. Readers cannot be expected to recall the referents for a multiplicity of acronyms in a document. Never reduce a case to an acronym.

§ 4:65 Spelling

[A] General preferences

Many words have two acceptable spellings. To achieve uniformity of usage for the Official Reports, Webster's Third New International Dictionary has been selected as the defining authority for preferred spellings of words. If Webster's gives more than one spelling, the first is preferred. For hyphenation rules see sections 4:43 and 4:44.

[B] "Er" and "or" endings

To achieve uniformity in the use of words ending with "er" or "or," the spellings indicated below are preferred and are followed in the Official Reports:

abettor	franchisor	offeror
adjuster	grantor	optionor
adviser	indemnitor	pledgor
bailor	inspector	promisor
condemner	insurer	relator
consignor	intervener	settlor
contemner	lender	supervisor
conveyor	libeler	supporter
distributor	lienor	surveyor
endorser	mortgagor	transferor
examiner	objector	vendor

§ 4:66 Footnote or endnote numbering and style

A footnote number should be placed as close as possible to the text that is footnoted, provided the placement will not seriously disrupt the natural flow of the sentence. For appellate opinions, the word processing footnote utility must be used. Footnotes are numbered consecutively within an opinion; majority and minority opinions are numbered independently. To refer to matter contained in an earlier footnote, use another footnote.

[4] See footnote 2, *ante,* page 10.

Footnotes are single-spaced and commence on the same page as the text to which they refer. The first line of each footnote should be indented, and there should be double-spacing between footnotes. Footnotes are governed by the same citation, abbreviation, and other style rules that apply to text; and they are treated as separate paragraphs of text. Font and font size should be the same for the footnote text and the body of the document.

A footnote to a direct quotation should generally be placed at the end of the quotation, and the footnote number is normally placed outside the closing quotation marks. For adding a footnote within a quoted sentence, see section 4:25.

The statement was "vital to the outcome."[1]

A footnote number at the end of a parenthetical expression or citation is placed after the closing parenthesis or citation.

(Plaintiff complained vociferously to the landlord.)[1]
We rejected this contention in another case. (*In re Williams* (1969) 1 Cal.3d 168 [81 Cal.Rptr. 784, 460 P.2d 984].)[11]

If the footnote refers to a particular citation in a series of citations within parentheses, the number should follow that citation.

> *(People v. Maddox* (1967) 67 Cal.2d 647 [63 Cal.Rptr. 371, 433 P.2d 163]; Gov. Code, § 37103;[4] 19 Ops.Cal.Atty.Gen. 153 (1952).[5])

An asterisk (*) is used with a footnote to note a parenthetical, editorial, or clarifying procedural matter before the text of the opinion starts. A second note of this type on any one page is identified by a dagger ([†]) and a third is identified by a double dagger ([‡]). An asterisk or dagger is used with reporter's notes. (See, e.g., *In re Spence* (1974) 36 Cal.App.3d 636, 642.)

§ 4:67 Trademarks

Avoid using product names if identification of a specific product is not critical to the discussion. A trademark is in the nature of a proper name, and when it is used in an opinion or court document, it should normally be capitalized. No trademark or registration symbol is required.

Trademark	Common name
Advil	ibuprofen
Anacin, Bufferin, etc.	aspirin, buffered aspirin
Coca-Cola, Pepsi	soft drink, cola drink
DissoMaster	child support computation software
Dumpster	large trash receptacle
Kleenex	tissue
Levi's	jeans, denim pants
Mace	irritant spray
Scotch tape	cellophane tape
7-Eleven	convenience store
Sheetrock	wallboard
Tylenol	acetaminophen
Valium	tranquilizer
Xerox	photocopy
Ziploc bag	plastic sandwich bag; baggie

CHAPTER 4
—Notes—

CHAPTER 4
—Notes—

CHAPTER 5

EDITORIAL POLICIES FOLLOWED IN OFFICIAL REPORTS

A. GENERAL RULES

§ 5:1   Racial, ethnic, and gender designations

[A] Racial and ethnic designations

The racial or ethnic identity of an individual should be mentioned only if relevant and necessary. References should normally track the identification terms found in the record (e.g., African-American, not Black, if the record consistently reflects that usage). When a racial or ethnic identification is necessary, be as specific as the context allows (e.g., Salvadoran or Central American, rather than Hispanic, if the record provides that information). Capitalize terms used to designate race and ethnicity, including Black and White.

> The defendant, who is Mexican-American, objected to the prosecutor's use of peremptory challenges to strike three Hispanic prospective jurors.
> Since defendant had demonstrated a bias against Asians, and the three assault victims are Korean, defendant was charged with violating Penal Code section 422.6, which prohibits an injury to a person because of a specified characteristic such as race or national origin.

For identification terms not based on the record, references should be based on a recognized authority (e.g., current government publications that report demographic data). Authorities providing comprehensive terms for racial or ethnic identification include: the annual California Statistical Abstract published by the California Department of Finance; the annual Vital Statistics of California published by the Department of Health Services; the annual Statistical Abstract of the United States published by the United States Department of Commerce; and the Standards for Maintaining, Collecting, and Presenting Federal Data on Race and Ethnicity published by the Office of Management and Budget, replacing Statistical Policy Directive No. 15.

Do not alter designations used in quoted authorities to reflect contemporary usage. Maintaining the integrity of the quoted matter is normally preferred.

[B] Gender-neutral style

When writing in general terms, use gender-neutral language. (See Cal. Rules of Court, rule 989.) This requires awareness that not all judges, lawyers, parties or witnesses are male, and avoidance of "he" as a generic pronoun. "He" becomes "he or she"; "him" becomes "him or her." Overuse of disjunctive pronouns to maintain gender neutrality can be distracting, but the following suggestions for maintaining a gender-neutral style will minimize use of disjunctive pronouns.

174

1. Repeat the noun instead of using the pronoun: "If title has passed from him to a third person . . ." becomes "If title has passed from the debtor to a third person . . . ."

2. Replace the possessive pronoun with an article: Use "the right to" instead of "his right to."

3. Replace the suffix "-man": Terms such as "fireman" and "policeman" can be replaced with other nouns, such as "firefighter" and "police officer."

4. Use the suffix "-er"/"-or": Terms such as "draftsman" and "workman," and archaic terms such as "adminstratrix" or "executrix," are replaced with "-er" and "-or" equivalents, such as "drafter," "worker," "administrator," or "executor."

5. Use the plural instead of the singular: "A defendant who retains his own counsel . . ." becomes "Defendants who retain their own counsel . . . ."

6. Recast the sentence to avoid using a pronoun altogether.

§ 5:2   Stylistic considerations

Instruction on what constitutes good legal writing is generally beyond the scope of this manual. Legal writers should, of course, strive for clarity, conciseness, and readability. A direct, economic style reduces the risk of ambiguity in opinions and other legal writings.

[A] Omit needless words

Avoid wordy constructions and wordy idioms. Thus, "he was aware of the fact that," is replaced by "he knew"; "because of the fact that" becomes "because"; and "in order to" can often be replaced by "to." Constructions such as "the important fact in this situation is that" can usually be omitted entirely without any change in the sentence's meaning.

[B] Use the active voice

In general, prefer the active voice to the passive voice. Observing this rule produces sentences that are clearer, more direct, and less wordy. Thus, "Appellant argued that the court should have applied the second rule" is more concise and vigorous than "It was argued by appellant that the second rule should have been applied by the court."

[C] Use verbs instead of nominalizations

Nominalization is the process, often unintentional, of turning verbs into nouns; though grammatically correct, it can import a host of needless words into a sentence. Legal writing, particularly writing consisting of long and complex sentences, can be enhanced by removing unwanted nominalizations and replacing them with their base verbs. For example, "The parties *stipulated* to dismiss" is shorter and more direct than "The parties *entered into a stipulation* to dismiss." Similarly, "He agreed to *sell* the house" is more direct than "He agreed to *the sale of* the house"; and "The court *referred* to" should replace "The court *made a reference* to."

[D] Collective nouns

Collective nouns like "the jury," "the majority," "the Legislature," "the committee," and "the board" are usually singular and take singular verbs and singular pronouns. "The court" is always singular.

> The faculty was badly divided on the tenure vote.
> The board has denied the application.
> The committee has the matter under submission.
> The jury returned its verdict.
> The court is unlikely to reverse its decision.

§ 5:3 Editorial format and enhancement of opinions for Official Reports

The State of California's publishing contract for the Official Reports requires that bound volumes and advance pamphlets be printed substantially in the appearance, manner, and style presently used in the fourth series. The format and styles, physical and editorial, prescribed in this manual are incorporated by reference in the publication contract to describe, in part, the publisher's editorial responsibilities.

§ 5.4 Furnishing lower court information

To provide the publisher with essential editorial information for publishing an opinion for the Official Reports, the court must designate the trial court and provide the trial and appellate court case numbers. The court must also list the appearances of counsel (see §§ 5:14–5:27) and the trial court judge or judges whose ruling or rulings are challenged (see §§ 5:28–5:32).

Typical editorial information examples follow.

CERTIFIED FOR PUBLICATION
IN THE COURT OF APPEAL OF THE STATE OF CALIFORNIA
SECOND APPELLATE DISTRICT
DIVISION FIVE

THE PEOPLE,	)	
Plaintiff and Respondent,	)	B012345
v.	)	(Super. Ct. No. A 654321)
HARRY HORN,	)	
Defendant and Appellant.	)	

APPEAL from a judgment [or order or summary judgment] of the Superior Court of Los Angeles County, Susan B. Miller, Judge. Affirmed.

Rodney H. Fan, under appointment by the Court of Appeal, for Defendant and Appellant.

Sidney L. Star, Attorney General, Linda Heard, Chief Assistant Attorney General, R. Leigh Locke, Assistant Attorney General, and Hans C. Strom, Deputy Attorney General, for Plaintiff and Respondent.

....

CERTIFIED FOR PUBLICATION
IN THE COURT OF APPEAL OF THE STATE OF CALIFORNIA
FIRST APPELLATE DISTRICT
DIVISION ONE

ANN A. SMITH et al.,	)	
Plaintiffs and Respondents,	)	A012345
v.	)	(Super. Ct. No. A 654321)
SOUTHERN PACIFIC COMPANY,	)	
Defendant and Appellant;	)	
PUBLIC EMPLOYEES RETIREMENT	)	
SYSTEM	)	
Intervener and Appellant.	)	

APPEAL from a judgment of the Superior Court of the City and County of San Francisco, Mary M. Mars, Judge. Affirmed.

John Jones and Douglas E. Severn for Defendant and Appellant.

Frank Forrest, Attorney General, June Jacobs, Assistant Attorney General, and Arthur Orr, Deputy Attorney General, for Intervener and Appellant.

No appearance for Plaintiffs and Respondents.

....

CERTIFIED FOR PUBLICATION
IN THE COURT OF APPEAL OF THE STATE OF CALIFORNIA
SECOND APPELLATE DISTRICT
DIVISION FIVE

JAMES CASTRO,)	
Petitioner,)	B012345
v.)	(Super. Ct. No. A 654321)
THE SUPERIOR COURT OF)	
SANTA BARBARA COUNTY,)	
Respondent;)	
CHARLES ENT et al.,)	
Real Parties in Interest)	

ORIGINAL PROCEEDINGS in mandate. Walter Murray, Judge. Petition denied.
Richard Roe for Petitioner.
No appearance for Respondent.
Flower, Flower & Martinez and Richard Martinez for Real Parties in Interest.

§ 5:5 Diagrams, photocopies, photographs, and other appendix material

If illustrative material necessary for understanding the opinion is included as an appendix, provide a copy that is clear and legible. Photocopies of poor quality are difficult or impossible to satisfactorily incorporate in the Official Reports. Computer-generated graphic image files are preferable when available. Appendix material consisting of text should be in the same word processing format as the opinion itself. If appendix material cannot be included with the computer version of a published opinion, that omission should be noted at the top of the first page of the computer version.

Photographs or other illustrative material are included as an appendix at the end of the opinion, with an appropriate reference in parentheses or in a footnote. If a case contains multiple opinions (e.g., a dissenting opinion), the appendix should follow the last opinion, even if only one of the earlier opinions refers to it.

> (A copy of plaintiff's letter of resignation is attached as appendix A, *post,* page 77.) *or*
> *See appendix A, *post*, page 123, for a diagram of the encroachment.

§ 5:6 Citing to sources not generally available—clerk's and reporter's transcripts

Opinion authors normally should not indicate the source or page for an excerpt or quotation from the record. Identify a document by referring to the document itself and not to the record. To signal that abstracted materials are from the record, use a general reference to the particular transcript as a whole and avoid using page references.

§ 5:7   Use of *supra, infra, ante,* and *post* for internal opinion references

Opinion authors should use *ante* (before) and its opposite, *post* (after) to refer to earlier or later parts, pages, or footnotes within an opinion. *Ante* is also used in a concurring or dissenting opinion to refer to the majority or lead opinion; *post* is used in a majority or lead opinion to refer to a concurring or dissenting opinion. By contrast, *supra* (above) is used in citations to signal that an authority external to the opinion has been cited previously, and also as a substitute for an earlier, more complete reference. Because *supra* is reserved for citations, and *infra* (below) is the opposite of *supra, infra* is not often used, and it should never be paired with *ante*.

> (*Ante*, fn. 1) or (At pp. 25–30, *post*)
> (Maj. opn. *ante*, at pp. 26–27)

§ 5:8   Abbreviated or short-form reference

To enhance readability and reduce repetition of long and unwieldy names, an abbreviated or short form reference is used. Like an acronym, it is a word or short phrase that stands for a longer phrase. Occasionally, the referent for a shortened form is clear and obvious (e.g., Standard Oil instead of Standard Oil of California). When it is not, expressly adopt the short form of reference by placing the short form in parentheses after the full title or name. Do not use quotation marks; the word "hereafter" is optional. After adoption, use the abbreviated reference only.

> The Teachers Union Manual of Practices and Goals (hereafter Manual) contains that statement.
> Defendant Acme Restaurant, Baking and Pastry Supplies and Services (Acme) filed a motion.

For abbreviated case titles, see section 1:1[C]; for codes, see section 2:5[B]; for treatises, see section 3:1[D]; for law review titles, see section 3:8[A]; for names of administrative agencies or geographical units, see sections 4:4[A] and 4:7; for statutes or acts, see section 4:10[B]; and for names of parties, see section 4:11.

B. PROTECTIVE NONDISCLOSURE OF IDENTITY

§ 5:9   Policy regarding nondisclosure of victim or minor

The Supreme Court has issued the following policy statement to all appellate courts: "To prevent the publication of damaging disclosures concerning living victims of sex crimes and minors innocently involved in appellate court proceedings it is requested that the names of these persons be omitted from all appellate court opinions whenever their best interests would be served by anonymity. Anonymity, however, is inappropriate for homicide victims, who are to be identified whenever possible." Thus, a homicide victim's name is not suppressed even if a sex crime was also committed against that victim.

Individuals entitled to protective nondisclosure are described by first name and last initial, or by referring to them by their status. Do not use middle names or middle initials, street addresses, or full birth dates. The name "Anonymous" and other fictitious names should be avoided absent a court order under Penal Code section 293.5 (Jane Doe or John Doe designation).

> Susan T.
> The complaining witness
> the 10-year-old child
> the victim (Mary)
> Anna B., *not* Anna Marie B. *or* Anna M. B.

§ 5:10 Application to minors, juvenile court law

The identity of minors involved in juvenile court proceedings, or innocently involved in appellate court proceedings, should be protected both in the title and in the body of an opinion, generally by using the first name and last initial. If a parent has the same last name as the minor, the parent's last name should be suppressed as well. If the minor's first name is so unusual as to defeat the objective of anonymity, only the minor's initials should be used.

> In re CHANTAL S., a Person Coming
> Under the Juvenile Court Law.
>
> RIVERSIDE COUNTY DEPARTMENT
> OF PUBLIC SOCIAL SERVICES,
>   Plaintiff and Respondent,
>   v.
> RANDALL S.,
> Defendant and Appellant.   [title]
>
> A petition charged John E., a minor, with burglary.
> The two minors, K.D. and J.D., were removed from their parents' home.
> Fred E. testified at the juvenile court hearing of his daughter Mary E.

The nondisclosure policy does not apply where the minor is held to answer as an adult in criminal proceedings. However, nondisclosure is followed when a minor *successfully* seeks relief in a collateral proceeding, such as a petition for a writ of mandate to compel the juvenile court to reconsider its determination that he or she was not amenable to treatment under juvenile law.

§ 5:11 Adult plaintiff's action for wrongdoing committed during plaintiff's minority

Protective nondisclosure should not be applied to an adult who is bringing an action for wrongdoing committed against him or her during the plaintiff's minority. (See, e.g., *Sellery v. Cressey* (1996) 48 Cal.App.4th 538; *Doyle v. Fenster* (1996) 47 Cal.App.4th 1701.)

§ 5:12 Jurors and witnesses

After a verdict in a criminal matter, court records containing juror personal identifying information are sealed, and that information remains confidential (Code Civ. Proc., §§ 206, 237). In such cases, care must be taken to ensure that protected jurors not be identified in opinions. Initials or juror identification numbers, or similar identification adopted by local court rules or policies, may be used instead of names.

Similarly, the identities of victims or witnesses in criminal matters may be subject to protective nondisclosure. (See, e.g., Pen. Code, § 1054.7.) Again, care must be taken to ensure that those persons not be identified in opinions.

§ 5:13 Lanterman-Petris-Short conservatees

Welfare and Institutions Code section 5325.1, subdivision (b), part of the Lanterman-Petris-Short Act (Welf. & Inst. Code, § 5000 et seq.) protects a conservatee's right to dignity, privacy, and care. Accordingly, the identity of such conservatees should not be disclosed. (See, e.g., *Conservatorship of Susan T.* (1994) 8 Cal.4th 1005.)

C. LISTING OF COUNSEL

§ 5:14 Collecting information; sources

To ensure accuracy in the listing of counsel for the Official Reports, it is essential that the opinion author's staff and other court personnel carefully examine all filings, appearances at oral argument, and pertinent correspondence in the original record.

§ 5:15 Listing of attorneys and firms

[A] In general; what constitutes appearance

An opinion published in the Official Reports lists the names of attorneys and law firms appearing of record on appeal. Where multiple parties on the same side are all represented by the same counsel, a single listing for those parties' counsel is sufficient. Where multiple parties on the same side have separate representation, however, the counsel listing should show which counsel represents which parties. For use of clients' names in counsel listing, see section 5:16.

Filing an appellate brief or other substantive document, adopting a filed brief, or participating at oral argument constitutes an appearance for listing purposes. When the Supreme Court reviews a Court of Appeal decision, counsel appearances in both courts are listed in any resulting Supreme Court opinion. Likewise, counsel appearances in both courts are listed if the Court of Appeal's opinion survives the Supreme Court's review, in whole or in part, and also when the Supreme Court dismisses review as improvidently granted and orders the Court of Appeal decision to remain published. Attorneys or firms appearing only in the trial court are not listed.

In general, give the names of individuals and firms as spelled in the briefs, except where there is an obvious error. If the briefs differ as to spelling, consult the California State Bar's online membership records <http://www.calsb.org>, a current edition of one of the California attorney directories, or the telephone directory. If the difference is merely that an attorney's name is spelled in full on one brief and abbreviated on another, use the full spelling. Examine all briefs and party files, as firm names and participating attorneys may change between briefs.

The counsel listing is not considered a substantive part of the opinion and may be clerically corrected without modification if errors are noted after filing.

[B] Names of law firms, law corporations, and legal services organizations

List the firm name first, then the attorneys appearing from that firm. The variety of firm names presents occasional challenges in striking the proper balance between brevity, fidelity to the firm name, and avoidance of unnecessary repetition. Firm names that are a combination of attorney names are listed that way. And names made up of a *single surname* plus words indicating association retain that full name (e.g., Gutierrez & Associates, Coudert Brothers, Becker Law Offices, Jacob Associates, and Goldman Law Firm). But words added to indicate corporate status or the form of association (such as "a Law Corporation," "LLP," and "APC") are omitted.

Firm names made up of one attorney's *full name* plus words indicating association will be listed as the firm name plus the attorney's name. For example, Law Offices of David King and David King, David King and Associates and David King, and David King Law Office and David King. If David King did not appear, the firm would be listed, in conjunction with the attorney or attorneys who personally appeared, as Law Offices of David King and John Smith, David King and Associates and Jane Minor, etc.

With some exceptions, follow the firm's punctuation. Most firms use the ampersand (&), but some firms use "and," and some use both, as Jones & Smith and Black. (Where the ampersand is used on one brief and the word "and" on another, use the ampersand.) Similarly, where a firm name omits commas, the commas should likewise be omitted from the counsel listing.

Nontraditional law firm names should also be listed, such as the ABC Law Group, provided the firm is authorized to act in that name (i.e., as a law corporation pursuant to the Law Corporation Rules of the State Bar). Court staffs should accept the record at face value and are not expected to verify, merely for the sake of the counsel listing, that a firm is authorized to act under its name. Legal services organizations, such as Neighborhood Legal Services, are also included as law firm names.

If a client changes firms, or an attorney changes firms, having appeared for the client during the appeal while at both firms, then both firms are listed. If a firm changes its name during the appeal and files appearances under different names, list both names. For example, if briefs were filed under "Smith & Jones," but by oral argument the firm name had changed to Smith Jones and Carter, then list both versions of the firm name. For example, Smith & Jones, Smith Jones & Carter. Do not include a name change occurring after the last appearance.

[C] Names of attorneys

List all attorney names that appear on the briefs; also list all attorneys who participate in oral argument. Include *all* attorneys who formally adopt a brief. Do not rely only on the list of attorneys on the first page of a brief, but include also the participating attorneys on the signature page at the back.

For example, the first page may list Black & Blue and John Blue for Plaintiff and Respondent, while the signature page lists Black & Blue and John Blue, by Fred Green. Fred Green's name must be added, and the listing would be Black & Blue, John Blue and Fred Green for Plaintiff and Respondent. Where a brief is signed "by" a member of the law firm, replace "by" with "and", and show counsel as "[Law Firm] and [Attorney] for [Party]."

In addition, consult the court's minutes for the date of oral argument, which must list names of attorneys who argued the case.

If an individual attorney has changed his or her name after the brief was filed, and the new correct name can be verified, use the attorney's name at the time the opinion is filed. Once an attorney has appeared of record in the reviewing court, his or her name is listed in reporting the decision and cannot be withdrawn at a later date either unilaterally or by stipulation. (See also § 5:26.)

Do not list nonattorneys (see § 5:24) unless the party appeared in propria persona (see § 5:23). Do not use the words "of counsel" in listing attorneys, even if those words appear on the briefs.

[D] Multiple parties with separate representation

Where there are multiple parties with the same trial and appellate designations, so that there is an "et al." in the title (e.g., all designated as Plaintiffs and Appellants), *but* they do not share the same counsel, list those parties' counsel separately, showing which parties each counsel represents. Where, however, several counsel represent several parties with the same designations, there is no need to break down representation on a party-by-party basis, and those counsel are all listed together.

> *Criminal appeal with several "et al." indigent criminal defendants, each represented by a sole practitioner. Listing shows defense counsel and party name and designation:*
>
> Leslie C. Sanchez, under appointment by the Supreme Court, for Defendant and Appellant Ernesto Ortega.
>
> Maureen J. Brady, under appointment by the Supreme Court, for Defendant and Appellant Brandon Conner.
>
> Richard D. Rosen, under appointment by the Supreme Court, for Defendant and Appellant Maurice Arendt.
>
> *Civil appeal with several plaintiffs/appellants, all represented by the same law firms and attorneys, and with defendants/respondents represented by separate firms and attorneys. Listing shows defendants' counsel separately, with defendants' names and designations; plaintiffs' counsel are categorized by party designation only:*
>
> Wasser, Cohen and Cassel, Charles R. Pearce, Gary J. Smith; Ghilotti & Cleese, Thomas J. Ghilotti and Justin A. Crown for Plaintiffs and Appellants.

Daniel E. Lungren, Attorney General, Lois Copeland, Assistant Attorney General, Paul Espinosa and Ramon Reilly, Deputy Attorneys General, for Defendant and Respondent California State Lottery Commission.

Lahr, Ripple & Ruvin, Melanie W. Grey, Greg S. French; Wilson and Connolly, David C. Wilson and Jeri E. Brown for Defendant and Respondent Account-tex, Inc.

An attorney appearing in propria persona and for other, but not all, defendants/appellants; counsel for remaining defendants/appellants, and other counsel, are categorized by party designation alone:

Jo Smith, in pro. per., and for Defendants and Appellants Acme Co. and Mary A. Le.

Douglas C. Benedict for Defendants and Appellants.

Forrest and Myers and Robert F. Forrest for Plaintiffs and Respondents.

[E] Semicolons in counsel listing

Use semicolons to separate a law firm and its attorneys (or a sole practitioner) from unrelated counsel representing the same party or parties. This allows readers to more clearly see affiliations of attorneys and their law firms. For example:

Two firms representing the only defendant/respondent:

Smith and Avakian, Mary R. Avakian, John P. Jackson; Clark & Ng and David T. Clark for Defendant and Respondent.

One firm and two sole practitioners representing the only defendant/respondent:

Lee, Mikami and Koh, Christopher Lee, Elizabeth Koh; Mark Golden; and John Baker for Defendant and Respondent.

§ 5:16 Use of clients' names in counsel listing

In counsel listings, the parties are generally identified by their trial and appellate status only (e.g., Plaintiff and Appellant, Defendant and Respondent, Intervener and Appellant, Petitioner (in an original proceeding in reviewing court), Respondent, and so on).

Where two or more parties have the same status (e.g., both are plaintiffs and appellants), and are represented by different counsel, follow the procedure outlined in section 5:15[D].

§ 5:17 Sequence of names; appeals

Regardless of whether the appellant was the plaintiff, defendant, intervener, and so forth, in the trial court, counsel are named in the following order:

1. Counsel for appellants.
2. Counsel for amicus curiae on behalf of appellants.

3. Counsel for respondents.
4. Counsel for amicus curiae on behalf of respondents.
5. Counsel for Minor, Conservatee, etc.

(See, e.g., *Ramirez v. Plough* (1993) 6 Cal.4th 539, 542; *In re Marriage of Perry* (1998) 61 Cal.App.4th 295 [counsel for minor].)

If the plaintiff and defendant both appeal, show first the counsel for the plaintiff and then the counsel for the defendant. If an intervener alone appeals, the intervener's counsel will be listed first as counsel for appellant. The same rule applies for a third party claimant, or a real party in interest, appealing alone.

Where there is no appearance for a party on appeal, that fact should be noted; for example, "No appearance for Defendant and Respondent." However, if a nonappearing party is listed in the title for the purpose of identification only, or if there is no appellate designation, omit any reference to that party in the counsel listing. (See, e.g., *Fairmont Ins. Co. v. Frank* (1996) 42 Cal.App.4th 457.)

Where the amicus curiae does not appear in support of any particular litigant's position or where the amicus curiae's support status is not clear (see § 5:19), list the amicus curiae counsel last.

§ 5:18 Sequence of names; original proceedings commenced in appellate court

For original proceedings commenced in appellate court, counsel are named in the following order:

1. Counsel for petitioner.
2. Counsel for amicus curiae on behalf of petitioner.
3. Counsel for respondent.
4. Counsel for amicus curiae on behalf of respondent.
5. Counsel for real party in interest.
6. Counsel for amicus curiae on behalf of real party in interest.

(See, e.g., *California State Auto. Assn. Inter-Ins. Bureau v. Superior Court* (1990) 50 Cal.3d 658.)

Where there is no appearance for a party, as is frequently the case where a court is a respondent, that fact should be noted; for example, "No appearance for Respondent."

Where the proceeding seeking a writ was commenced in the trial court and the pending matter is an appeal from the trial court ruling, follow the rules for the listing of counsel in appeals (see § 5:17).

§ 5:19 Amicus curiae

If an amicus curiae (friend of the court) brief is filed in support of a party to the appeal, list the name of amicus curiae counsel, the amicus curiae entity or individual, and the trial and appellate status of the party on whose behalf the amicus curiae brief was filed. Where counsel does not appear in support of any particular litigant's position or where the amicus curiae's support status is not clear, the listing omits reference to any party to the appeal. The listing should also indicate when an individual appears as an amicus curiae at the court's invitation.

> Chung & Golden and Dennis T. Chung for Timber Harvest Association as Amicus Curiae on behalf of Defendant and Respondent.
> Shearman & Stickland, Jason F. Doten and Shirley S. Gutman for Majority Systems, Inc., as Amicus Curiae on behalf of Plaintiff and Respondent.
> Jennifer S. Parks for Youth and Children's Fund as Amicus Curiae on behalf of Real Party in Interest.
> Alma S. Rodriguez for Coastal Arts Foundation as Amicus Curiae.
> Karen Harris as Amicus Curiae, upon the request of the Supreme Court.
> or . . . upon the request of Chief Justice Black.
> or . . . upon the request of the Court of Appeal.

If two or more individuals or entities file an amicus curiae brief, use the plural, Amici Curiae. If these individuals or entities all share the same counsel, no separate counsel listing is needed. If the amici curiae are separately represented (i.e., multiple amicus curiae briefs are filed), then separate counsel listings should indicate which counsel represent which amicus curiae (see § 5:15[D]). And if an amicus curiae brief is filed on behalf of one party, but there are other parties on the same side, then the counsel listing should also identify which party the brief was filed for.

> Sanches and Singh and Lester R. Sanches for 97 California Cities and the California Association of Counties as Amici Curiae on behalf of Defendant and Respondent.
> O'Malley and Rossi and John P. Rossi for Save the Lakes Foundation and Fresh Air Foundation as Amici Curiae on behalf of Plaintiff and Respondent Mountain Homeowners Association.

If amici curiae counsel are attorneys for the state, a city, or a county (see § 5:20), that designation should be shown; for example, Attorney General, Deputy Attorney General, City Attorney, District Attorney, County Counsel, and so on. For such public entity counsel, place the name of the city or county in parentheses after the designation of each chief officer, but not after the names of the deputies, as follows:

> Casey J. Smith, Attorney General, Jody S. Jacobs, Deputy Attorney General, John P. Jones, District Attorney (Tulare), Thomas Reilly, Deputy District

> Attorney, Mary Pollak, District Attorney (Merced) and Edward P. Apple,
> District Attorney (Kern), for Counties as Amici Curiae on behalf of
> Defendant and Appellant.
> (See, e.g., *Rider v. County of San Diego* (1991) 1 Cal.4th 1, 5; *California
> Fed. Savings & Loan Assn. v. City of Los Angeles* (1991) 54 Cal.3d 1, 5.)

§ 5:20 Official titles of public attorneys

In order to avoid space-consuming recitations of the frequently changed and often lengthy titles of attorneys for state, county, city, and other governmental agencies, the Official Reports does not list those formal titles. A limited number of short titles, more descriptive than official, are, however, listed. These are: Attorney General, District Attorney, City Attorney, Public Defender, and County Counsel.

List assistants and deputies of these officers as follows: Assistant Attorney General, Deputy Attorney General, Deputy Public Defender, Chief Deputy State Public Defender, Deputy State Public Defender, Principal Deputy County Counsel, and so on. If more than one assistant or deputy appears, use one pluralized designation: Assistant Attorneys General, Deputy District Attorneys, Deputy Public Defenders. Because "counsel" is both singular and plural, two or more deputies should be referred to as Deputy County Counsel. Public attorneys are listed before private attorneys in each paragraph listing counsel.

> John Bruce, Attorney General, Mary Thorton, Chief Assistant Attorney
> General, N. Fred Green, Assistant Attorney General, Edmund Redding
> and Charles Bluff, Deputy Attorneys General, for Plaintiffs and
> Appellants.
> Ben Fujiyama, State Public Defender, Betty Gee and Barry Brown, Deputy
> State Public Defenders, for Defendant and Appellant.
> Martha Moore, County Counsel, Douglas Nguyen and Mark Rodrigo,
> Deputy County Counsel, for Defendant and Respondent.
> Barnes and Ruggieri and Francis R. Ruggieri, City Attorney, for Defendant
> and Respondent.

§ 5:21 Change of public attorney during pendency of appellate court proceedings

If a new public attorney takes office while an action is pending in the appellate courts, list both new and old officeholders only if both *appeared* of record. Filing a brief, adopting a filed brief, or participating at oral argument constitutes an appearance for purposes of the counsel listing; merely holding a government position as public attorney during the pendency of the appeal, however, does not. For example:

1. Where a brief was filed by Attorney General John First, but no subsequent appearance is made by new Attorney General Jane Second (or her deputies), then only Attorney General John First and the participating deputies would be listed as counsel, even if the case is decided while Jane Second is Attorney General.
2. Where *both* Attorneys General, through their deputies, file briefs, then both are listed. An example of proper designation would be John First and Jane Second, Attorneys General, Helen Help and Harry Support, Chief Assistant Attorneys General, Mary Smart and William Bright, Deputy Attorneys General, for Plaintiff and Respondent. (See, e.g., *People v. Cooper* (1991) 53 Cal.3d 1158, 1160.)
3. Where Attorney General John First files a brief and Attorney General Jane Second files no brief but she (or a deputy) argues the case, that is considered to be an appearance and both Attorneys General are then listed, with any participating assistants and deputies.
4. Where an appeal or other appellate court proceeding was commenced while Attorney General John First was in office, but no appearance for the public entity was made during that period, then Attorney General First should not be listed.
5. A waiver of oral argument is not considered an appearance.

§ 5:22 Criminal cases; court-appointed counsel

Where counsel is appointed by an appellate court in a criminal case, the fact of appointment is noted. A law firm cannot be listed as appointed counsel, nor can any of the appellate projects that work with appellate courts to provide and support appointed counsel. Only the individual attorney's name is listed.

> Judith Jacobs, under appointment by the Supreme Court, for Defendant and Appellant.
> Lisa Green and John Robinson, under appointments by the Court of Appeal, for Defendants and Appellants.

When the same attorney is appointed in both the Court of Appeal and the Supreme Court, use: "Caroline Tom, under appointment by the Supreme Court, for Defendant and Appellant." But where the Supreme Court appoints a new attorney to represent the defendant in that court, and does not appoint previous counsel to continue representation in the Supreme Court, use: "Caroline Tom, under appointment by the Supreme Court, and Joe Oakes, under appointment by the Court of Appeal, for Defendant and Appellant."

Where the State Public Defender is appointed, note the fact of appointment as follows:

> Eric Smith, State Public Defender, under appointment by the Supreme Court [or Court of Appeal], and Victoria Torres, Deputy State Public Defender, for Defendant and Appellant.

If the participating attorney is a panel attorney working with the State Public Defender's Office, but is not a staff member of that office, list his or her name after that office's participating members. Where the State Public Defender is not appointed by the court but a defendant is nevertheless represented by that office, follow the style noted in section 5:20. (Gov. Code, § 15421.)

§ 5:23 Party in propria persona

When a party appears as his or her own attorney, or appears for herself or himself and others, or as executor, receiver, and so forth, the party is listed in the counsel listing, with the words "in pro. per." Only an individual can be listed as "in pro. per." Do not use this designation for a law firm that is representing itself.

> William S. Teller, in pro. per., for Defendant and Appellant.

Where a party appears as his or her own attorney, and counsel is later retained or appointed by an appellate court, the forms are as follows:

> Linda O'Donnell, in pro. per.; and Jerome Luna for Plaintiff and Respondent. [*Retained.*]
>
> Sammy Khayat, in pro. per.; Floyd & Foster and Nathan L. Foster for Petitioner. [*Retained.*]
>
> Karen Green, in pro. per.; and James Rudnicki, under appointment by the Supreme Court [or Court of Appeal], for Defendant and Appellant. [*Appointed.*]

If a party appearing in pro. per. is also represented by counsel, the name of the party in pro. per. is listed first, to show that he or she alone is appearing in propria persona.

> James Sharp, in pro. per.; Hillier, Riven & Dale and Harvey Dale for Plaintiffs and Respondents.
>
> Mason B. Kiddie, in pro. per.; Bogart & DiFilippo and Michael DiFilippo for Petitioners.
>
> Jane R. Heath, in pro. per., and for Defendants and Appellants.

§ 5:24 Nonattorneys

Except for parties in propria persona (§ 5:23), do not list nonattorneys (such as certified law students), even though they may have argued a case with the appellate court's permission or assisted other attorneys in preparing appellate court briefs.

§ 5:25 Opinion covering two cases

If necessary to avoid confusion as to representation where an opinion covers two or more cases, include the pertinent appellate court docket number in the counsel listing. For example: "for Plaintiff and Respondent in No. B012345" or "for Plaintiff and Appellant in No. B012399," and so forth. (See, e.g., *Rosenberg v. Superior Court* (1998) 67 Cal.App.4th 860.)

§ 5:26 Substitution of attorneys

Where an attorney has filed a brief or otherwise appeared in the appeal, but thereafter there is a substitution or withdrawal of attorneys under California Rules of Court, rule 48(b), list as counsel *both* the retiring attorney and the new attorney. A substitution of attorneys does not negate an appearance by the retiring attorney prior to the substitution or withdrawal.

§ 5:27 Counsel on intervention

A person seeking to intervene in an action is called a "Movant" until permission to intervene is granted. Counsel will thus be shown as "for Movant" if permission has been denied and as "for Intervener" if permission has been granted. (See, e.g., *Sinclair Paint Co. v. State Bd. of Equalization* (1997) 15 Cal.4th 866 [permission granted]; *Mar v. Sakti Internat. Corp.* (1992) 9 Cal.App.4th 1780 [permission denied].)

D. DESIGNATION OF TRIAL JUDGE

§ 5:28 General rule and exceptions

The trial judge's name is provided to identify the source of the ruling or action from which the appeal or other review is sought. A typical listing would be: Superior Court of Lassen County, No. 12345, Sandra A. Dart, Judge (see sample opinion title page, § 5:4). Where the appeal is from several rulings made by different judges, include the names of all judges whose decisions are challenged: Superior Court of Kern County, No. 12345, Mary Whyte and Fred Bogosian, Judges. However, do not include a judge whose ruling is not being contested, as, for example, where he or she merely continued the matter or sat on an immaterial preliminary motion.

The trial judge's name is also provided for original proceedings in the appellate court arising from a lower court, including grant or denial of a writ by a lower court. For writ proceedings in the Court of Appeal that do not arise from a trial judge's ruling, no trial judge is designated. Also, rulings of the Workers' Compensation Appeals Board, the Alcoholic Beverage

Control Appeals Board, the Public Employment Relations Board, and the Agricultural Labor Relations Board have no trial court number or judge.

§ 5:29 Trial judges in counties with unified courts (Cal. Const., art. VI, § 23.)

Superior courts of counties whose courts have unified under California Constitution, article VI, section 23, are still denominated Superior Court of _____ County, and not "Consolidated Court" or "Unified Court," or similar denomination. (Cal. Const., art. VI, §§ 4, 23, subds. (b), (c).)

§ 5:30 Trial judges sitting under assignment

Information that the trial judge was sitting under assignment should be provided in the filed opinion, usually in a parenthetical note after the judge's or justice's name. Also include the judge or justice's regular superior court and county or Court of Appeal district and note whether the judge or justice is retired. Include a retired appellate justice's former appellate district, but not division. In the Official Reports, this information appears in an unnumbered footnote.

> Superior Court of Marin County, No. 665168, Robert Fairley, Judge. (Retired Judge of the Marin Sup. Ct. assigned by the Chief Justice pursuant to art. VI, § 6 of the Cal. Const.) [*Do not use the word "County" in the parenthetical.*]
> Superior Court of Orange County, No. 98765, Janet Jefferson, Judge. (Judge of the Mun. Ct. for the L.A. Jud. Dist. assigned by the Chief Justice pursuant to art. VI, § 6 of the Cal. Const.)
> Superior Court of Los Angeles County, No. YC002229, Mark Jacobson, Judge. (Retired judge of the L.A. Sup. Ct. assigned by the Chief Justice pursuant to art. VI, § 6 of the Cal. Const.)

Other designations indicating retired judges or justices sitting under assignment are: Retired judge of the municipal court; Retired judge of the former municipal court; Retired Associate Justice of the Supreme Court; Retired Associate Justice of the Court of Appeal, Second District. (See, e.g., *Flatt v. Superior Court* (1994) 9 Cal.4th 275; *Pro-Family Advocates v. Gomez* (1996) 46 Cal.App.4th 1674.)

For appellate justices sitting under assignment, see section 5:37.

§ 5:31 Temporary judges sitting by stipulation

Where a court commissioner, referee, retired judge or justice, or other attorney is sitting as a temporary judge by stipulation of the parties, use the designation Temporary Judge, not judge pro tem. or pro tempore (see Cal. Const., art. VI, § 21), with a parenthetical notation. Information as to a retired judge or justice's former court is not listed for individuals sitting as a temporary judge. In the Official Reports, this information will appear in an unnumbered footnote.

> Superior Court of Butte County, No. 12345, Ann Forrest, Temporary Judge. (Pursuant to Cal. Const., art. VI, § 21.)
> (See *Howard v. Thrift Drug & Discount Stores* (1995) 10 Cal.4th 424; *Hsu v. Abbara* (1995) 9 Cal.4th 863; Cal. Rules of Court, rules 244, 532.)

§ 5:32 Commissioners and referees without stipulation

Where a court commissioner or referee who has not been qualified by stipulation to serve as a temporary judge is nevertheless empowered to perform subordinate judicial duties or to decide uncontested actions and proceedings, and the determination in such situations is challenged, use Commissioner, Juvenile Court Referee, or similar designation, but without the parenthetical notation referred to in section 5:31; for example, Keith Stone, Commissioner; Marsha Murray, Juvenile Court Referee. (See *In re Joseph D.* (1993) 19 Cal.App.4th 678; *In re Marriage of Grissom* (1995) 30 Cal.App.4th 40; *Freedom Newspapers, Inc. v. Orange County Employees Retirement System* (1993) 6 Cal.4th 821; Cal. Const., art. VI, § 22; Code Civ. Proc., §§ 259, 638–645.1; Cal. Rules of Court, rule 532.2.)

E. NAMES OF JUSTICES ON OPINIONS

§ 5:33 General guidelines

Under the California Constitution, a valid judgment generally requires concurrence of a qualified majority of the justices present at oral argument—four out of seven justices in the Supreme Court, and two out of three justices in the Court of Appeal. (Cal. Const., art. VI, §§ 2, 3.) The parties may, however, stipulate to a decision by fewer justices than heard the argument; also, oral argument may be waived and the cause deemed submitted on the briefs. Thus, the names of all participating justices are given with the opinion. Additionally, every opinion requires designation of the Chief Justice (or Acting Chief Justice) for Supreme Court opinions, and of the Presiding Justice (or Acting Presiding Justice) for Court of Appeal opinions.

The Official Reports does not list the names of participating justices in the same manner as the as-filed versions of opinions. In the as-filed opinion, the author's name is placed at the end, followed by the names of those who concurred and dissented, in seniority sequence. In the Official Reports, the author's name is placed at the start of the opinion, and the concurring justices are listed at the end, followed by the word "concurred." For example, Jones, P. J., and Smith, J., concurred.

If a concurring or dissenting justice authors an opinion, participating justices are noted in the same fashion as in the majority opinion.

§ 5:34 Single or majority opinion

For a single (unanimous) or majority opinion, provide the justices' last names, in capital letters, followed by C. J., P. J., or J., as the case may be. If a justice is acting as Chief Justice or as Presiding Justice, use the form "JONES, Acting C. J." or "JONES, Acting P. J." There is one space between the "C." and "J." and the "P." and "J." In the as-filed opinion, list the authoring justice immediately after the opinion, followed by the words "WE CONCUR" or "I CONCUR," then the name(s) of the concurring justice(s) in order of seniority.

If two justices sitting on the same appellate court have the same last name, distinguish them by inserting the first name or initials in parentheses after the last name, as in STONE (S. J.), P. J.; VOGEL (MIRIAM A.), J. Use this form only when omitting the name or initials may cause confusion. The name of a trial court judge assigned to an appellate court should be distinguished in the same fashion, to avoid confusion with another judge with the same last name sitting at the same trial or appellate court level.

If the opinion is by the court, with no specified authoring justice, use THE COURT (not Per Curiam or By the Court). The names of the participating justices are then listed in an unnumbered footnote, including the designation of Presiding Justice or Chief Justice.

§ 5:35 Concurring and dissenting opinions

If a justice files a concurring or dissenting opinion, the justice's name is placed at the beginning of that opinion, followed by the word, "Concurring" or "Dissenting." For example: JONES, J., Dissenting. If the opinion *commences* with the words "I concur" or "I dissent" it is unnecessary to insert the additional words "Concurring" or "Dissenting." If the opinion is both a concurring and a dissenting opinion and that fact does not appear from the first sentence of the opinion, use JONES, J., Concurring and Dissenting.

Note, however, that if one of three Court of Appeal justices on a panel dissents, and one of the remaining two use the designation "concurred in the result," the opinion could be problematic. (See *Amwest Surety Ins. Co. v. Wilson* (1995) 11 Cal.4th 1243.)

The name of any justice who concurs in a concurring or dissenting opinion is placed at the end of that opinion in the same style as for concurrence in the main opinion (see § 5:33).

When several justices join as *authors* of a dissenting or concurring opinion, all the names are listed in full capital letters in the order of seniority. (See *Treu v. Kirkwood* (1954) 42 Cal.2d 602, 621; *Estate of Dow* (1957) 48 Cal.2d 649, 654.)

§ 5:36 Order of opinions

When a decision has two or more opinions, the order of opinions, unless otherwise directed by the court, is: main opinion, concurring opinion, concurring and dissenting opinion, and dissenting opinion. If there are two opinions in the same category, for example, two separate concurrences, the sequence is based on the author's seniority with the court.

The main opinion may be a majority opinion, a plurality opinion, or a lead opinion. A majority opinion is signed by more than half of the justices; a plurality opinion is signed by the greatest number of justices, but not by a majority. A lead opinion occurs when two or more opinions have the same number of signatures, but less than a majority (e.g., if the justices are divided 3-3-1, 2-2-2-1, or 1-1-1). In such instances, the court selects which opinion reflects the court's disposition, and that is designated as the lead opinion.

§ 5:37 Justices sitting under assignment

If a participating justice has been assigned from another division, another appellate district, or a trial court, an unnumbered footnote after the justice's name should contain the justice's usual court and the fact of assignment. If the assigned justice is retired, give that information as well. (An assigned justice may not sit as Acting Presiding Justice in his or her temporary assigned division.)

BLACK, J.*

---

*Retired Associate Justice of the Supreme Court, assigned by the Chief Justice pursuant to article VI, section 6 of the California Constitution.

HALLORAN, J.*

---

*Retired Associate Justice [*or* Presiding Justice] of the Court of Appeal, First Appellate District, assigned by the Chief Justice pursuant to article VI, section 6 of the California Constitution.

When the assignment is made by the Acting Chief Justice, the footnote should read: *Assigned by the Acting Chief Justice pursuant to article VI, section 6 of the California Constitution.

When an assignment is made to the Supreme Court, the designation includes the title of the justice and the court *and division*—for example: Presiding [or Associate] Justice of the Court of Appeal, First Appellate District, Division Two, assigned by the Chief Justice pursuant to article VI, section 6 of the California Constitution. A presiding justice of a Court of Appeal who is assigned to the Supreme Court sits there as a justice rather than as a presiding justice.

For trial judges sitting under assignment, see section 5:30.

§ 5:38 Supreme Court; order of names

The names of the justices of the Supreme Court, when listed as concurring or dissenting, should be given in the order of seniority, with the exception that the Chief Justice always heads the list when included therein. When a justice is Acting Chief Justice, list that name first regardless of the justice's normal position in the order of seniority.

If an assigned justice participates (see § 5:37), that name is shown at the end of the list with an appropriate footnote.

§ 5:39 Disqualification or nonparticipation

If a justice is disqualified, or deems himself or herself disqualified, that fact is sometimes noted in a separate paragraph after the main opinion and the names of the concurring justices and before any dissenting opinion. The wording is usually taken from the court's minutes. The following forms have been used:

> Jones, J., being disqualified, did not participate therein.
> *or* Jones, J., deeming himself disqualified, did not participate.
> *or* Smith, J.,* sat in place of the Chief Justice, who deemed herself
> disqualified. [*Footnote then notes Smith's assignment, see § 5:37.*]

If a justice does not participate for a reason other than disqualification, the assignment information is usually sufficient, but if the justice wishes to note the absence from participation, the following are examples for doing so:

> Jones, J., did not participate therein.
> *or* Jones, J., did not participate in the hearing or determination of this
> matter.

F. MODIFICATION OF OPINIONS

§ 5:40 Formal order required

[A] In general; time limitations

All modifications of opinions, whether by addition, deletion, or substitution, must be made before the decision becomes final in the modifying court. Modifications must be made by formal court order, with the concurrence of a qualified majority of the court, and entered in the court's minutes. Although a qualified majority must concur in the modification, modification orders are often signed only by the presiding justice.

Upon filing, modification orders for published opinions are made available on the judicial branch's Web site at <http://www.courtinfo.ca.gov>. It is then either incorporated into the opinion before publication (see § 5:41), or published separately in the advance pamphlets (see § 5:42).

A formal modification order has traditionally been filed for changes that alter the written opinion as to substance, argument, or authority cited, or that would add to or omit any consequential portion of the as-filed opinion. Clerical corrections may be made without formal order. If there is a doubt and the court still retains jurisdiction, the better practice is to make a formal order of modification.

[B] Sample modification order

When adding, deleting, or substituting material in the original opinion, note these guidelines:

1. When the opinion is published in the advance sheets, refer to that version to identify the page and language affected, rather than to the as-filed opinion.
2. Identify the affected paragraph, line, language, or footnote as precisely as possible, using quotation marks to identify the words or phrases to be changed. If the words to be changed are themselves in quotation marks in the opinion, it is better to repeat the entire passage as adjusted to avoid any ambiguity.
3. Preferably, indicate the new language by indenting or otherwise setting it off on the modification page.
4. Prominently indicate the publication status (certified for publication, certified for partial publication, or not for publication) of the opinion modified.
5. Note whether or not the modification changes the judgment; a change to the judgment extends the time for finality. (Cal. Rules

of Court, rule 24(a), (b).) It is commonplace to state that the judgment has been affected anytime there is any change to an opinion's dispositional language.

CERTIFIED FOR PUBLICATION
IN THE COURT OF APPEAL OF THE STATE OF CALIFORNIA
SECOND APPELLATE DISTRICT
DIVISION ONE

LINDSAY HARRIS,
   Plaintiff and Respondent,
 	
         v.
 	
XYZ INSURANCE COMPANY,
   Defendant and Appellant.
	)
	) B012345
	) (Super. Ct. No. 54321)
	) ORDER MODIFYING OPINION
	) AND DENYING REHEARING,
	) CERTIFYING OPINION FOR
	) PUBLICATION
	) [NO CHANGE IN JUDGMENT]
	) *or*
	) [CHANGE IN JUDGMENT]

THE COURT:

It is ordered that the opinion filed herein on November 1, 1998, be modified as follows:

1. On page 1, second sentence of the first full paragraph, the word "limited" is changed to "absolute" so the sentence reads:

   The absolute liability issue is moot.

2. On page 2, the second full paragraph, beginning "The question of" is deleted and the following paragraph is inserted in its place:

   Without concluding that the questioned instructions are a paragon of clarity, we do deduce that, taken together, they correctly state the law.

3. On page 3, line 3 of footnote 10, the word "material" is to be inserted between the words "only" and "evidence" so that the sentence reads:

   The only material evidence on that issue was the engineer's report.

4. At the end of the last paragraph on page 4, after the sentence ending "as revealed by company records," add as footnote 12 the following footnote, which will require renumbering of all subsequent footnotes:

   [12] Statements filed on July 1, 1994, disclosed this.

5. The paragraph commencing at the bottom of page 5 with "The jury had" and ending at the top of page 6 with "for the court" is modified to read as follows:

   The jury had the policy before it as an exhibit and could refer to it if necessary. However, the interpretation of the policy was entirely a matter for the court.

6. On page 8, at the end of footnote 16, after the word "mind" add the following:

(See *Cozens v. Superior Court* (1973) 31 Cal.App.3d 441.)

[There is no change in the judgment.] *or* [This modification changes the judgment.]

Respondent's petition for rehearing is denied.

The opinion in the above-entitled matter filed on November 1, 1988, was not certified for publication in the Official Reports. For good cause it now appears that the opinion should be published in the Official Reports and it is so ordered.

In the preceding example, if the opinion had already appeared in the advance pamphlet when the modification order was filed, the initial paragraph would so indicate, and the page references would be to the Official Reports pagination rather than to the original as-filed pagination, as follows:

It is ordered that the opinion filed herein on November 1, 1996, and reported in the Official Reports (50 Cal.App.4th 100) be modified in the following particulars:

1. On page 123, line 14 of the first full paragraph, . . .

If the modification order refers to the as-filed opinion pagination and the modification is published on an "a" page in the advance pamphlet (see § 5:42), the publisher will automatically adjust the references to fit the Official Reports pagination.

§ 5:41 Modification before advance pamphlet publication

When a modification order is received in time, the changes can be incorporated into the opinion for publication in the advance pamphlet. A boldface legend on the opinion's inception page states that the advance pamphlet opinion is printed as modified; for example, "[As modified Nov. 1, 1996]." In the bound volume, the fact of modification is noted at the end of the opinion, along with any other history notations.

§ 5:42 Modification after advance pamphlet publication; the "a" page

If a modification order is received too late for changes to be incorporated for the advance pamphlet, and if it is short enough not to affect the opinion's pagination, the order is published separately in the next available advance pamphlet as an "a" page following the reported cases. For example, if the last reported opinion ends on page 567 of an advance pamphlet, a modification order for an opinion in a previous pamphlet would begin on page 567a and continue on 567b, 567c, and so forth. The modification is then incorporated into the opinion for publication in the Official Reports bound volume, and the opinion's original citation stays the same. In the bound volume, the fact of modification is noted at the end of the opinion with any other history notations.

If the modification's length affects the opinion's pagination, then the entire modified opinion is reprinted in a later advance pamphlet, with a different citation. In the bound volume, the opinion is omitted from its original location, and a note directs readers to turn to a later page or volume. Pending publication of the affected bound volumes, the case is listed in the Cumulative Subsequent History Table in the advance pamphlets, to alert researchers to refer to the later version of the opinion (see § 1:20).

To minimize such reprintings, it is suggested that appellate court staffs consider advising the Reporter of Decisions when a lengthy modification is forthcoming. With advance knowledge of a lengthy modification, reprinting the opinion in its entirety at a new location can generally be avoided.

§ 5:43 Notation that opinion was modified

All modification orders, even those directing that a few words or a short passage be added, deleted, or modified, are noted immediately following the opinion in the bound volume and in computer versions. (See, e.g., *Andres v. Young Men's Christian Assn.* (1998) 64 Cal.App.4th 85, 93.)

§ 5:44 Correction of clerical errors

Although an opinion must be modified on formal order before it becomes final, a clerical error may be corrected even after the opinion is final. If the error is discovered before the advance pamphlet publication cutoff date, normally the first seven court days after filing, advising the Reporter of Decisions will often permit a clerical correction before publication.

G. PARTIAL PUBLICATION

§ 5:45 General guidelines; retaining enough material for interpretation of opinion

A majority of the court rendering a decision may certify the opinion for partial publication by having the authoring justice note at the top, CERTIFIED FOR PARTIAL PUBLICATION.* The author's unnumbered footnote (the page 1 footnote) advises the reader that only certain portions of the opinion meet the publication standards of California Rules of Court, rule 976(b), and that, accordingly, only those portions are published and citable. (See Cal. Rules of Court, rules 976.1, 977(a).) The published part of the opinion must retain enough facts and procedural history to enable the reader to understand the rule of law set forth. (Cal. Rules of Court, rules 976, 976.1.) The court's disposition must be included in the published part. If protective nondisclosure is appropriate (see §§ 5:9–5:13), it should be used in both the published and nonpublished portions.

The page 1 footnote must clearly indicate which parts of the opinion are not to be published. This is generally done by referring to the opinion's internal structure (i.e., the outline structure). A typical page 1 footnote, therefore, might read:

> *Pursuant to California Rules of Court, rules 976(b) and 976.1, this opinion is certified for publication with the exception of parts III and V. *or*
>
> *Parts III and V of this opinion are not certified for publication. (See Cal. Rules of Court, rules 976(b), 976.1.) *or*
>
> *Parts 4 and 6 through 8 are not ordered published, as they do not meet the standards for publication contained in rule 976(b) of the California Rules of Court. *or*
>
> *Under California Rules of Court, rules 976(b) and 976.1, only the Factual and Procedural Background, parts I, IV, and X of the Discussion, and the Disposition are certified for publication.

§ 5:46 Omitting major segments of opinion

When a major segment of an opinion is not to be published, the outline number or letter identifying this material is nonetheless included, with the author's heading, if any. An unnumbered footnote at that point refers the reader back to the "page 1 footnote" that explains the omission (see § 5:45). The omitted material is then represented by a single line of dots. Where, however, consecutive segments are to be omitted, their headings are not printed unless the author advises the Reporter of Decisions to include them. The omitted material is again represented by a single line of dots, as shown in the following example. (For additional examples, see *Jordy v. County of Humboldt* (1992) 11 Cal.App.4th 735, 747; *People v. Lopez* (1992) 11 Cal.App.4th 844, 851.)

C. DELAY AND DUE PROCESS OF LAW* [*or* V.-VII.*]

....

---

*See footnote, *ante*, page 1.

§ 5:47 Omitting subparts or unstructured segments of opinion

More complex omissions from publication may require more detailed instructions. Some authors designate the omitted material by using bracketed statements in the text of the as-filed opinion; for example: [The portions of this opinion that follow (parts V-VIII) are deleted from publication.] If later portions are to be published, another bracketed sentence might note: [The remainder of this opinion is to be published.].

Where the portions to be omitted from publication are not entire parts or major segments of the opinion, a footnote direction in the style of an opinion modification may be used.

CERTIFIED FOR PARTIAL PUBLICATION*

―――――――

*Pursuant to California Rules of Court, rules 976(b) and 976.1, this opinion is certified for partial publication. The portions directed to be published follow.†

―――――――

†Note to the Reporter of Decisions: This opinion is to be published in full with the following exceptions:

(1) Omit the last full paragraph commencing at the bottom of page 7 beginning with "The trial court held" and all subsequent paragraphs and related footnotes through the first full paragraph at the top of page 11 ending with the words, ". . . was adversely affected."

(2) At the end of the first full paragraph on page 14, omit the third sentence, beginning with the words, "He was later detained . . . ."

§ 5:48 Retaining footnote numbering

In partial publication, when an unpublished part of the opinion contains footnotes, do not renumber any subsequent published footnotes. Not only is this task unnecessary, but renumbering can also cause confusion when footnote references are made by minority opinion authors or by counsel in their petitions for rehearing and review. Additionally, the accuracy of the author's internal cross-references is at risk when original sequences are changed. Readers will recognize that the broken footnote numbering is the result of the omission of parts of the opinion.

§ 5:49 Retaining numbering and lettering for topic headings

Do not renumber or reletter to give the partial opinion the appearance of sequential continuity; the published opinion must clearly indicate omissions (see § 5:46).

§ 5:50 Minority opinions

Where part of the minority opinion is directed to unpublished portions of the majority or lead opinion, the minority opinion should omit from publication those portions relating to unpublished portions of the majority opinion. Where the minority opinion speaks only to the unpublished portions of the main opinion, it should generally be omitted in its entirety. (See *People v. Delgado* (1983) 149 Cal.App.3d 208.) The majority opinion's partial publication instructions should not be employed to inhibit publication of a minority opinion in the cause.

§ 5:51 Partial publication ordered by Supreme Court

"After granting review, after decision, or after dismissal of review and remand as improvidently granted, the Supreme Court may order the opinion of the Court of Appeal published in whole or in part." (Cal. Rules of Court, rule 976(d).) The Reporter of Decisions and the publisher will follow the Supreme Court's partial publication instructions in the same manner described in the foregoing sections, except that the opinion's heading statement will read, ORDERED PARTIALLY PUBLISHED* rather than CERTIFIED FOR PARTIAL PUBLICATION.* The accompanying unnumbered footnote will then describe the Supreme Court's order of partial publication.

> * Pursuant to California Rules of Court, rule 976(d), the Supreme Court by order dated January 10, 1999 [or, by opinion filed January 10, 1999 (if that is the case)], directed this Court of Appeal opinion to be published with the exceptions of parts III and V.

H. PUBLICATION PROCEDURES FOR OFFICIAL REPORTS

§ 5:52 Procedures for rule 976(e), California Rules of Court

The Official Reports publication contract obligates the State of California, through the Reporter of Decisions Office, to provide computer versions of published opinions to the publisher on the day of filing (or the day a postfiling publication order is filed), as close to the actual filing time as is practical. This requirement also facilitates making published opinions available to the public on the judicial branch Web site <http://www.courtinfo.ca.gov>. Also, California Rules of Court, rule 976(e) provides that "[t]wo copies of each opinion of the Supreme Court, and two copies of each opinion of a Court of Appeal or of an appellate [division] of a superior court which the court has certified as meeting the standard for publication specified in [rule 976] subdivision (b) shall be furnished by the clerk to the Reporter of Decisions. The Reporter of Decisions shall edit the opinions for publication as directed by the Supreme Court. Proof sheets of each opinion in the type to be used in printing the reports shall be submitted by the Reporter of Decisions to the court which prepared the opinion for examination, correction and final approval." Courts must also forward a copy of the opinion, and of any modification, directly to the Official Reports publisher.

§ 5:53 Proofreading, answering queries, returning corrected proofs of opinions

Pursuant to California Rules of Court, rule 976(e), each opinion is edited for publication by the Reporter of Decisions. The Reporter of Decisions Office makes necessary revisions, additions, and adjustments to the editorial materials and notes style, printing and other errors perceived on galley proofs, which are then submitted as adjusted to the authoring court for examination, proofreading, correction, and final bound volume approval. Due to the high volume of published opinions, not all the printing and other errors that a slower reading would disclose are caught. Therefore, the Reporter of Decisions must rely on careful proofreading by each justice's staff to ensure fidelity of publication.

A due date for return of a galley proof is prominently noted on the title page of an edited opinion forwarded to the originating court. Timely return of a submitted galley proof is essential to meet contract-based commitments to the Official Reports publisher, but accommodations are almost always possible if a court requires extra time and so advises the Reporter of Decisions Office.

Although no substantive changes may be made during the editing process described by rule 976(e), California Rules of Court, the proofreading and correction process affords opinion authors a final opportunity to resolve ambiguities, correct grammatical lapses, and make other changes within the bounds of clerical correction.

§ 5:54 Procedures for superior court appellate division opinions

In addition to the editorial information that must be furnished with all appellate court opinions certified for publication (see § 5:4), an appellate division opinion submitted for publication must indicate that it was certified for publication within the time that the appellate division retained jurisdiction. When available, computer versions of appellate division opinions that are to be published should be sent to the Reporter of Decisions along with file-stamped paper copies. This may be done by electronic mail. The opinion should specify that a copy was also forwarded to the appropriate Court of Appeal after the judgment became final in the appellate division, to allow the Court of Appeal to elect to transfer the cause to itself. (See Cal. Rules of Court, rules 62(a), (b), 106, 107(b), 976(c).)

When the period for transfer by the Court of Appeal on its own motion has expired (see Cal. Rules of Court, rule 62(b)), or before that if the Court of Appeal has actually denied transfer, the clerk of the appellate division should forward to the Reporter of Decisions a letter indicating (1) that a copy of the opinion stamped "Certified for Publication" was submitted to the appropriate Court of Appeal, noting the date submitted; (2) that the Court of Appeal received the opinion, noting the date received; and (3) that the Court of Appeal either filed an order declining to transfer the case, noting the date of such order, or that the Court of Appeal has not transferred it within the jurisdictional time.

Upon receipt of such a letter from the clerk, the Reporter of Decisions will then proceed with publication procedures. If, however, the Court of Appeal has transferred the cause to itself, the appellate division clerk should advise the Reporter of Decisions of that fact. These opinions are published in the Official Reports on supplemental pages, or Supp. pages, at the end of volumes containing opinions of the Court of Appeal.

§ 5:55 Memorials; procedure for publication

On occasion, a bound volume of the Official Reports is dedicated to the memory of a justice or other distinguished member of the legal community.

Memorials are published, upon court direction, in the next bound volume of the Official Reports on completion of the publication procedures. Where a justice was in office at the time of his or her death, the memorial is normally published in the bound volume in which that justice's final opinions will appear. The "In Memoriam" is published immediately following the last reported opinion of the particular volume. The justice's name is indexed in the table of cases as "Jones, Hon. John J., Memorial for" and "In Memoriam—Hon. John J. Jones."

Customarily the In Memoriam is introduced editorially by a dated history of all courts on which the justice sat, a notation of the date and place of the memorial, and an identification of the clerk, reporter, and bailiff in attendance. (See, e.g., 43 Cal.3d 1421; 203 Cal.App.3d 1531.)

To prepare the memorial for publication, the originating court should collect all the editorial information noted above, edit the memorial for publication, then forward the memorial and editorial information to the Reporter of Decisions. The Reporter of Decisions then prepares the memorial for galley publication. When the memorial is printed, a sufficient number of preliminary galleys will be returned to the originating court so that the court can distribute one galley to each of the parties participating in the memorial service for approval. When the court has obtained the approval of all parties, a dated galley with all adjustments indicated is returned to the Reporter of Decisions with the notation, "O.K. to print as adjusted."

CHAPTER 5
—Notes—

CHAPTER 5
—Notes—

CASE TITLES

C. SPECIFIC TITLES

§ 6:21 Adoption proceedings

§ 6:22 Arbitration proceedings

§ 6:23 Conservatorship proceedings

§ 6:24 Criminal proceedings

§ 6:25 Disciplinary proceedings against attorneys

§ 6:26 Disciplinary proceedings against judges

§ 6:27 Estates, conservatorships, and guardianships

    [A] Double titles

    [B] Single titles

§ 6:28 Extraordinary writ proceedings

    [A] Original proceedings in appellate court

    [B] Appeal from original proceedings in trial court

§ 6:29 Family Code proceedings

    [A] Appellate designations in general

    [B] Appeals concerning joined parties

§ 6:30 Forfeiture of bail

§ 6:31 Guardianship proceedings

§ 6:32 Habeas corpus proceedings

§ 6:33 In rem proceedings

    [A] Escheat

    [B] Forfeiture of illegally used property

§ 6:34 Interpleader

§ 6:35 Intervention

§ 6:36 Juvenile court proceedings

    [A] Direct appeals

    [B] Writ proceedings

§ 6:37 Nonadversary proceedings

§ 6:38 Parental rights termination proceedings

§ 6:39 Probate proceedings

    [A] Estate administration

    [B] Will contests

A. GENERAL RULES

§ 6:1   Purpose of title

The opinion title is an important informational aid for noting the type of proceeding and identifying parties and their roles in the litigation. It is not necessarily an index to all the parties, a complete description of each party's status (as executor, trustee, etc.), or a definitive statement of each party's respective litigation position (as plaintiff, defendant, cross-defendant, appellant, etc.). Generally, the appellate opinion title identifies parties appearing before the reviewing court, parties who will be affected by the reviewing court's judgment, or parties whose identification is essential to understanding the action.

While the primary purpose of this chapter is to assist court staffs, the Reporter of Decisions Office, and the Official Reports publisher in styling titles, these rules are also intended to assist attorneys in filing appellate briefs and papers with properly styled appellate titles.

In contrast to appellate titles, the complaint in the trial court must include the names of all parties, but in subsequent pleadings or other filings, it is sufficient to state the name of the first party on each side with an appropriate indication of other parties. (Code Civ. Proc., § 422.40.) (For the use of "et al.," see § 6:3.)

§ 6:2   Types of titles

The full appellate title appears in the caption of the opinion. An abbreviated version appears at the top of each page of the Official Reports version of the opinion. This "running head" title is ordinarily used for citation purposes (see also § 1:1[A]). While running head or otherwise abbreviated titles may employ a variety of standard abbreviations (e.g., "&," "Co.," "Ins."), full titles use abbreviations only if they are part of a party's true legal name. (See *Vikco Ins. Services, Inc. v. Ohio Indemnity Co.* (1999) 70 Cal.App.4th 55.)

§ 6:3   Format of title

The party who initiated the action in the trial court (the plaintiff, petitioner, or cross-complainant) is listed first (i.e., above the "v."), regardless of which party appeals. In an appeal by both the plaintiff and defendant, both are called "Appellant" and neither is called "Respondent"; it is implicit that both are respondents to each other's appeal. (*The terms "cross-appellant" and "cross-respondent" are never used in appellate titles and should be avoided in the body of opinions.*) When there are several parties with identical trial and appellate court designations, only the first party is named for title purposes. The designation "et al." signals that there are additional parties. (For exceptions in death penalty cases and workers' compensation proceedings, see §§ 6:24 and 6:48.)

In titles, include "The" when it is the first word of a party's proper name, but note that "The" is disregarded for tabling and indexing purposes (e.g., "The Ajax Company" would be tabled as "Ajax Co." for the Official Reports).

When a surname contains an intermediate capital, with a prefix that is the equivalent of "the," "of," "son of," etc. (e.g., LaMarr, De Forrest, MacDonald, etc.), the initial letter is a full capital, and the rest of the prefix is in small capitals (e.g., LAMARR, DE FORREST, MACDONALD). Use this form regardless of whether the surname is written as one or two words. Do not use personal degrees or titles (C.P.A., M.A., M.D., Dr., Rev., Hon., etc.) in opinion titles.

In addition to identifying the parties, identify the appellate court and list the appellate docket number or numbers and the trial court docket number or numbers, if any, in the caption portion of the opinion. For computer versions of opinions that will not show the court's dated file stamp, insert the filing date in the upper left corner of the first page, using the following style: Filed 1/2/00. If the opinion includes an appendix that is not available in the same format as the computer version, include a statement to that effect following the file date. A notation indicating the publication status of opinions must also be part of the main title for opinions of the Courts of Appeal and superior court appellate divisions (see Cal. Rules of Court, rule 976). The customary language is "CERTIFIED FOR PUBLICATION," "CERTIFIED FOR PARTIAL PUBLICATION*" and "NOT TO BE PUBLISHED." (For partially published opinions, the asterisk footnote provides the publication instructions.) Because all Supreme Court opinions are published, a publication status notation is not used. (See also §§ 1:25, 5:40[B]4, 5:45 et seq.)

Typical title pages are:

Filed 1/2/00

IN THE SUPREME COURT OF CALIFORNIA

THE PEOPLE,	)	
Plaintiff and Respondent,	)	S012345
v.	)	Ct.App. 2/3 B012345
JOSEPH GREEN,	)	(Super. Ct. No. A-54321)
Defendant and Appellant.	)	

Filed 12/2/99   Appendix not available electronically

CERTIFIED FOR PUBLICATION *[or]*
CERTIFIED FOR PARTIAL PUBLICATION* *[or]*
NOT TO BE PUBLISHED

IN THE COURT OF APPEAL OF THE STATE OF CALIFORNIA
FIRST APPELLATE DISTRICT
DIVISION FOUR

WILLIAM G. LITTLE,)	
Plaintiff and Appellant,)	A012345
v.)	(Super. Ct. No. A 54321)
SMITH PLUMBING, INC., et al.,)	
<u>Defendants and Appellants.</u>)	

....

Filed 4/24/00

CERTIFIED FOR PUBLICATION

APPELLATE DIVISION OF THE SUPERIOR COURT
OF THE STATE OF CALIFORNIA FOR THE COUNTY OF LOS ANGELES

THE PEOPLE,)	Super. Ct. Crim. A.
Plaintiff and Respondent,)	No. 12345
v.)	(Municipal Court for the Los Angeles
CHRIS LEE,)	Judicial District of Los Angeles
<u>Defendant and Appellant.</u>)	County No. 54321)

....

Filed 7/6/00

CERTIFIED FOR PUBLICATION

IN THE COURT OF APPEAL OF THE STATE OF CALIFORNIA
SECOND APPELLATE DISTRICT
DIVISION TWO

MARIA GONZALES et al.,)	
Plaintiffs and Appellants,)	B012345
v.)	(Super. Ct. No. 54321)
ACME COMPANY,)	
<u>Defendant and Respondent.</u>)	
MARIA GONZALES et al.,)	
Petitioners,)	B0123456
v.)	
THE SUPERIOR COURT OF)	
LOS ANGELES COUNTY,)	
Respondent;)	
ACME COMPANY,)	
Real Party in Interest.)	

....

214

For title styles when multiple cases are consolidated or coordinated for disposition by a single opinion, see section 6:5.

§ 6:4   Appeals involving multiple parties at trial

If the first person or entity named as plaintiff or defendant appeals, name that party (with "et al." if others also appeal); generally ignore those who do not appeal. When the first plaintiff or defendant does not appeal from an adverse decision, but others do, omit the first name and substitute the next named party who does appeal.

In the following examples, assume that the plaintiffs in the trial court were A, B, and C and that the defendants were D, E, and F.

1. If the decision below is in favor of defendants and only A appeals, the title is:

A, Plaintiff and Appellant, v. D et al., Defendants and Respondents.

2. If the decision below is in favor of defendants but only C appeals, the title style is:

C, Plaintiff and Appellant, v. D et al., Defendants and Respondents.

3. If the judgment below allows a recovery by the first plaintiff (A) but denies relief to the other plaintiffs, who then appeal, the title is:

B et al., Plaintiffs and Appellants, v. D et al., Defendants and Respondents.

4. If the judgment below is in favor of plaintiffs and the first defendant (D) does not appeal, the title is:

A et al., Plaintiffs and Respondents, v. E et al., Defendants and Appellants.

5a. If B and C appeal a partial summary judgment in favor of D and D also appeals, assuming there is only one appellate docket number (see § 6:5), the title is:

B et al., Plaintiffs and Appellants, v. D, Defendant and Appellant.

[or]

5b. If D's appeal is directed against A as well as B and C:

A, Plaintiff and Respondent; B et al., Plaintiffs and Appellants, v. D, Defendant and Appellant.

6. Same scenario as 5a, but there are separate appellate docket numbers assigned to the initial appeal by D and the subsequent appeal by B and C (see also § 6:5); the titles are:

B et al., Plaintiffs and Respondents, v. D, Defendant and Appellant.
B et al., Plaintiffs and Appellants, v. D, Defendant and Respondent.

7. Assuming an action was dismissed as to the first defendant (D) and only B appeals D's dismissal from the case and assuming also the remaining defendants appeal an adverse judgment in favor of all of the plaintiffs, if there is one appellate docket number, the title is:

A et al., Plaintiffs and Respondents; B, Plaintiff and Appellant, v.
D, Defendant and Respondent; E et al., Defendants and Appellants.

8. Same scenario as 7, but there are separate appellate docket numbers assigned to the initial appeal by B and the subsequent appeal by E and F (see also § 6:5); the titles are:

B, Plaintiff and Appellant, v. D, Defendant and Respondent.
A et al., Plaintiffs and Respondents, v. E et al., Defendants and
    Appellants.

The foregoing examples eliminate from the main title the names of persons who are not parties to the appeal. The style does not, however, eliminate the names of parties who will be *affected* by the appeal merely because they fail to make an appearance in the reviewing court. For example, if A appealed from a judgment in favor of defendants D, E, and F, it would make no difference whether D filed a brief, joined in a codefendant's brief, or failed to appear; in each instance the title is:

A, Plaintiff and Appellant, v. D et al., Defendants and Respondents.

On the other hand, parties who generally would be excluded from the title will remain in the title if they make an appearance on appeal or if they are essential for the identification of the proceedings. For instance, if plaintiffs A and B obtain a favorable judgment and plaintiff C appeals an adverse judgment, ordinarily A and B would be omitted from the appellate title. If B nevertheless files a respondent's brief on appeal, B's appearance must be reflected in the title as follows:

B, Plaintiff and Respondent; C, Plaintiff and Appellant, v.
D et al., Defendants and Respondents.

For retention of parties for identification purposes, see sections 6:34, 6:41, 6:45, 6:46.

§ 6:5 Consolidated and coordinated cases

[A] Consolidated cases

When separate cases are consolidated for trial or for appellate review, a multiple title is required setting out each case's title unless the titles are completely identical in every respect. If, for example, plaintiff A is an appellant in one case and a respondent in another, separate titles will be required for each case and the titles are to be listed in chronological order by docket number. Likewise, if A is the plaintiff and appellant in the first case and B is the plaintiff and appellant in the second case, separate titles are required even if D is the defendant and respondent in both cases; it is not appropriate to combine the cases using a title of "A et al." But if the identity of the parties and their respective litigation designations are identical in each case on appeal, only a single title is used, with all applicable trial or appellate court docket numbers listed for the consolidated cases. Whenever there are multiple docket numbers from either the trial court or the appellate court, the necessity of multiple titles should be considered. Multiple titles will never be appropriate, however, if there is only one docket number each from both the trial and appellate courts.

> MERVYN'S, Plaintiff and Appellant, v.
> ANGELINA REYES, as City Clerk, etc., et al., Defendants and Respondents;
> SHERMAN L. LEWIS III, Real Party in Interest and Respondent.
> --
> MERVYN'S, Plaintiff and Appellant, v.
> ANGELINA REYES, as City Clerk, etc., et al., Defendants and Respondents;
> SHERMAN L. LEWIS III, Real Party in Interest and Appellant.
> (*Mervyn's v. Reyes* (1998) 69 Cal.App.4th 93 [both titles listed due to different appellate designations for Real Party in Interest].)

> GENERAL MOTORS CORPORATION, Plaintiff and Appellant, v.
> CITY AND COUNTY OF SAN FRANCISCO, Defendant and Respondent.
> (*General Motors Corp. v. City and County of San Francisco* (1999) 69 Cal.App.4th 448 [multiple cases consolidated in appellate court; identical titles].)

> PEGGY ANN BUCKLEY et al., Plaintiffs and Respondents, v.
> CALIFORNIA COASTAL COMMISSION, Defendant and Appellant.
> --
> PEGGY ANN BUCKLEY et al., Cross-complainants and Respondents, v.
> CALIFORNIA COASTAL COMMISSION, Plaintiff, Cross-defendant and
>   Appellant.
> (*Buckley v. California Coastal Com.* (1998) 68 Cal.App.4th 178 [two cases consolidated in trial court with single appellate case number; appeal from judgments on main complaint in the first case and cross-complaint in the second case].)

> (See also *Cairns v. County of Los Angeles* (1997) 62 Cal.App.4th 330 [three actions consolidated in the trial court]; *Putnam v. Clague* (1992) 3 Cal.App.4th 542 [three appeals consolidated in the Court of Appeal].)

Where there are more than four actions with distinct titles, use only the title of the first case with a bracketed reference to the remaining actions.

List the running-head-type titles and trial or appellate court docket numbers for the additional cases in an asterisk footnote. For example:

> MARK K., Plaintiff and Appellant, v. ROMAN CATHOLIC ARCHBISHOP OF LOS ANGELES, Defendant and Respondent.
>
> [And four other cases.*]
>
> ---
>
> *John K. v. Roman Catholic Archbishop (No. BC153772); Michael M. v. Roman Catholic Archbishop (No. KC023297); Christopher D. v. Roman Catholic Archbishop (No. NC019503); Scott G. v. Roman Catholic Archbishop (No. NC019504).
>
> (See *Mark K. v. Roman Catholic Archbishop* (1998) 67 Cal.App.4th 603 [multiple trial court cases]; *Rosenberg v. Superior Court* (1998) 67 Cal.App.4th 860 [multiple appellate cases].)

[B] Coordinated cases

Under coordination procedures, separate actions with common issues that are pending in several different counties or courts may be transferred to one court and coordinated for trial (Code Civ. Proc., §§ 404–404.9; Cal. Rules of Court, rules 1500–1550). In appeals of such coordinated actions, use the title assigned by the Judicial Council, such as "Cases Relating to Crash of Flight 1040" or "Consolidated Toxic Tort Actions," in lieu of the typical adversary titles. Also list the Judicial Council coordination proceeding number as "CJJP No. 1234" in addition to the other trial and appellate court docket numbers. (See *In re Complex Asbestos Litigation* (1991) 232 Cal.App.3d 572, except that adversary portion of the title would now be omitted.)

If there is no subject matter title assigned by the Judicial Council, follow the guidelines listed in section 6:5[A] for consolidated cases. (See *20th Century Ins. Co. v. Garamendi* (1994) 8 Cal.4th 216 [adversary titles used for three coordinated actions]; *California School Employees Assn. v. Del Norte County Unified Sch. Dist.* (1992) 2 Cal.App.4th 1396 [first case title listed with four other cases from various jurisdictions identified in asterisk footnote].)

§ 6:6 Grouping litigants in cases with cross-complaints

In a case with a cross-complaint, group all parties with identical trial and appellate designations together and list each group separately. If an appeal concerns only the ruling on the cross-complaint, name the cross-complainant first, above the "v.," and drop the trial court designations of "Plaintiff" and "Defendant." A single action with cross-complaints or complaints in intervention is still just one action, with a single title, assuming there is only one docket number in both the trial and appellate courts.

For example, assume A sues D, E, and F. F then cross-complains against A, D, and E, and additionally names G et al. as cross-defendants:

1. If defendant F appeals adverse judgments on both A's complaint and F's cross-complaint, the title is:

> A, Plaintiff, Cross-defendant and Respondent, v. D et al., Defendants, Cross-defendants and Respondents; F, Defendant, Cross-complainant and Appellant; G et al., Cross-defendants and Respondents.

2. If plaintiff A appeals an adverse judgment on A's complaint and F appeals an adverse judgment on F's cross-complaint, assuming there is only one appellate docket number, the title is:

> A, Plaintiff, Cross-defendant and Appellant, v. D et al., Defendants, Cross-defendants and Respondents; F, Defendant, Cross-complainant and Appellant; G et al., Cross-defendants and Respondents.

3. If plaintiff A appeals an adverse judgment on A's complaint, and F loses on the cross-complaint but elects not to appeal, the title reverts to the simple A v. D style because the cross-complaint is not involved in the appeal:

> A, Plaintiff and Appellant, v. D et al., Defendants and Respondents.

4. If F obtains a favorable judgment against A, D, and E on the cross-complaint but appeals the judgment insofar as it denies recovery against G et al., assuming that is the only ruling challenged on appeal, the title is:

> F, Cross-complainant and Appellant, v. G et al., Cross-defendants and Respondents.

In rare instances, a cross-complainant may be listed above the "v." along with the plaintiff. For example, assume plaintiff A sues defendant D; D cross-complains against A, G, and H; and A in turn cross-complains against D, G, and H and joins J and K as additional cross-complainants (see Code Civ. Proc., § 389). If A, J, and K appeal, the title is:

> A, Plaintiff, Cross-defendant and Appellant; J et al., Cross-complainants and Appellants, v. D, Defendant, Cross-complainant and Respondent; G et al., Cross-defendants and Respondents.

In the preceding example, note that J et al. are listed above the "v." along with the plaintiff only because they were (1) joined as cross-complainants (2) by the plaintiff. Both of those very specific requirements must be met before a cross-complainant qualifies to be listed above the v. when a party designated as a plaintiff is also listed in the same title. Note also that A's additional designation of "Cross-complainant" and D's additional designation of "Cross-defendant" are not listed in the title above due to the prohibition of listing more than three designations for a party or similarly situated group of parties. Generally, drop the latest trial court designation or designations when there are more than three; always retain the party's appellate designation.

> (See *Aerojet-General Corp. v. Transport Indemnity Co.* (1997) 17 Cal.4th 38; *Wilson, McCall & Daoro v. American Qualified Plans, Inc.* (1999) 70 Cal.App.4th 1030; *California Pacific Homes, Inc. v. Scottsdale Ins. Co.* (1999) 70 Cal.App.4th 1187; *Gordon v. Hamm* (1998) 63 Cal.App.4th 1324.)

B. LITIGATION DESIGNATIONS

§ 6:7   Use of party designation in text and titles

In briefs and opinions, generally use the trial designations or personal names in referring to the parties (i.e., do not use "Appellant" and "Respondent"). Ordinarily, the issues arose in the trial court and are more easily followed by retaining those designations. Occasionally, it may be simpler to use appellate designations if the issues relate to proceedings in the reviewing court. Be consistent, however, in how parties are designated. Do not refer to the same party successively, for example, as "Plaintiff," "Respondent," and "Board."

Some lower court designations are "Petitioner" and "Respondent," for example, in marital dissolution actions, trust administration proceedings, and writ proceedings. To avoid a confusing combination with appellate designations, the lower court designations are either dropped (see § 6:29) or adjusted (see §§ 6:28, 6:42) for appellate court titles. Accordingly, the use of trial designations in those opinions is discouraged.

§ 6:8   Class actions

When a party files a class action lawsuit, it is not necessary to identify the other plaintiffs as a class, and the title follows the style of an ordinary action, using "et al." (See Code Civ. Proc., § 382; *StorMedia Inc. v. Superior Court* (1999) 20 Cal.4th 449; *Granberry v. Islay Investments* (1995) 9 Cal.4th 738.)

§ 6:9   Corporations

A corporation has all the powers of a natural person in carrying out its business activities (Corp. Code, § 207), including the capacity to sue and be sued. (See also Corp. Code, § 17003, subd. (b) [powers of limited liability corporation].) Do not abbreviate any word of a corporate name in an opinion title unless the abbreviated form is part of the corporation's legal name.

Do not note that an entity is "a corporation" or "a California corporation," since that fact is usually apparent from the title or will appear in the body of the opinion. Also, do not add "etc." after a corporate name.

§ 6:10 Government officers

When suit is brought by or against a government officer in his or her official capacity, the title should so note: "A, as City Treasurer, etc.," or "as County Auditor, etc.," or "as Insurance Commissioner, etc.," or "as Attorney General, etc.," or "as Director of Finance, etc." Do not list "offices" or "positions" such as Office of the Attorney General, Attorney General, or Director of the Department of Motor Vehicles in titles.

AMERICAN ACADEMY OF PEDIATRICS et al., Plaintiffs and Respondents, v.
DANIEL E. LUNGREN, as Attorney General, etc., et al., Defendants and Appellants.
(*American Academy of Pediatrics v. Lungren* (1997) 16 Cal.4th 307.)

THE PEOPLE ex rel. BILL LOCKYER, as Attorney General, etc., Plaintiff and Respondent, v.
SHAMROCK FOODS COMPANY, Defendant and Appellant.
(*People ex rel. Lockyer v. Shamrock Foods Co.* (1999) 73 Cal.App.4th 1396.)

RICHARD LAKE, Plaintiff and Appellant, v.
SALLY R. REED, as Director, etc., Defendant and Respondent.
(*Lake v. Reed* (1997) 16 Cal.4th 448.)

For substitution of parties when a government officer changes during pendency of an appeal, see section 6:19; for quo warranto proceedings, see section 6:40.

§ 6:11 Government bodies

Generally state any geographic description before the name of a particular body; e.g., use "Riverside County Board of Supervisors" not "Board of Supervisors of Riverside County." Courts are the exception; they are listed in the following manner: "The Superior Court of Fresno County," "The Superior Court of the City and County of San Francisco," or "The Municipal Court for the East Los Angeles Judicial District of Los Angeles County."

When an action involves a state board or department rather than the State of California itself, the title should show the name of that particular body, not the State of California. (See, e.g., *Yamaha Corp. of America v. State Bd. of Equalization* (1998) 19 Cal.4th 1; *California Correctional Peace Officers Assn. v. State Personnel Bd.* (1995) 10 Cal.4th 1133; cf. § 6:20 for suits in name of state or People.) Look to the California Constitution or codes to determine if "California" or "State" is part of the state body's actual name. If there is no specific agency, board, commission, department involved, the style is "City of," "County of," or "State of." (See *Rider v. City of San Diego* (1998) 18 Cal.4th 1035.)

Note that the specific divisions of the Department of Industrial Relations are listed after the department itself, as follows: Department of Industrial Relations, Division of Labor Standards Enforcement. (See *C & C Partners, Ltd. v. Department of Industrial Relations* (1999) 70 Cal.App.4th 603.)

An "office," e.g., "Office of the Governor," is generally a mere description, and it is not to be used as a party name. An exception exists where "Office" is part of the official name of an agency created by law, e.g., the Office of Statewide Health Planning and Development (see Health & Saf. Code, § 127000).

§ 6:12 Individuals doing business under fictitious names; sole proprietorships

When a party is doing business under a fictitious name, as with a sole proprietorship, ignore that fact for title purposes. Do not use descriptions such as "DBA," "doing business as," or "etc." to indicate the fictitious name. Thus, if defendant D is sued as "D, doing business under the name of D's Realty Co.," the title is:

A, Plaintiff and Appellant, v. D, Defendant and Respondent.

For designation of partnerships and unincorporated associations, see section 6:14.

§ 6:13 Natural persons; aliases

Except as otherwise provided by statute, an action must be prosecuted in the name of the real party in interest. (Code Civ. Proc., § 367.) Therefore disregard the fact that a person has used an alias or is "also known as" a different name. When it appears from the pleadings or other reliable documentation that a person is suing or being sued under an alias, or that his or her name is misspelled, use the correct name, not the alias or the inaccurate spelling. Do not use "AKA" to indicate the alias or explanations like "erroneously sued as" in titles.

§ 6:14 Partnerships or associations

Any partnership or other unincorporated association may sue and be sued in the name it has assumed. (Code Civ. Proc., § 369.5, subd. (a); see Corp. Code, §§ 15048 [registered limited liability partnerships], 15054 [foreign limited liability partnerships]; see also Corp. Code, §§ 16101, subds. (4), (6) & (7), 16111, 16307, subd. (a) [governing partnerships formed on or after Jan. 1, 1997, and governing all partnerships on and after Jan. 1, 1999].)

Do not parenthetically note that an entity is "a partnership" or "an association," since that fact is usually apparent from the title or will appear in the body of the opinion. Do not add "etc." after a partnership or association name.

When the partnership or association is named first, followed by its members' names, use the firm's name and "et al." (e.g., AJAX PROPERTIES et al.). If the first named party is a member of the entity, it is not necessary to note that a partnership or association is involved (e.g., TOM SMITH et al.). (See *San Mateo Community College Dist. v. Half Moon Bay Limited Partnership* (1998) 65 Cal.App.4th 401.)

§ 6:15 Persons acting in representative capacity

If a party is involved in an action in a representative capacity, indicate that capacity in the title. Use "etc.," after the person's status (e.g.,"JOHN JONES, as Administrator, etc.," "as Executor, etc.," "as Personal Representative, etc.," "as Trustee, etc.," "as Trustee in Bankruptcy, etc.," "as Special Administrator, etc.," "as Supervisor, etc.," "as Judge of the Superior Court, etc.," and so forth. Trusts and estates, for example, generally cannot appear in their own right. The trustees, executors, or personal representatives, in their representative capacities, must be the named parties (see §§ 6:27, 6:47).

If a person appears in both a representative and an individual capacity, the designation is "JOHN JONES, Individually and as Executor, etc." But if the person appears individually and as guardian ad litem of a minor or an incompetent person; "et al." is used to describe representation of the unnamed minor or legally incompetent person; no notation of representation is otherwise made in the title.

§ 6:16 Minors

Minors lack capacity to sue or be sued and must be represented either by a guardian ad litem or guardian of the estate. (See Code Civ. Proc., § 372, subd. (a); Fam. Code, § 6500 ["minor" is an individual under 18 years of age].) Although the guardian appears for the minor, the minor is the party and is named as such. In the title, "etc." is used in place of "by _____, his guardian ad litem." (See 4 Witkin, Cal. Procedure (4th ed. 1997) Pleading, § 62, pp. 119–120.) The title therefore is:

MICHAEL RANDALL, a Minor, etc., et al., Plaintiffs and Respondents, v.
ORANGE COUNTY COUNCIL, BOY SCOUTS OF AMERICA, Defendant
and Appellant.
(*Randall v. Orange County Council* (1998) 17 Cal.4th 736.)

For protective nondisclosure, see section 6:18; for adoption proceedings, see section 6:21; for conservatorship and guardianship proceedings, see sections 6:23 and 6:31; for habeas corpus proceedings involving minors, see section 6:32; and for juvenile court proceedings, see section 6:36.

§ 6:17 Incompetent persons

An incompetent person must appear either by a guardian or conservator of the estate, or by a guardian ad litem appointed by the court. (Code Civ. Proc., § 372, subd. (a).) Usually, the incompetent person, not the guardian, is the party and is named as such. (See 4 Witkin, Cal. Procedure (4th ed. 1997) Pleading, § 62, pp. 119–120.) In the title, "etc." is used in place of "by _____, her guardian." When the issue before the appellate court is whether the party is or is not incompetent, do not use the designation "an Incompetent Person" following the individual's name. When competency is not an issue, typical titles are:

JOSE CALDERON, an Incompetent Person, etc., Plaintiff and Respondent, v.
ELOISE ANDERSON, as Director, etc., Defendant and Appellant.
(*Calderon v. Anderson* (1996) 45 Cal.App.4th 607.)

REGENCY HEALTH SERVICES, INC., Petitioner, v.
THE SUPERIOR COURT OF LOS ANGELES COUNTY, Respondent;
LOIS FAYE SETTLES, an Incompetent Person, etc., Real Party in Interest.
(*Regency Health Services, Inc. v. Superior Court* (1998) 64 Cal.App.4th 1496.)

For conservatorship and guardianship proceedings, see sections 6:23 and 6:31.

§ 6:18 Protective nondisclosure for titles

Publication of the names of innocent victims of sex crimes and the names of minors who, without blame, are caught up in the type of case in which damaging disclosures are made serves no useful legal or social purpose. Thus, the Supreme Court has issued the following policy memorandum to all appellate courts: "To prevent the publication of damaging disclosures concerning living victims of sex crimes and minors innocently involved in appellate court proceedings it is requested that the names of these persons be omitted from all appellate court opinions whenever their best interests would be served by anonymity." Protective nondisclosure is also used in titles concerning individuals found to be gravely disabled within the definition of the Lanterman-Petris-Short Act (Welf. & Inst. Code, § 5000 et seq.), which governs the involuntary treatment of the mentally ill in California. (Protective nondisclosure is treated more fully in §§ 5:9–5:13.)

The prevailing California appellate court practice is to not disclose the identity of minors in either the title or body of opinions reviewing juvenile court proceedings. (See *In re Cindy L.* (1997) 17 Cal.4th 15; *In re Tracy L.* (1992) 10 Cal.App.4th 1454.) The preferred reference style is to identify a minor by first name and last name initial, although the use of initials alone is acceptable. If the minor's first name is so unusual as to defeat the objective of anonymity, then the minor's initials alone should be used. (See *T.N.G. v. Superior Court* (1971) 4 Cal.3d 767, 770, fn. 1.) To carry out this nondisclosure policy, it is necessary to also suppress the identity of parents and others bearing the minor's last name (cf. § 6:24). The terms "Anonymous," "John Doe," and "Jane Doe" are not used.

Protective nondisclosure for minors does not apply when a minor is prosecuted as an adult in a criminal proceeding. (See *People v. Macias* (1997) 16 Cal.4th 739; but see *People v. Joe T.* (1975) 48 Cal.App.3d 114, 121 [criminal proceeding was a nullity and the matter was remanded to the juvenile court].) When a minor seeks relief in a collateral proceeding, such as a petition for reconsideration of the court's determination that the minor was not amenable to treatment and must be prosecuted under the general criminal law, and relief is denied, the protective nondisclosure style is not used. (Compare *Jimmy H. v. Superior Court* (1970) 3 Cal.3d 709 [relief granted] with *Bryan v. Superior Court* (1972) 7 Cal.3d 575 [relief denied].) Likewise, where the People successfully challenge a ruling finding a minor amenable to treatment under the juvenile court law, the minor's full name is used. (See *People v. Superior Court (Jones)* (1998) 18 Cal.4th 667.)

§ 6:19 Substitution of parties

When one party is formally substituted for another because of death, transfer of interest, bankruptcy, liquidation, receivership, or other reason, the original party's name is dropped from the title and the new party's name is inserted. (See *San Mateo Community College Dist. v. Half Moon Bay Limited Partnership* (1998) 65 Cal.App.4th 401.) When litigation is continued by a substituted party in a representative capacity, the status of the representative should be shown. (See *Sullivan v. Delta Air Lines, Inc.* (1997) 15 Cal.4th 288; *Plattner v. City of Riverside* (1999) 69 Cal.App.4th 1441; §§ 6:15, 6:27[A].)

When a party has transferred his or her interest in the subject matter of an action, and the successor continues the action in the original party's name, there is no need to change the case title. (See *Stark v. Shaw* (1957) 155 Cal.App.2d 171, 182.)

When a public official is a party in his or her official capacity (see § 6:10), the officeholder on the date the opinion is filed is named as the party, not a predecessor who may have held office at the time of trial. No formal substitution is required when there is a change in office for a public official being sued in his or her official capacity. (See *Weadon v. Shahen* (1942) 50 Cal.App.2d 254, 259–260.)

§ 6:20 Suits in name of the state or the People

When litigation is initiated by a private individual, governmental official, or branch of the state, in the name of the state or the People, the relator's name is given, with "ex rel."

> THE PEOPLE ex rel. DEPARTMENT OF TRANSPORTATION, Plaintiff and Appellant, v. MARY MOOR, Defendant and Respondent.

> THE PEOPLE ex rel. JOHN JONES, as Attorney General, etc., Plaintiff and Respondent, v. COUNTY OF SAN MATEO et al., Defendants and Appellants.

> (See *People ex rel. Gallo v. Acuna* (1997) 14 Cal.4th 1090; *State of Cal. ex rel. State Lands Com. v. Superior Court* (1995) 11 Cal.4th 50.)

An appearance in intervention in the name of the state or the People by a private individual, governmental official, or branch of the state is styled in the same fashion. (See *Friends of Cuyamaca Valley v. Lake Cuyamaca Recreation & Park Dist.* (1994) 28 Cal.App.4th 419.)

C. SPECIFIC TITLES

§ 6:21 Adoption proceedings

For an appeal from an order or judgment after a petition for adoption, the usual form of double title is:

> Adoption of JOHN INFANT, a Minor. EDITH ADOPTER, Plaintiff and Appellant, v. SONYA MOTHER, Defendant and Respondent.

If the opinion contains damaging disclosures, the appellate policy of protective nondisclosures applies (see § 6:18), resulting in the use of an anonymous title, with corresponding anonymous party references in the text of the opinion as well:

> Adoption of JOHN I., a Minor. EDITH A., Plaintiff and Appellant, v. SONYA M., Defendant and Respondent.

The vast majority of adoption cases use protective nondisclosure. (See *Adoption of Zachariah K.* (1992) 6 Cal.App.4th 1025; *Adoption of Lindsay C.* (1991) 229 Cal.App.3d 404.)

If relief from an adoption ruling is sought by a petition for a writ of habeas corpus, mandate, or prohibition, the usual titles for such proceedings are followed. (See §§ 6:28, 6:32; see also *Los Angeles County Dept. of Children etc. Services v. Superior Court* (1998) 62 Cal.App.4th 1 [mandate]; *San Diego County Dept. of Pub. Welfare v. Superior Court* (1972) 7 Cal.3d 1 [prohibition, mandate, and habeas corpus]; *In re Richard M.* (1975) 14 Cal.3d 783 [habeas corpus proceeding to obtain custody].)

§ 6:22 Arbitration proceedings

In the superior court, arbitration proceedings should use an adversary title. The "In re" form, which implies an in rem or ex parte proceeding, is not appropriate. The title should follow the general rules for ordinary appeals in civil actions. (See, e.g., *Law Offices of Ian Herzog v. Law Offices of Joseph M. Fredrics* (1998) 61 Cal.App.4th 672.)

Proceedings commenced in the appellate courts seeking relief by writ, as, for example, for a writ of mandate .to set aside a trial court order granting a motion to compel arbitration or vacating an arbitration award, follow the title styles applicable to original writ proceedings. (See § 6:28; see also *Sobremonte v. Superior Court* (1998) 61 Cal.App.4th 980.)

§ 6:23 Conservatorship proceedings

A double title is used in conservatorship proceedings (see § 6:27 for distinction between double and single titles). The conservatorship is described first, followed by the adversary title. "Petitioner" and "Objector" are the trial court designations used for the parties in the adversary title. Conservatorships may be of the person, of the estate, or both.

> Conservatorship of the Estate [*or* Person, *or* Person and Estate] of JANE SPADE. RALPH BROWN, as Conservator, etc., Petitioner and Appellant, v. MARY CLARK, Objector and Respondent.

Do not use lengthy conservatorship titles, such as "In the Matter of the Conservatorship of JANE SPADE," or "In re the Matter of Conservatorship of the Estate of JANE SPADE."

> Conservatorship of the Person and Estate of ANGELA D.
> ROBERT D. et al., as Coconservators, etc., Petitioners and Respondents, v. ANGELA D., Objector and Appellant.
> (*Conservatorship of Angela D.* (1999) 70 Cal.App.4th 1410 [appeal by conservatee].)

Conservatorship of the Estate of LEWIS MICHAEL GEIGER.
GERALD M. GEIGER, as Conservator, etc., Petitioner and Appellant, v.
UNITED STATES DEPARTMENT OF JUSTICE, Objector and Respondent;
BIRGIT CARLSEN GEIGER, Intervener and Appellant.
(*Conservatorship of Geiger* (1992) 3 Cal.App.4th 127 [case involving
intervener].)

(See also *Conservatorship of Coombs* (1998) 67 Cal.App.4th 1395; *O'Brien
v. Dudenhoeffer* (1993) 16 Cal.App.4th 327 [civil action brought by
conservator to void the transfer of real property].)

For persons acting in a representative capacity, see section 6:15; for
minors and incompetent persons, see sections 6:16 and 6:17; for guardianship proceedings, see section 6:31.

§ 6:24 Criminal proceedings

In ordinary criminal prosecutions and appeals, the plaintiff's name is
"The People." Defendants are designated in the same manner as in ordinary
civil actions. (See Pen. Code, §§ 684, 685.) "Et al." is used for multiple
defendants charged in the same complaint if all are involved in the appeal.
In death penalty cases, however, where multiple defendants sentenced to
death are involved in the appeal, all of their names are listed in the title; "et
al." is not used. (See *People v. Champion* (1995) 9 Cal.4th 879.) If the first
named defendant does not appeal, that name is omitted, and the title will
show instead the name of the first defendant who does appeal (see § 6:4).
When the prosecution uses an alias in the initial pleadings and the defendant's true name is discovered later, the main title should carry the true
name (see § 6:13). Similarly, the use of protective nondisclosure for criminal defendants is not appropriate. Typical title styles are:

THE PEOPLE, Plaintiff and Respondent, v. JOHN JONES, Defendant and
Appellant.

THE PEOPLE, Plaintiff and Respondent, v. JANE SMITH et al., Defendants
and Appellants.

A *coram nobis* or *coram vobis* proceeding is regarded as part of the
original action rather than a new adversary action; thus it takes the title of
the original case. (See *People v. Chaklader* (1994) 24 Cal.App.4th 407; *Betz
v. Pankow* (1993) 16 Cal.App.4th 931, fn. 5.)

(See also *People v. Fernandez* (1999) 70 Cal.App.4th 117 [appeal from an
order extending a prisoner's commitment pursuant to the Mentally
Disordered Offender Act (Pen. Code, § 2960 et seq.)]; *People v. Mercer*
(1999) 70 Cal.App.4th 463 [appeal from civil commitment under the
Sexually Violent Predators Act (Welf. & Inst. Code, § 6600 et seq.)]; but see
Hubbart v. Superior Court (1999) 19 Cal.4th 1138 [challenge to civil
commitment by petition for writ of prohibition].)

§ 6:25 Disciplinary proceedings against attorneys

The form of title for opinions concerning review of discipline imposed by the State Bar Court is:

In re ASHLEY ATTORNEY on Discipline.

This general form is used regardless of the specific type of discipline imposed by the State Bar Court (e.g., disbarment, suspension, interim suspension, or reprimand).

For nondisciplinary State Bar proceedings, see section 6:43.

§ 6:26 Disciplinary proceedings against judges

When a disciplinary determination by the Commission on Judicial Performance is reviewed by the Supreme Court, the style of title is:

JOHN JONES, a Judge of the Superior Court, Petitioner, v.
COMMISSION ON JUDICIAL PERFORMANCE, Respondent.

(See *Oberholzer v. Commission on Judicial Performance* (1999) 20 Cal.4th 371.)

§ 6:27 Estates, conservatorships, and guardianships

[A] Double titles

Since all estate administration cases (i.e., conservatorship, guardianship, and probate cases) and will contests have a dual aspect, two titles are necessary: a description of the conservatorship, decedent's estate, or guardianship involved, followed by the title of the adversary proceeding between the parties.

Estate of EVELYN J. CONDON, Deceased.
MICHAEL R. CONDON et al., Petitioners and Respondents, v.
CAROLINE M. McHENRY, Objector and Respondent.
(*Estate of Condon* (1998) 65 Cal.App.4th 1138.)

For specific probate titles, see section 6:39; for conservatorship and guardianship titles, see sections 6:23 and 6:31.

[B] Single titles

When the action brought by or against the executor, conservator, or other representative is not part of the probate or conservatorship proceeding, but rather is an independent civil action, such as a complaint to enforce a contract between the decedent and third parties, the title style is:

RUSSELL RUOFF, Individually and as Conservator, etc., Plaintiff and
Appellant, v.
HARBOR CREEK COMMUNITY ASSOCIATION et al., Defendants and
Respondents.
(*Ruoff v. Harbor Creek Community Assn.* (1992) 10 Cal.App.4th 1624.)

MICHAEL O'BRIEN, as Conservator, etc., Plaintiff and Appellant, v.
JACK DUDENHOEFFER et al., Defendants and Respondents.
(*O'Brien v. Dudenhoeffer* (1993) 16 Cal.App.4th 327.)

(See also *Freedom Newspapers, Inc. v. Superior Court* (1992) 4 Cal.4th 652
[executor substituted for party who died during pendency of appeal];
Transamerica Homefirst, Inc. v. Superior Court (1999) 69 Cal.App.4th 577
[public guardian involved on behalf of conservatee].)

An estate is not recognized as a legal entity and cannot sue or be
sued. The executor or personal representative for the estate is the named
party (see § 6:15). It is improper to name "The Estate of A" as a party. (See 4
Witkin, Cal. Procedure (4th ed. 1997) Pleading, § 59, pp. 116–117; *Tanner
v. Estate of Best* (1940) 40 Cal.App.2d 442, 445; see also Code Civ. Proc., §
369, subd. (a)(1).) An exception exists under Probate Code sections 550
and 552 when a claim involves a decedent who was insured against liability.
(See *Escobedo v. Estate of Snider* (1997) 14 Cal.4th 1214.)

§ 6:28 Extraordinary writ proceedings

[A] Original proceedings in appellate court

In an original proceeding commenced in an appellate court, designate the parties as "Petitioner," "Respondent," and "Real Party in Interest."
(See Cal. Rules of Court, rule 56(a); Code Civ. Proc., § 1107.)

ELBERT ERNEST DAVIDSON et al., Petitioners, v.
THE SUPERIOR COURT OF FRESNO COUNTY, Respondent;
CITY OF MENDOTA, Real Party in Interest.
(*Davidson v. Superior Court* (1999) 70 Cal.App.4th 514.)

[B] Appeal from original proceedings in trial court

On appeal from a trial court decision on an application for a writ in
an original proceeding, the parties are redesignated as "Plaintiff" and
"Defendant." The name of the real party in interest is added when appropriate and all parties are given appellate designations:

DRY CREEK CITIZENS COALITION et al., Plaintiffs and Appellants, v.
COUNTY OF TULARE et al., Defendants and Respondents;
ARTESIA READY MIX CONCRETE, INC., Real Party in Interest and
Respondent.
(*Dry Creek Citizens Coalition v. County of Tulare* (1999) 70 Cal.App.4th 20.)

CALIFORNIA CASUALTY INSURANCE COMPANY, Plaintiff and Appellant, v. THE MUNICIPAL COURT FOR THE CULVER JUDICIAL DISTRICT OF LOS ANGELES COUNTY, Defendant and Respondent;
CHARLOTTE ANNE EMILE, Real Party in Interest and Respondent.
(*California Casualty Ins. Co. v. Municipal Court* (1998) 66 Cal.App.4th 1410.)

This style was adopted to avoid the confusion that would otherwise result when a party is a "Respondent" in the lower court and a "Respondent" or "Appellant" on appeal. For example, if the respondent below appeals, the appellate title designation, if not adjusted, would be "Respondent and Appellant." And if the respondent below is the respondent on appeal, the unadjusted designation would be "Respondent and Respondent."

For designations in special proceedings, see section 6:42.

§ 6:29 Family Code proceedings

[A] Appellate designations in general

The party initiating a proceeding under the Family Code generally is the petitioner, and the other party is the respondent. (Cal. Rules of Court, rules 1210, 1281.) But confusion would result by designating a party as "Respondent" in the lower court and "Appellant" and "Respondent" on appeal. Thus, opinion and brief titles for this type of case drop the lower court designations of "Petitioner" and "Respondent" entirely, retaining only appellate court descriptions.

List first the party who initiated the trial court proceedings, regardless of whether that party is appellant or respondent on the appeal (see § 6:3). If a party has changed his or her name, use the current name for the adversary title, but retain the name used during the marriage for the "In re the Marriage of _____" part of the title. If both the former husband and wife appeal and are described as "Appellant," the counsel listing should identify counsel as "for Appellant Jane Jones" and "for Appellant Fred Jones," respectively.

In re the Marriage of JANE and FRED JONES.
JANE JONES, Respondent, v. FRED JONES, Appellant.

In re Marriage of FRED SIMPSON and JANE JONES.
FRED SIMPSON, Respondent, v. JANE JONES, Appellant.

In re the Marriage of MARY L. and JON E. HOKANSON.
MARY L. PALMER, Appellant, v. JON E. HOKANSON, Appellant.
(*In re Marriage of Hokanson* (1998) 68 Cal.App.4th 987.)

[B] Appeals concerning joined parties

California Rules of Court, rules 1250–1256 allow the joinder of parties who claim an interest in a Family Code proceeding. The usual style of title on an appeal involving joined parties is:

> In re the Marriage of JANE and FRED JONES.
> JANE JONES, Respondent, v. FRED JONES, Respondent;
> NORMA HEATH et al., Appellants.

> In re the Marriage of MARY K. and JAMES M. ODDINO.
> MARY K. ODDINO, Appellant, v. JAMES M. ODDINO, Respondent;
> HUGHES AIRCRAFT COMPANY NON-BARGAINING RETIREMENT PLAN,
> Respondent.
> (*In re Marriage of Oddino* (1997) 16 Cal.4th 67.)

> In re the Marriage of JANE and FRED JONES.
> MARY GRANDPARENT et al., Appellants, v. JANE JONES et al.,
> Respondents.

§ 6:30 Forfeiture of bail

In an appeal from a proceeding to forfeit bail posted in a criminal matter, or to set aside forfeiture (see Pen. Code, § 1305), the usual style of title is:

> THE PEOPLE, Plaintiff and Respondent, v.
> FRONTIER PACIFIC INSURANCE COMPANY, Defendant and Appellant.
> (*People v. Frontier Pacific Ins. Co.* (1999) 69 Cal.App.4th 1093.)

The proceeding does not take the title of the criminal action to which it is collateral. Forfeiture proceedings of this type ordinarily are civil in nature. (See *People v. North Beach Bonding Co.* (1974) 36 Cal.App.3d 663.)

For titles in forfeiture actions of illegally used property, see section 6:33[B].

§ 6:31 Guardianship proceedings

The double titles in guardianship proceedings consist of a guardianship title describing the type of guardianship involved and an adversary title (see also § 6:27 for distinction between double and single titles). The guardianship title also describes the person's incapacity with one of the following notations: a Minor, an Incompetent Person, *or* an Insane Person.

> *When only the guardianship of the estate is involved, use:*
> Estate of ADAM JONES, a Minor [*or* an Incompetent Person, *or* an Insane Person].

When only the guardianship of the person is involved, use:
Guardianship of ADAM JONES, an Insane Person.

When the guardianship of both the person and estate is involved, use:
Guardianship of the Person and Estate of ADAM JONES, an Incompetent Person.

When multiple wards are involved:
Guardianship of the Persons and Estates of ADAM JONES et al., Minors.

Never use "In re the" or "In the Matter of the" as a preface to the guardianship title. The adversary title, using "Petitioner" and "Objector" for the trial court party designations, follows after the guardianship title.

Guardianship of Z.C.W. et al., Minors.
KATHLEEN C., Petitioner and Appellant, v.
LISA W., Objector and Respondent.
(*Guardianship of Z.C.W.* (1999) 71 Cal.App.4th 524 [protective nondisclosure used].)

Guardianship of SYDNEY SIMPSON et al., Minors.
ORENTHAL J. SIMPSON, Petitioner and Respondent, v.
LOUIS BROWN et al., Objectors and Appellants.
(*Guardianship of Simpson* (1998) 67 Cal.App.4th 914.)

Guardianship of the Person and Estate of ETHAN S., a Minor.
WAYNE S. et al., Petitioners and Respondents, v.
LEWIS HEADRICK, as Guardian, etc., Objector and Appellant.

WAYNE S., Plaintiff and Respondent, v.
LEWIS HEADRICK, Defendant and Appellant.
(*Guardianship of Ethan S.* (1990) 221 Cal.App.3d 1403 [consolidated cases].)

For persons acting in representative capacity, see section 6:15; for minors and incompetent persons, see sections 6:16 and 6:17; and for protective nondisclosure, see section 6:18.

§ 6:32 Habeas corpus proceedings

Use a single title, without a secondary adversary title for every habeas corpus proceeding, regardless of whether it is an original proceeding for relief or an appeal from the grant or denial of relief and regardless of whether the proceeding is criminal or civil. (See *In re Mikhail* (1999) 70 Cal.App.4th 333 [original proceeding]; *In re Rhodes* (1998) 61 Cal.App.4th 101 [appeal].) Never use "Ex Parte," "In the Matter of the Application of," "On Application of," or "Petition of." The title for an adult is: "In re JOHN JONES on Habeas Corpus."

When the writ is sought by or on behalf of a minor and it is collateral to a juvenile court proceeding or contains damaging disclosures, use protective nondisclosure for the minor (see §§ 6:16, 6:18): for example, "In re MARY S., a Minor, on Habeas Corpus."

§ 6:33 In rem proceedings

[A] Escheat

Usually, the form of title in escheat actions is the adversary form used in civil actions generally.

> KENNETH CORY, as State Controller, Plaintiff and Appellant, v.
> CROCKER NATIONAL BANK, Defendant and Respondent.
> (*Cory v. Crocker National Bank* (1981) 123 Cal.App.3d 665 [action against a corporate defendant for accounting, escheat, and report and delivery of unclaimed property].)

But if the state seeks the escheat of property of an estate or if an heir files a claim to an escheated estate, and the action is taken in the probate court, the title will follow the double-title rules for probate proceedings (an estate title and an adversary title):

> Estate of FRED BORN, Deceased.
> THE STATE OF CALIFORNIA, Petitioner and Respondent, v.
> TOM SMITH, as Executor, etc., Objector and Appellant.

> Estate of GEORGE SUPECK, Deceased.
> NICK SUPECK et al., Petitioners and Appellants, v.
> THE STATE OF CALIFORNIA, Claimant and Respondent.
> (*Estate of Supeck* (1990) 225 Cal.App.3d 360 [erroneous party designations corrected in this example].)

[B] Forfeiture of illegally used property

In actions to declare a forfeiture, the first named defendant is usually the thing proceeded against. Although the thing proceeded against cannot take action as a respondent or appellant, it should continue to be designated as defendant for the purpose of identifying the case. On a separate title line, the person asserting an ownership or possessory interest in the property is designated as defendant (not claimant) along with the appropriate appellate designation of appellant or respondent.

> THE PEOPLE, Plaintiff and Appellant, v. ONE PURSE SEINE NET, Defendant; JOHN MELVILLE, Defendant and Respondent.

> THE PEOPLE, Plaintiff and Respondent, v. $5,000 UNITED STATES CURRENCY, Defendant; IRENE SMITH, Defendant and Appellant.

THE PEOPLE, Plaintiff and Respondent, v. ONE 1986 TOYOTA PICKUP, Defendant; ROBERTO DE LA TORRE, Defendant and Appellant.

THE PEOPLE, Plaintiff and Respondent, v. MENDOCINO COUNTY ASSESSOR'S PARCEL NO. 056-500-09, Defendant; RAFAEL PRIETO TARRADAS, Defendant and Appellant.

(See *People v. 6344 Skyway, Paradise, California* (1999) 71 Cal.App.4th 1026; *People v. One 1986 Cadillac Deville* (1999) 70 Cal.App.4th 157; *People v. $241,600 United States Currency* (1998) 67 Cal.App.4th 1100; *People v. Parcel No. 056-500-09* (1997) 58 Cal.App.4th 120; *People v. Ten $500 etc. Traveler's Checks* (1993) 16 Cal.App.4th 475.)

§ 6:34 Interpleader

In interpleader cases the plaintiff interpleader is usually a stakeholder, who delivers money or property as directed by the court below and is then discharged. (See Code Civ. Proc., § 386.) In preparing the appellate title, identify and distinguish rival defendants. The plaintiff interpleader's name is retained, without an appellate designation, to identify the procedural origin of the appeal.

MICHAEL D. BRADBURY, as District Attorney, etc., Plaintiff, v.
JACK D. KAISER et al., Defendants and Respondents;
FRANCHISE TAX BOARD, Defendant and Appellant.
(*Bradbury v. Kaiser* (1992) 3 Cal.App.4th 1257.)

If the plaintiff interpleader is not fully discharged (e.g., when the plaintiff is discharged only to the extent of the funds or property delivered and remains liable for a deficiency, or when the court requires additional deposits, or when the validity of the order of discharge is challenged), its name is retained on appeal with an appellate designation.

OLD FAITHFUL INSURANCE CO., Plaintiff and Respondent, v.
TOM SMITH, Defendant and Appellant;
JACK BLACK, Defendant and Respondent.

When the interpleader action is commenced by a defendant's cross-complaint (see Code Civ. Proc., § 386), the same principles apply. If the defendant is fully discharged below, retain the name for identification only; if the defendant remains a party, provide an appellate designation as well. (See, e.g., *City of Glendale v. Roseglen Constr., Inc.* (1970) 10 Cal.App.3d 777; for cross-complaint titles, see § 6:6.)

§ 6:35 Intervention

In cases of intervention, the terms "Plaintiff in Intervention" and "Defendant in Intervention" are not used, and the order of names on appeal is plaintiff, defendant, and intervener:

WESTERN TELCON, INC., et al., Plaintiffs and Appellants, v.
CALIFORNIA STATE LOTTERY, Defendant and Respondent;
CALIFORNIA-NEVADA INDIAN GAMING ASSOCIATION, Intervener and
Respondent.
(*Western Telcon, Inc. v. California State Lottery* (1996) 13 Cal.4th 475.)

AMWEST SURETY INSURANCE COMPANY, Plaintiff and Respondent, v.
PETE WILSON, as Governor, etc., et al., Defendants and Respondents;
CHARLES QUACKENBUSH, as Insurance Commissioner, etc., Defendant
and Appellant;
VOTER REVOLT, Intervener and Appellant.
(*Amwest Surety Ins. Co. v. Wilson* (1995) 11 Cal.4th 1243.)

The party moving to intervene is a "Movant" until the motion is granted. In the example above, if Voter Revolt had appealed from an order denying leave to intervene, it would have been designated "Movant and Appellant" instead of "Intervener and Appellant."

RILEY O'DELL et al., Plaintiffs and Respondents, v.
FREIGHTLINER CORPORATION, Defendant and Respondent;
ROLLINS LEASING CORPORATION, Movant and Appellant.
(*O'Dell v. Freightliner Corp.* (1992) 10 Cal.App.4th 645.)

Occasionally an appeal is taken from a judgment determining the movant or intervener's rights, and either the plaintiff or defendant is not actively involved in the appeal. That party's name and trial designation should nevertheless appear in the title for identification purposes.

LEE R. STAFFORD et al., Plaintiffs and Appellants, v.
TOAN MACH, Defendant;
ALLSTATE INSURANCE COMPANY, Intervener and Respondent.
(*Stafford v. Mach* (1998) 64 Cal.App.4th 1174.)

APISAMA NASONGKHLA et al., Plaintiffs and Respondents, v.
GEORGE GONZALEZ et al., Defendants;
STATE FARM MUTUAL AUTOMOBILE INSURANCE COMPANY, Movant
and Appellant.
(*Nasongkhla v. Gonzalez* (1994) 29 Cal.App.4th Supp. 1.)

Where the appellate court permits intervention in a pending original proceeding, the intervener is listed last in the title.

DEPARTMENT OF ALCOHOLIC BEVERAGE CONTROL, Petitioner, v.
ALCOHOLIC BEVERAGE CONTROL APPEALS BOARD et al., Respondents;
ANHEUSER-BUSCH, INC., Real Party in Interest;
CALIFORNIA BEER AND BEVERAGE DISTRIBUTORS, Intervener.
(*Department of Alcoholic Beverage Control v. Alcoholic Beverage Control
Appeals Bd.* (1999) 71 Cal.App.4th 1518.)

For titles concerning third party creditor claims and third party lien claims, see sections 6:45 and 6:46.

§ 6:36 Juvenile court proceedings

[A] Direct appeals

An appeal from a juvenile court order or judgment uses a double title. To avoid confusion, replace the trial designations used in the proceedings below ("Petitioner," "Respondent") with "Plaintiff" and "Defendant" for the appellate title. The first title identifies the minor, using protective nondisclosure (see § 6:18); the adversary title follows.

The identity of the initiating party in the adversary title depends on the kind of proceeding involved. A Welfare and Institutions Code section 300 proceeding, to declare a neglected or abused minor a "dependent" of the court, is filed in the name of the county's chief probation officer or the county welfare department, and it usually names the parent or guardian as the responding party. (See Welf. & Inst. Code, §§ 215, 272; Cal. Rules of Court, rules 1405(c), 1406(b).)

> In re CINDY L., a Person Coming Under the Juvenile Court Law.
> LOS ANGELES COUNTY DEPARTMENT OF CHILDREN AND FAMILY
> SERVICES, Plaintiff and Respondent, v.
> EDGAR L., Defendant and Appellant.
> (*In re Cindy L.* (1997) 17 Cal.4th 15.)

A Welfare and Institutions Code section 601 or section 602 proceeding, to declare a delinquent child a "ward" of the court, usually names the minor as the responding party. A section 601 proceeding is filed in the name of the county's chief probation officer, whereas a section 602 proceeding is filed in the name of the People. (See Welf. & Inst. Code, § 650, subds. (a) & (c); Cal. Rules of Court, rule 1406(b); see also Welf. & Inst. Code, § 650, subd. (b) [truancy proceeding under Welf. & Inst. Code, § 601.3 filed by probation officer or district attorney].)

> In re MANUEL G., a Person Coming Under the Juvenile Court Law.
> THE PEOPLE, Plaintiff and Respondent, v.
> MANUEL G., Defendant and Appellant.
> (*In re Manuel G.* (1997) 16 Cal.4th 805.)

Supplemental proceedings after a section 601 or 602 wardship proceeding may be commenced under Welfare and Institutions Code sections 777 and 778; the title on appeal is adjusted accordingly. The respondent normally is the person or public entity with custody of the juvenile when the supplemental petition is filed. For example, a parent may petition the juvenile court under section 778 to set aside one of its orders. In an appeal after that petition, the basic form of title is:

In re MARY C., a Person Corning Under the Juvenile Court Law.
SUSAN C., Plaintiff and Appellant, v.
SAN BERNARDINO COUNTY WELFARE DEPARTMENT, Defendant and
Respondent.

By contrast, a supplemental proceeding under Welfare and Institutions Code section 777 is initiated by the probation officer or prosecutor. (See *In re Marco A.* (1996) 50 Cal.App.4th 1516; *In re Babak S.* (1993) 18 Cal.App.4th 1077.)

[B] Writ proceedings

Petitions to test juvenile court orders by application for writ of mandate, prohibition, or habeas corpus follow the title styles for such proceedings (see §§ 6:42, 6:46). Titles in writ proceedings do not use the nonadversary "In re MARY C., a Person Coming Under the Juvenile Court Law." title.

SAN DIEGO COUNTY DEPARTMENT OF SOCIAL SERVICES, Petitioner, v.
THE SUPERIOR COURT OF SAN DIEGO COUNTY, Respondent;
SYLVIA A., a Minor, et al., Real Parties in Interest.
(*San Diego County Dept. of Social Services v. Superior Court* (1996) 13 Cal.4th 882.)

ELIJAH R., Petitioner, v.
THE SUPERIOR COURT OF LOS ANGELES COUNTY, Respondent;
LOS ANGELES COUNTY DEPARTMENT OF CHILDREN AND FAMILY
SERVICES et al., Real Parties in Interest.
(*Elijah R. v. Superior Court* (1998) 66 Cal.App.4th 965.)

§ 6:37 Nonadversary proceedings

Several types of cases, somewhat similar in nature to probate proceedings, originate in a lower court as nonadversary proceedings but later become contested. For these, use a double title, with the nonadversary title followed by the adversary title.

In re Establishment of SAN DIEGO COMMERCE as a Newspaper of General Circulation.
SAN DIEGO COMMERCE, Petitioner and Respondent, v.
SAN DIEGO DAILY TRANSCRIPT, Contestant and Appellant.
(*In re San Diego Commerce* (1995) 40 Cal.App.4th 1229.)

In re MISSION INSURANCE COMPANY et al. in Liquidation.
CHARLES QUACKENBUSH, as Insurance Commissioner, etc., Plaintiff and
Respondent, v.
IMPERIAL CASUALTY AND INDEMNITY COMPANY, Defendant and
Appellant.
(*In re Mission Ins. Co.* (1995) 41 Cal.App.4th 828.)

In re JOHN BEAN to Establish Fact of Death of MARY BEAN, Deceased.
JOHN BEAN et al., Petitioners and Respondents, v.
JOSEPH SPROUT, as State Controller, Objector and Appellant.
(See, e.g., *In re Lewis* (1969) 271 Cal.App.2d 371.)

Similar double title styles are used with voluntary dissolution, liquidation, and conservation statutory proceedings involving entities such as banks, building and loan associations, charitable associations and corporations, insurance companies, etc. (See, e.g., *In re American Reserve Ins. Co.* (1983) 138 Cal.App.3d 906 [liquidation]; *In re Metropolitan Baptist Church of Richmond, Inc.* (1975) 48 Cal.App.3d 850 [voluntary dissolution]; *In re Cole's Check Service, Inc.* (1963) 215 Cal.App.2d 332 [trust funds set aside pursuant to Fin. Code, § 12300.3].)

§ 6:38 Parental rights termination proceedings

A proceeding initiated by an individual to have minors declared free from parental custody and control, under Family Code section 7820, takes the following title style:

In re BRYCE C., a Minor.
VERNON S., Petitioner and Appellant, v.
JEROME C., Objector and Respondent.
(*In re Bryce C.* (1995) 12 Cal.4th 226 [stepfather's petition to declare a minor free of the father's custody and control].)

Challenges to terminations of parental rights instituted by a county department of social services are titled in accordance with section 6:36.

For protective nondisclosure, see section 6:18.

§ 6:39 Probate proceedings

[A] Estate administration

Probate proceedings generally take double titles (see § 6:27 for distinction between double and single titles). First list the nonadversary title (e.g., Estate of MARCIA JONES, Deceased), followed by an adversary title. As shown below, use "Estate of A, Deceased." for the first title. Ignore lengthier descriptions, such as "In the Matter of the Estate of A, Deceased," which may appear on printed forms and transcripts.

The first party named in the adversary title is the one who initiated the particular proceeding (i.e., the party seeking relief or court confirmation by filing the first petition, application, or motion that is directly involved in the appeal). The initiating party is designated as "Petitioner" and the adversary party is identified as "Objector" or "Claimant," depending on which designation most nearly reflects the facts. Normal appellate court designations are added, and appearances in a representative capacity should be noted (see § 6:15).

> Estate of GEORGE RAYMOND GILKISON, Deceased.
> JAMES L. GILKISON, as Executor, etc., Petitioner and Respondent, v.
> C. RUSSELL KING, Claimant and Respondent.
> (*Estate of Gilkison* (1998) 65 Cal.App.4th 1443.)

> Estate of DORIS C. McCRARY, Deceased.
> HELEN L. CARNAHAN, as Executor, etc., Petitioner and Respondent, v.
> STANTON M. ALWARD et al., Objectors and Appellants;
> ELIZABETH S. JOCHIM, Claimant and Respondent.
> (*Estate of McCrary* (1997) 54 Cal.App.4th 100.)

For guardianship estates, see section 6:31.

[B] Will contests

Actions to contest a will also require a double title, as described in [A]. The adversary title depends on the nature of the will contest (e.g., contests before probate, after probate, or by complaint in intervention).

Will contests before probate:

On trial of the contest under Probate Code section 8250, the contestant is in effect the plaintiff and the petitioner seeking probate is the defendant. Nevertheless, use "Petitioner" for the proponent of the will (normally the party seeking appointment as executor or administrator) and "Contestant" for the party challenging its admission into probate.

> Estate of A, Deceased.
> B, Petitioner and Appellant, v.
> C, Contestant and Respondent.
> (See *Estate of Smith* (1998) 61 Cal.App.4th 259; *Estate of Crabtree* (1992) 4 Cal.App.4th 1119.)

> Estate of A, Deceased.
> B, Petitioner and Appellant, v.
> C, Contestant and Respondent;
> D et al., Claimants and Appellants. [*Other parties appearing in support of the will are generally designated "Claimants and Appellants."*]

Will contests after the will is admitted to probate:

Normally the initiating party, who files a petition to revoke the will from probate, is denominated the "Contestant" (see Prob. Code, § 8270), and the proponent is described as "Claimant" or "Objector," depending on which of these terms most nearly fits the facts. (See § 6:15 as to representative capacity.)

When some parties do not share identical trial and appellate court designations, list each nonidentical group separately (see § 6:4). The following example is for an appeal following the probate court's revocation of a will where the contestant (C) petitioned to revoke; the beneficiaries (B et al.) appeared in support of the will; and others (D et al.), who will take if the will fails, but who did not initiate the contest, appeared in support of revocation.

> Estate of A, Deceased.
> C, Contestant and Respondent, v.
> B et al., Claimants and Appellants;
> D et al., Claimants and Respondents.

> (See also *Estate of Hermon* (1995) 39 Cal.App.4th 1525.)

Intervention:

When a party with sufficient interest to contest a will intervenes in a pending will contest, the title style is:

> Estate of A, Deceased.
> B, Petitioner and Respondent, v.
> C et al., Contestants and Appellants;
> TOM SMITH, Intervener and Appellant.

§ 6:40 Quo warranto proceedings

When the action is commenced by the Attorney General, follow the style noted in section 6:10 for public officers. Actions brought in the name of the state or the People upon the relation of a private party follow the style noted in section 6:20. (See, e.g., *People ex rel. Fund American Companies v. California Ins. Co.* (1974) 43 Cal.App.3d 423.)

Occasionally a quo warranto proceeding will be instituted by a legislative body of a county, city and county, or municipal corporation. (See Code Civ. Proc., § 811.) The style of title for such a proceeding is:

> COUNTY OF RIVERSIDE ex rel. BOARD OF SUPERVISORS, Plaintiff and Appellant, v. JOHN GREEN et al., Defendants and Respondents.

§ 6:41 Sanction awards against nonparties

On review of a sanction award against nonparties, such as a litigant's attorney, generally no respondent is named unless sanctions are to be paid to a party instead of the court. The names of the plaintiff and defendant are retained, however, to identify the underlying case. The name of the person sanctioned, the trial court designation of "Objector," and the appropriate appellate designation (usually "Appellant") are added to the title of the action in which sanctions were awarded. (See, e.g., *Trans-Action Commercial Investors, Ltd. v. Firmaterr, Inc.* (1997) 60 Cal.App.4th 352.)

A, Plaintiff, v.
B, Defendant;
MALCOLM ATTORNEY, Objector and Appellant.

§ 6:42 Special proceedings

The Code of Civil Procedure defines a "special proceeding" negatively: "An action is an ordinary proceeding in a court of justice by which one party prosecutes another for the declaration, enforcement, or protection of a right, the redress or prevention of a wrong, or the punishment of a public offense." (Code Civ. Proc., § 22.) "Every other remedy is a special proceeding." (Code Civ. Proc., § 23; see generally Code Civ. Proc., § 1063 et seq.) Ordinarily, parties to "special proceedings" in the trial court are designated as "Plaintiff" and "Defendant." (Code Civ. Proc., § 1063.) The appellate title customarily uses "Appellant" and "Respondent" (see § 6:7).

In some special proceedings, however, the initiating party in the trial court is designated "Petitioner" and the opponent is the "Respondent." On appeal from such a proceeding, it would be confusing if the party designations below were used in conjunction with appellate designations (e.g., designations like "Petitioner and Respondent," "Respondent and Respondent," or "Respondent and Appellant"). To avoid this result, the petitioner in the trial court is characterized as "Plaintiff" and the respondent in the trial court is listed as "Defendant" (see §§ 6:28, 6:47).

§ 6:43 State Bar nondisciplinary proceedings

Titles of Supreme Court opinions reviewing decisions and determinations described in California Rules of Court, rule 952(d) use the typical civil adversary title style. Typical titles for such opinions are:

LEW WARDEN, Plaintiff and Appellant, v.
THE STATE BAR OF CALIFORNIA et al., Defendants and Respondents.

RAYMOND L. BROSTERHOUS et al., Plaintiffs and Appellants, v.
THE STATE BAR OF CALIFORNIA et al., Defendants and Respondents.

(See *Warden v. State Bar* (1999) 21 Cal.4th 628; *Brosterhous v. State Bar* (1995) 12 Cal.4th 315; *Johnson v. State Bar* (1993) 12 Cal.App.4th 1561.)

Review of determinations concerning admission to the State Bar are titled as follows.

In re JOSEPH MENNA on Admission.
(*In re Menna* (1995) 11 Cal.4th 975.)

For titles in attorney disciplinary proceedings, see section 6:25.

§ 6:44 Supersedeas writs

When a petition for a writ of supersedeas is filed to stay proceedings pending appeal, the petition and any opinion rendered must bear the same title as the appeal. It should not be entitled in the name of the applicant against the trial court. The proper form of title is:

> THOMAS PECSOK et al., Plaintiffs and Appellants, v.
> SAMUEL BLACK et al., Defendants and Respondents.
> (*Pecsok v. Black* (1992) 7 Cal.App.4th 456.)

§ 6:45 Third party creditor claims

In creditor attachment cases, a third party may enter the litigation and claim a prior right to the property attached. Though this is in the nature of intervention, the third party is designated as "Third Party Claimant."

> KAICHEN'S METAL MART, INC., Plaintiff and Appellant, v.
> FERRO CAST COMPANY, Defendant and Respondent;
> ROHR INDUSTRIES, INC., Third Party Claimant and Respondent.
> (*Kaichen's Metal Mart, Inc. v. Ferro Cast Co.* (1995) 33 Cal.App.4th 8.)

Even if the dispute on appeal is only between the plaintiff (or defendant) and the third party, retain the uninvolved party's name and trial court designation in the title for identification purposes.

> ROBERT M. CASSEL, Plaintiff and Respondent, v.
> THEODORE A. KOLB et al., Defendants;
> UNION BANK OF CALIFORNIA, N.A., Third Party Claimant and Appellant.
> (*Cassel v. Kolb* (1999) 72 Cal.App.4th 568.)

For titles with intervening parties, see section 6:35.

§ 6:46 Third party lien claims

In some situations, a third party may seek to establish a lien on a cause of action or on any judgment subsequently obtained. For example, a judgment creditor may seek a lien on the debtor's cause of action or, in a personal injury action, a medical insurer may seek reimbursement, from the anticipated judgment, of medical expenses incurred by the injured plaintiff. These claims are in the nature of intervention, but "Claimant" is used to designate the third party in this type of action. The terms "judgment creditor" and "judgment debtor" are not used in titles.

Generally, the dispute on appeal will involve only the plaintiff or the defendant in addition to the third party; retain the uninvolved party's name and trial court designation in the title for identification purposes.

VICTOR TAPIA, a Minor, etc., Plaintiff and Respondent, v.
WENDY LAURIE POHLMANN, Defendant;
COUNTY OF SAN DIEGO, Claimant and Appellant.
(*Tapia v. Pohlmann* (1998) 68 Cal.App.4th 1126.)

For titles with intervening parties, see section 6:35.

§ 6:47 Trusts

Similar to estates (see § 6:27), trusts are not recognized as legal entities and cannot sue or be sued. Only trustees can be named as parties, thus it is improper to name "The ABC Trust" as a party. (See Prob. Code, §§ 17200, subd. (a), 17200.1; see also Code Civ. Proc., § 369, subd. (a)(1).) Additionally, the description "Trustee of the ABC Trust" is not properly listed as a party name; the trustee's name is listed followed by "as Trustee, etc." "Trustees of the California State University" is an official board name, not a description, so it is properly used in titles (see Ed. Code, § 66600).

Trust administration cases do not use a nonadversary title, such as "In re the Matter of the Charles G. Adams Trust," to identify the trust. In addition, the lower court designations of "Petitioner" and "Respondent" are changed to "Plaintiff" and "Defendant" in accordance with section 6:42.

BERNARD A. LECKIE, as Trustee, etc., Plaintiff and Appellant, v.
COUNTY OF ORANGE et al., Defendants and Appellants.
(*Leckie v. County of Orange* (1998) 65 Cal.App.4th 334.)

MARTHA B. NOGGLE et al., Plaintiffs and Respondents, v.
BANK OF AMERICA NT & SA, as Trustee, etc., Defendant and Appellant.

MARTHA B. NOGGLE et al., Plaintiffs and Appellants, v.
BANK OF AMERICA NT & SA, as Trustee, etc., Defendant and Respondent.
(*Noggle v. Bank of America* (1999) 70 Cal.App.4th 853.)

Proceedings under the California Uniform Transfer to Minors Act (Prob. Code, § 3900 et seq.) are titled like trust cases except that the fiduciary party description is "as custodian, etc."

For representative capacity, see section 6:15.

§ 6:48 Workers' compensation proceedings

Because the Workers' Compensation Appeals Board and the same insurance companies are involved in a great many of these cases, the name of a respondent in addition to the board is always used in opinions reviewing Workers' Compensation Appeals Board decisions.

STATE FARM FIRE AND CASUALTY COMPANY, Petitioner, v.
WORKERS' COMPENSATION APPEALS BOARD and PATRICK A.
LEONARD, JR., Respondents.
(*State Farm Fire & Casualty Co. v. Workers' Comp. Appeals Bd.* (1997) 16
Cal.4th 1187.)

Use the term "et al." only if there are three or more respondents.

JENNIFER HENRY, Petitioner, v.
WORKERS' COMPENSATION APPEALS BOARD, MAMMOTH
MOUNTAIN SKI AREA et al., Respondents.
(*Henry v. Workers' Comp. Appeals Bd.* (1998) 68 Cal.App.4th 981.)

CHAPTER 6
—Notes—

INDEX